WORDS 2000
FOR TODAY

Notes for daily Bible reading

INTERNATIONAL BIBLE READING ASSOCIATION

Cover image – Friendship across cultures
Photograph by Mark Howard
Editor – Maureen Edwards

Published by:
The International Bible Reading Association
1020 Bristol Road
Selly Oak
Birmingham
B29 6LB

Charity No 211542

ISBN 0-7197-0935-0
ISSN 0140-8275

Typeset by Avonset, Bath
Printed and bound in Great Britain by
Caledonian International Book Manufacturing Co.

CONTENTS

Acknowledgements and abbreviations

GNB *Good News Bible* (The Bible Societies/Collins Publishers) – Old Testament © American Bible Society 1976; New Testament © American Bible Society 1966, 1971, 1976.

NIV Scripture quotations taken from *The Holy Bible, New International Version* © 1973, 1978, 1984 by International Bible Society. Used by permission of Hodder & Stoughton Limited. All rights reserved. 'NIV' is a registered trademark of International Bible Society. UK trademark number 1448790.

NJB Taken from the *New Jerusalem Bible*, published and copyright 1985 by Darton, Longman and Todd Ltd and Doubleday & Co Inc, and used by permission of the publishers.

NRSV *New Revised Standard Version* © 1989, Division of Christian Education of the National Council of Churches of Christ in the United States of America.

REB *Revised English Bible* © Oxford University and Cambridge University Presses 1989

RSV *The Holy Bible, Revised Standard Version* © 1973, Division of Christian Education of the National Council of Churches of Christ in the United States of America.

BCE Before the Common Era. BCE and CE are used by some writers instead of BC and AD.

EDITORIAL

Are the challenges of the new Millennium any greater than the last? What is our vision for the future? These are questions we have sought to address in this year's notes. We live in an ever-changing world. Although we put our trust in God, who in one sense doesn't change, we are aware that this God leads us on to new situations and wider horizons. All of these, though they frighten us, belong to the excitingly varied world that God is still creating and drawing together. As with Abraham, God calls us to leave behind what is familiar and comforting – to venture out to discover that there is more to learn from the many ways God is revealed to people of different faiths and cultures – all of them a part of God's creation and design.

The Bible's timeless words continue to speak to and disturb peoples and nations, offering the same choice – life or death. The way to life is clearly there in the Torah, the sharp challenges of the prophets, and the words and example of Jesus. It's a way that breaks down barriers and dispels bitterness between nations, ethnic groups, people of different faiths, rich and poor, lenders and debtors, women and men, young and old, people with differing 'disabilities', humankind and the rest of creation... It's a way that takes us back to the roots of our faith, and to a deeper awareness of all that we have learned and received of God's infinite love, for there is our inspiration. And there is the inexhaustible source of the 'water of life' upon which we draw.

We welcome to our pages writers with a wide experience of life and the world, Jews and Christians. There is so much to learn from one another. I discovered this during the seven years I lived and worked in Kenya. Through the insights and experience of Kenyan friends, I came to see the gospel and the world through another window, and my life changed. As you encounter new and surprising insights, don't dismiss them, but allow the Holy Spirit to help you explore them further and discover new ways of relating to people around you and learning from them. So may you discover the grace and vision to share fully in God's mission to bring healing, reconciliation and peace to our communities and the earth itself, for this is the exciting challenge of these significant days in which we are privileged to live.

Maureen Edwards

Maureen Edwards – Editor

MORNING PRAYERS

Lord God, we come to you with hearts that are cold,
that they may be warmed by your selfless love.
We come to you with hearts that are sinful,
that they may be cleansed by the Saviour's precious blood.
We come to you with hearts that are weak,
that they may be strengthened by your Holy Spirit.
We come with hearts that are empty,
that they may be filled with your divine presence,
Father, Son and Holy Spirit. Amen

St Augustine of Hippo (354-420)

Almighty God, make all things within us new this day.
Renew our faith and hope and love.
Renew our wills that we may serve you
　　more gladly and watchfully than ever.
Renew our delight in your word and your worship.
Renew our joy in you.
Renew our longing that all may know you.
Renew our desires and labours to serve others,
and so take care of us, your people,
　　who embrace the Cross of your Son
　　and want to walk in the light and power of your Spirit,
now and for always, through Jesus Christ our Lord. Amen

The Assembly Worship Book, World Council of Churches,
Harare 1998

May the God who brings hope
to the shepherds of the fields,
to the fisherfolk of the seas,
to the beggars of the streets,
empower and strengthen our faith
to do powerful deeds of justice and peace.

The Philippines (source unknown)

Make us Bibles, Lord, so that those who cannot read the
Bible can read it in us.　　　　　　　　　　　　*China*

EVENING PRAYERS

Thou hast led me through my crowded travels of the day
    to my evening's loneliness.
I wait for its meaning through the stillness of the night.
Rabindranath Tagore

If you fail to see the person but only the disability,
who is blind?
If your heart and mind do not reach out to your neighbour,
who is handicapped?
If you cannot hear your brother's cry for justice,
who is deaf?
Tony Wong, Jamaica

God, you often take us by surprise;
you do not tell us your name.
You make yourself known to us
    in the events that happen along the way.

Give us courage to take risks
to build a highway in the desert
    when we do not see how we can possibly move forward.
Give us courage to believe that you are there,
    and will be ahead of us when we dare not move.
Give us courage to believe that we will find you there,
    to honour the things we dare to do,
when we are prepared to take the risk
    and carry the first rock to build the highway. Amen
The Assembly Worship Book, World Council of Churches,
Harare 1998

O Lord, our palm trees can no longer hide us
from the world. Strengthen our hearts
that we may look with confidence to the future.
Tahiti

How to use 'a quiet time'

Have a visual focus – a cross, a plant, interesting stones... create a prayer table on which to display them with other symbols. Place on it pictures or articles from the daily news.

Use silence Relax and empty your mind of all that's going on around you. Know that God's loving presence encircles you, your family, your community and the world. Learn to enjoy God's presence. If, because of personal problems, you cannot free your mind of the day's concerns, remember that these are your prayers and offer them to God. Know that you are loved and valued, and seek the strength and peace God offers.

Read the Bible passage for the day and then the notes. Read the verses again, allowing the words to fill your mind. Try to discover their message for you and the world around you. Refer back to other readings in the theme, so that you can see how the thoughts link together. If the writer of the week's notes comes from a different culture or background from yours, ask yourself what is new and fresh. What surprising insights have come to you from his or her perspective?

Listen Remember that the most important part of prayer is to hear what God is saying to us. God speaks to us through the words of Scripture, the daily news, and often through people around us – our children, our friends, our neighbours, the person who asks for help, the stranger... Frequently the voice of God disturbs our complacency, and calls us to 'Go out' and do something we've never done before!

Include the world Hold the news of each day in your mind. Enter the situation of those you hear or read about and try to pray alongside them – with them. In a wonderful way, prayer transcends the thousands of miles between us. Through prayer we draw strength from the mysterious fellowship that binds us to one another and to God.

Pray without ceasing Remember that prayer is not only 'the quiet time' we set aside. It becomes part of the whole of life, a continuous dialogue between God and ourselves, through all that we do and think and say: a growing awareness of the loving presence of God who travels with us and never leaves us.

THE MILLENNIUM DAWNS
1. Vision

Notes based on the New Jerusalem Bible by
Sheila Cassidy

Sheila Cassidy works as a specialist in Psycho-social Oncology at the Plymouth General Hospital (UK). In her spare time she preaches, lectures, broadcasts and writes books. Her writing is deeply influenced by her involvement with suffering, both in cancer wards and in her personal experience of imprisonment, torture and solitary confinement in Chile.

The last few years have been so full of talk about the significance of the new Millennium: people have booked places on cruises or planned special parties. Restaurant owners have worried how much they would pay their waiters on 'THE NIGHT', or whether the possibility of being let down is so great that it would be better to close and lose their rich pickings. Church people have pondered upon the spiritual significance of this, the two thousandth anniversary of the birthday of Jesus, and have protested with more or less vigour that the world is planning a massive birthday party but has forgotten whose birthday it is.

This, then is the challenge: to listen to Christ here and now, present in each of our lives. We remember Jesus the Nazarene and marvel that his name is remembered two thousand years after his death, but it is to the risen Christ that we turn to hear our message for the new Millennium.

Saturday January 1   *Ephesians 1.3-14**
Moving forward
So! How does it feel to be a Christian on this the first day of the new Millennium? I'm assuming my readers have recovered from their end of year celebrations and that they are in pensive mood. My first thought is one of enormous gratitude and of hope, for surely to be a Christian is to be a person of hope. I feel gratitude for my life, for my health, friends and family. I am especially grateful for my gifts as a doctor and for work which has given my life such meaning over the years. If it doesn't sound too pious, I'm grateful for the privilege of being called to serve: because, for me, to serve others is a central part of following Christ.

What, I wonder, would St Paul make of our world today? Would his view have broadened with the times? Would his concept of the 'chosen people of God' have included a multi-faith dimension? My guess is that he would have mellowed and grown in understanding of Jesus' message that the Creator God, whom Paul calls Father, is a God who loves all men, women, children and young people, weak and strong, good and evil.

> For the love of God is broader
>   than the measure of man's mind,
> And the heart of the Eternal
>   is most wonderfully kind.'   *Frederick W Faber (1814-63)*

In this passage from Ephesians, Paul waxes lyrical over what some people would call 'the Cosmic Christ': the power of God behind the universe, drawing all things, all people together. It is this Christ whom Paul describes as 'the image of the unseen God' (Colossians 1.15), and who, with the Father and the Spirit, is involved in the birth process and pain of the whole created world and humankind who long to be set free (Romans 8.21-25). This is our common call: to labour with Christ for the freedom of all people: for freedom from oppression, hunger, homelessness, greed and despair. With this call comes Christ's promise that he will be with us as we labour, laughing, weeping, planning, resting, until we meet, face to face.

✳ *Holy God, Father and Mother of us all,*
widen our hearts to accept your love
that we may be worthy to be your followers,
in this new Millennium.

Sunday January 2   *Revelation 21.1-6a**

A God for a new world

There is a sense of newness in the air, of new beginnings, of hope that things will be better because we have passed from one moment to another. Part of me is a bit sceptical of all this, for life will go on and those who celebrated on New Year's Eve will have to go back to work and carry on where they left off. The patients are still in their hospital beds as they were on December 31st, though some have died, and some have gone home; and there is a fresh crop of babies to greet the dawn, and a chaos in the computer world as yesterday's technology baulks at a set of unfamiliar digits!

These words of St John, however, are just as mysterious and as important as they were two thousand years ago. John, the mystic, had, as mystics do, hit the nail on the head when he summed up

God's covenant with his people: our God is a God who has moved in with us, pitched his tent amongst us, rented a flat in the heart of the city. We may have forgotten about God, but that doesn't mean that he is not here. The fact that the churches are half empty should not fool us: God is alive and well, taking soup to the homeless, tending a handicapped child or an old woman with Alzheimer's. She is counselling and comforting the rape victim, working late in the office and having a drink in the pub with friends and including the lonely drinker. We may try to turn over a new leaf, wipe the slate clean for the Millennium, but God will carry on, unchanged and unchanging, for more millennia than we can imagine.

✳ *Changeless God, ever with us:*
give us vision for this new Millennium.
More than anything, give us ears to hear you,
and eyes to see you ever loving, ever present, in our midst.

Monday January 3   *Matthew 25.31-46**

Love one another

This is such a familiar passage and yet we forget it so easily. It contains within it what I understand to be the heart of the Christian message: that we should love one another.

It is important to look, too, at what Jesus did not say in this parable. He did not say, 'You didn't fall into temptation,' or 'You went regularly to church...' He didn't say anything about those who sang in the choir, or spent a lifetime in an unhappy marriage because they had promised to do so. Sometimes I think that Jesus' notion of righteousness is a bit different from ours. I am not suggesting for one moment that our individual attempts to do the right thing are not pleasing to God, but I find it interesting that the message in the Bible is more about kindness and justice than about sexual morality and church attendance. Jesus praised those who put themselves out for others: those who fed the hungry, comforted the widow, and looked after the orphan.

Could it be that God has compassion upon our foolishness, and understands the longings of our hearts and the weakness of our flesh? The more I understand what God is like, the more I think how lucky we are not to have the fire and brimstone deity whom so many people believe they must worship.

✳ *Gentle, just and loving God,*
forgive us our trespasses and help us to forgive one
another.

Seek justice

What a stunningly beautiful passage this is. After three years of monastic living and daily chanting of the psalms I am most familiar with the Gelineau version:

'May the mountains bring forth peace for
    the people and the hills, justice.
May he defend the poor of the people
    and save the children of the needy
    (and crush the oppressor)...
In his days justice shall flourish
    and peace till the moon fails.'   *The Grail Psalms*
                            (HarperCollins © 1963, 1986)

I love the cadence of the last two lines: there is something magical about the phrase 'peace till the moon fails'. But we must be wary that the beauty of this psalm does not blind us to its prophetic content. The poor of our time are those who most irritate us: they are the mentally ill, the men and women of London's cardboard city, the street children of Rio de Janeiro and Honduras. They are those who are hooked on heroin or strong cider, coke or cheap sherry. They are hungry and dirty, and they rattle the gates of our heart.

I live in the South West of England where there are few beggars in the streets, but in London I am all too familiar with the young schizophrenic who looks pitifully up at me from his pitch outside London Bridge Station. Jesus said the poor will be always with us: but that does not mean we should ignore them. The poor of the developing world are hungry and thirsty: hungry for food, thirsty for clean water; hungry for love, thirsty for justice. Justice, of course, is not an abstract concept but a way of dealing with wealth and with people which involves sharing the earth's resources. And, if the poor have more, we'll get less: less food, money, land, possessions. There's the crunch.

✳ *O scary God, may you judge your people in justice
    and your poor in right judgement.*

Wednesday January 5   *Jeremiah 31.7-14**

The faithful remnant

This theme of the faithful remnant of Yahweh is a favourite one in the Old Testament. It is tempting to think of this remnant as the 'elect', the virtuous ones who have not sinned (and number ourselves among them), but I think of the remnant as the *anawim,* the little people, the sick, the blind and the lame; the young and the very old. These are the people of whom Yahweh says: 'I have loved you with an everlasting love and so I still maintain my faithful love for you.' This curious phrase 'faithful love' is one of the key attributes of Yahweh, of our Creator God. 'Faithful love' is *hesed,* God's covenant love for his people. We find it again and again throughout the Scriptures: God has made a covenant, a treaty, with those he loves most: with the sick and the little people.

The Roman Catholic priest, the late Father Michael Hollings, who was Chaplain when I was at university, was a living example of this kind of covenant love for the poor. His home was open house to us when we were students, which was lovely for us. When he moved to London to a poor multi-racial parish he kept open house there too, and it was not always a comfortable place to visit. There are those who say that Michael was considered for a bishopric and perhaps to be a cardinal: he was wise and holy, and a good organizer. He was passed over, however, because such radical Christianity makes people nervous. Who knows, he might have turned the Archbishop's house into a refuge for the homeless, or started throwing about the furniture in the temple when he got in a rage about justice!

✳ *Incarnate Word, in whom all nature lives:*
Cast flame upon the earth.
Raise up contemplatives among us,
men who walk with the fire,
of ceaseless prayer, impetuous desire.

James McAuley, Australia

Epiphany, Thursday January 6   Matthew 2.1-12 *

The Epiphany

It's all there in the Christmas story, the key themes of humankind: birth and death, baby worship and infanticide, poverty and riches, humility and the lust for power. Herod schemed to kill Jesus because he saw him as a threat to his power, just as today's rulers plot to kill their rivals to 'take them out' as the latest military jargon has it. Herod wanted to take Jesus out so that there would be no threat to the stability of the nation he was governing: but he failed, because an angel warned Joseph, and he and Mary fled with the child into Egypt.

It's a lovely story, but familiarity dulls the message, the central message of Christianity: that the unseen Creator God took on our human condition and came to live among us. So far so good: as Christians we believe and celebrate that. Harder to accept is the ongoing life of Christ, ever present, *Emmanuel,* 'God with us', at home, in the office, and abroad. As Matthew tells us, it's Christ there trying to scrounge money off us in the street, Christ in the pompous lawyer or clergyman who irritates us so much and, of course, Christ in the refugee. If we don't understand this and try to live it, we might as well give up pretending to be Christians. Without this link with the here and now, the Nativity story loses its meaning. As it says on one of my Christmas cards this year:

'When the song of the angels is stilled,
When the star in the sky is gone,
When the kings and princes are home,
When the shepherds are back with the flocks,
The work of Christmas begins:
To find the lost,
To heal the broken,
To feed the hungry,
To release the prisoner,
To rebuild the nations,
To bring peace among people,
To make music in the heart.'   *Source unknown*

✳ **Loving God, help us to make Jesus' mandate our own.**
Fill us with a passion for justice
and a love that overflows like your own.

Friday January 7   *Matthew 2.13-18*
Rachel weeping for her children

This story of the massacre of the infants is one of the most distressing in the Gospels: for the death of children is always an outrage. For the past twenty years I have worked with the dying and the bereaved, but it is only in this past year that I have begun to understand what it means to a mother to lose a young child. As humans, we share with the animals an enormously powerful bond with our young: a God-given, built-in instinct which leads to the mother's powerful protection of her baby, and thus to the survival of the race. The murder of a child, therefore, attacks the mother's deepest instinct and wounds her in a way which is different from any other loss.

Just as Christ's life continues in our midst, so does Herod's slaughter of the innocents. In Latin America, the secret police 'exterminate' the street children whom they see as vermin, raiding the dustbins, thieving and sleeping under the bridges. In war-torn Bosnia whole families are wiped out because they follow the 'wrong religion', while here in the UK, little children are abducted, sexually violated and murdered, lest they betray their attacker.

Nothing changes, does it? The lust for power infects all manner of men and women who then become blind to the divine spark in themselves and in their victims.

Will the third millennium be different? Probably not. We must learn to live together, wheat and tares, working for peace and binding up broken hearts.

✳ *O God who suffers with those who mourn,*
  comfort the bereaved, especially
  those desperate women who have lost a child.

Saturday January 8   *Isaiah 65.17-25*

Dreams for peace

Christianity is a faith for dreamers and pragmatists: as one wise man put it, 'Blessed are those who dream dreams – and are ready to pay the price to make them come true.' In this passage, the prophet dreams of how life would be if oppression and cruelty were things of the past and everyone had their own land, their own home, and enough for themselves and their families. For some of us, life is like that now. Although we may complain that life is hard, our pay too low and taxes too high, we have food and shelter, work for ourselves, school for the children... We build our homes and live in them, plant gardens and eat their fruit. We do not toil in vain, nor do we bear children destined to disaster.

Alas, however, not everyone is so lucky. There are beggars on the streets of London and refugees driven from their homes the world over. What hope have they, what vision for the new Millennium? They can dream, but it's up to us to make those dreams come true. Can we ask our leaders to forgive the debts of the desperate nations of the earth: especially those doubly tormented by natural disaster? Can we increase our personal contributions to the Aid agencies, and give time to working with those who need our help?

What do we think about land-mines, pollution, AIDS, the tragic bread and butter of so many millions? Are we ready to pay the price to make the prophets' words come true: 'No more will the sound of weeping be heard there, nor the sound of a shriek...' (Isaiah 65.19).

* *God of all who weep and dream,*
give us courage and generosity
to make the dreams of the poor come true.

FOR REFLECTION – alone or with a group

- What dreams do you have for yourself, your family and the community?
- What is your vision for the world?
- Why is it important to have a vision for the future?

FOR ACTION

How will you begin to seek to make your vision a reality?

FINDING OUR WAY TOGETHER series

- For leaders of house fellowships, Bible study groups and worship groups
- A unique opportunity to explore world issues and contemporary themes in the light of the Bible
- Each book includes background notes, ways to lead groups, contemporary stories, activities for adults, questions for discussion, suggestions for prayer and ideas for action
- Uses the same passages and themes as *Words for Today* and *Light for our Path*
- Book 3 is based on the readings for the year 2000

Books 1 – 3 UK price £6.00 each

Order through your IBRA representative or from the appropriate address inside the front cover.

THE MILLENNIUM DAWNS
2. Repentance

Notes based on the Revised English Bible by
John Carden

Formerly working as an Anglican priest for the Church Mission Society, first in Pakistan and then as its Asia Secretary, John Carden later served as incumbent of a parish in Bath, and finally cared for a small international congregation in Jordan. He edited the WCC Ecumenical Prayer Cycle 'With All God's People' and more recently compiled 'A Procession of Prayers' (WCC/Cassell). Apology and forgiveness are recurring themes in both of these publications.

Although the Greek word *metanoia* (meaning 'to turn around') occurs only fifty times in the New Testament, the need of individuals and of nations to seek forgiveness – to turn around, to rectify what has gone amiss and to make a new beginning – is a familiar biblical theme. As peremptory a command as 'Repent!' sounds on the lips of John the Baptist, and clearly there are related words in the Old Testament which predate the call of John to *metanoia,* as well as those in the New Testament which accompany it.

1st Sunday after Epiphany, January 9   *Mark 1.1-8**
Make way
'Let there be respect for the earth,
peace for its people,
love in our lives,
delight in the good,
forgiveness of past wrongs and,
from now on, a new start.'

Though not so dramatic as the striking metaphors used in the Gospels to describe John the Baptist's task preparatory to the inauguration of the first Millennium – way making, road levelling, obstacle removing, rubbish burning – this resolution proposed for use throughout Britain in the year 2000 suggests tasks and concerns for individuals and communities closely resembling those advocated by John.

One very practical response to the need for a new start in our life together could be the simple act, traditionally enjoined upon

Muslims, of stooping down to remove the discarded can or other obstacle lying in the path of a neighbour. An annual response in Dresden, on the night of 13 December – the night when the city was devastated by bombs – is to gather together groups of children, to disarm them of small toys of war, and to help them to take them apart and rebuild them into more useful objects with which to welcome the Prince of Peace.

In South Africa, provision is made at evangelistic meetings for a special tent in which stolen property may be surrendered in response to a change of heart. Another environmental approach marks the beginning of an evangelistic campaign in a town of Uganda, which starts with a rubbish collection, accompanied by the fervent use of prayer.

✳ *My God, clean my heart*
as I clean my town.

Turning and returning

Used as a picture of God's constant love for his people, the story of Hosea's love for his wayward wife Gomer, and his willingness to go to any length to facilitate her return, movingly illustrates the Old Testament understanding of acts of turning and returning in the practice of repentance.

Hosea's steadfast trust in God and the language he uses in urging Gomer's restoration are reminiscent of those equally plain words, used by the anonymous 14th century author of *The Cloud of Unknowing* in another of his writings. He bids the wayward and ailing folk of his generation with the words of the prayer offered below.

Hospitalized for a prolonged period this last year and helplessly on the receiving end of a great many 'plasters' for this and that, I found the frequent saying of this prayer a constant reminder of the comforting and restorative power of the good, gracious God, and of his presence with me in making a necessarily re-ordered lifestyle. A kind of turning around or, if you like, another instance of repentance.

✳ *'Take good gracious God as he is*
plat and plain as a plaster
and lay it unto thy sick self
as it is.'

Tambourines and tears

The Pharisees featured in today's reading were deadly serious in their insistence that repentance was something that had to be worked for hard and long. And I use the word 'deadly', because they saw no chance of these conditions ever being met by the kind of men and women of dubious occupation and virtue with whom Jesus seemed to have surrounded himself.

Their murmur of disapproval in verse 2 should probably read, 'This man takes pleasure in tax collectors and sinners and feasts with them', suggesting that Jesus positively enjoys their company. This infers that in the presence of Jesus, his table companions are already beginning to taste and savour that saving closeness from which a sense of unworthiness and repentance follows, rather than the other way around. In this act of reversal it is these people, rather than the actively religious, who are responding to his presence and joyfully receiving the gift of forgiveness.

In the early days of the Salvation Army it was the custom to trawl public houses to rescue lost souls for Christ, and to bring them with tears and tambourines to the penitential bench. The story is told of a man approaching the bench, his face wreathed in smiles, only to be reproved by a senior officer. 'What,' the man replied, 'Do you mean to tell me that a man can't laugh when he is having his sins forgiven?' Today's reading suggests that Jesus would be right by his side, tambourine in hand!

✱ *O Lord, raise us out of the paralysis of guilt*
  into the freedom and energy of forgiven people.

World Council of Churches

What must be done?

Seeing before his eyes those immediate and fickle crowds who had cried 'Hosanna' on Palm Sunday and 'Crucify' only a few days later, Peter boldly upbraids the people of Jerusalem for their complicity in the death of Jesus. Thus confronted they are 'cut to the heart' (verse 37), and in a question reminiscent of the one asked of John the Baptist they ask what must be done.

Peter's reply is equally reminiscent of that given by John. They must first repent, and then be baptized, and thus receive the assurance of God's forgiveness and the gift of the Spirit. But

Peter goes further than John, and the 3000 are committed to the care of the Body of Christ in the steady ongoing life of the Christian community described in verse 42, so the reader must read on!

This steady ongoing life, following on perhaps from more exciting times, is in striking contrast to the immediacy often expected in much religious experience. 'The immediate person' expects that God should hear and respond to what is being asked, whereas, according to Kierkegaard, the true relationship between the believer and God lies in continued waiting, praying and listening. 'The immediate person makes demands, the true man or woman of God attends.' It is to this life of attending – to the mind of God, to the apostles' teaching, to the breaking of bread, to the prayers and to the common life – that the apostle Peter summons us today.

✳ *O Lord, stablish, strengthen and settle*
all who commit their lives to you in penitence and in
baptism.

Thursday January 13   Luke 16.19-31
The body in chains
This vivid story of the rich man and Lazarus greatly influenced the life of Dr Albert Schweitzer who, identifying Africa as the beggar lying at Europe's door, founded, and himself worked in, Lambarene Hospital in French Equatorial Africa. He did this as an act of atonement for his country's neglect of its responsibilities towards the needy in its colonial territories. More recently, increasing sensitivity towards the needs of many modern-day Lazaruses – in aboriginal communities, victims of racism, and other exploited people – has led to a number of apologies by individuals and communities, sometimes accompanied by acts of restitution.

In connection with the *Jubilee 2000* campaign, urging the relief of unpayable Third World debt, a modern sculpture, made entirely of chains, depicts a figure closely resembling the posture of Lazarus lying at the door of the rich man. This powerful figure is carried around our cathedrals as a focus for concern and penitence and action. Clearly, the breaking of such chains and the healing of the wounds they have inflicted upon people and communities is a complex process involving far-reaching repentance of a kind almost beyond our comprehension, let alone our practice.

✳ *To ponder:*
'*In sin we are all bound together. I must repent back into the family, into the clan, into the race, back to God.*'

Søren Kierkegaard, Denmark (1813-55)

Friday January 14   Luke 17.1-4

Forgiveness reaches deep

The warning of verses 1-2, to those who offend against the smallest and most vulnerable members of our human family, reinforces the common sentiment that although almost every other sin may be condoned, this one is beyond human power to forgive.

Continuing widespread abuse of children at the hands of individuals, in institutions, and by unjust political systems seems to bear out our Lord's warning that, this being a fallen world, such causes of stumbling are likely to continue. Uncomfortably, however, the 'Woe!' pronounced by our Lord is addressed not only to paedophiles, child abusers and perpetrators of genocide in far-away places, but to all of us who, secure at home, sit back and allow our negotiators to get good deals and to buy at the expense of God's little ones.

The wonder, however, as in the painfully borne fruit of our Lord's own suffering, is in the manner in which those 'Woes' have sometimes been undone by the very little ones most offended against. I have in mind 12-year old Kim Phue who, miraculously surviving appalling burns, as a grown woman offered forgiveness to the American commander who ordered the napalming of her village; the peace cranes launched across the world by Sadako Sasaki, child victim of atomic radiation in Hiroshima; and the scrawled words left by a child who perished in Ravensbruck concentration camp:

✳ '*And when we come to the final judgement, let all the fruits that we have borne be their forgiveness.*'

Saturday January 15   Revelation 2.1-7

Recovery from a body blow

Sent by the Elder John at the bidding of the exalted Christ, this letter is the first of seven addressed to groups of churches in different areas of Asia.

Ephesus was an important city, and perhaps included a number of Christian congregations in the area. John writes warmly and appreciatively of the toil and fortitude of the church, of their orthodoxy and high standard of morality (no mean attainments in a place like Ephesus); but he then delivers what can only be described as a body blow in the words of the single sentence of verse 4 which has continued to be a source of soul searching for Christians down the centuries. Without giving them time to recover he moves on immediately to the remedy in verse 5.

But this, his chosen remedy for lost love, takes time. Lancelot Andrewes makes the point that often we are in such a hurry that we take away the fruits of repentance before they come. And so we need a second repentance to repent of our first inadequate one. Having said that, returning to our first love via penitence does not rest on recapturing past feelings associated with our initial following of Christ. Instead it rests in 'doing what we once did' – picking ourselves up again and again, and living from that same generous forgiveness which drew us in the first place.

✳ *Blessed be God, who is always renewing his Church by his Holy Spirit, making young again what had grown old.*
Vatican II

FOR REFLECTION and ACTION – alone or with a group

- Look at other passages of Scripture (Isaiah 9.4-5; Matthew 3.1-12) relating to rubbish burning and ground clearing, envisaged as preparatory to the inauguration of the First Millennium. List those things in our individual and communal life that might be consigned to a similar fate to mark the beginning of this Millennium.
- Discuss the Salvation Army story (January 11) in the light of Evelyn Underhill's words: 'Every soul that appeals to God's forgiveness is required to move over to his side, and share the compassionate understanding, the unmeasured pity, with which he looks on human frailty and sin...'
- If you have not already done so, find out about *Jubilee 2000*.
- Look at some of the penitential prayers used in our churches, and ask how far they do justice to Søren Kierkegaard's quotation used with the reading on January 13.

THE MILLENNIUM DAWNS
3. Following

Notes based on the New Revised Standard Version by
Michael King

Michael King both studied and taught in West Africa as well as teaching in comprehensive schools in Britain for over 20 years. He is now Mission Education Secretary (World) for the Methodist Church in Britain, and lives in Hertfordshire with his GP wife and two children.

Following Jesus is never straightforward! The journey can be geographical or spiritual. Will the journey take me further into myself or lead me beyond my comfort zone? The readings for this week give us vision, but also challenge us to follow ever more closely in the footsteps of our Lord. God continually calls us, but we need to be willing to listen – and act.

2nd Sunday after Epiphany, January 16   *John 1.43-51**
Where are we going?

What is your vision of 'heaven opened' (verse 51)? And are we not impatient to see the vision fulfilled? Sometimes I wonder if, in our searching, we fail to see what should be so clear, right in front of our eyes. 'Can anything good come out of (your own town, village or situation)?'

Last summer, at an event called 'World Village', walking down a narrow alley, I heard the most wonderful noise of sheer joyful laughter. It was fully half a minute before I was able to see the reason or who was responsible, but it was a wonderful moment when I looked around the corner. Children of different nationalities from all over the world, as part of their programme, were playing with a parachute silk. An adult, who was laughing as much as the children, was apparently in charge. Their enjoyment was infectious and people who were passing stopped to look – and joined in their obvious delight.

We might just have glimpsed heaven. God's there. Let's follow.

✳ *God of joy and laughter,*
help us to follow you
by building communities who value each other's contributions
and enjoy each other's company.
May this enjoyment be a gift we bring to the new Millennium.

Obedience

This is a wonderfully personal Psalm. The writer has obviously no doubts whatsoever about his relationship with God and delights in it. God's total knowledge of him brings joy. It also, of necessity, results in obedience.

After the first morning of ski instruction, the final task was to negotiate a terrifyingly steep slope. Well, that's what it looked like to me at the top! Excuse the pun, but I froze.

The ski instructor realized my predicament and told me that I could do it, but probably not alone! All I had to do was follow her: place my skis in exactly the same path as hers, turn where she did (and when she said so), and keep my eyes fixed on her back.

Can you imagine the sense of pride that I felt when I got to the bottom of the slope, not having fallen? She had known what I could do, and what I could not do alone.

Obedience resulted in joy. How much more does God know us, for he is at the heart of our creative process. Obedience to our Creator brings joy, to both God and ourselves.

✳ *God at the very source of our being,*
help us to discern your will and way for us –
and help us to respond obediently.
May this obedience be a gift we bring to the new Millennium.

Challenge

Our mission as followers of Jesus is to be faithful to his life and teaching. In John 6, Jesus makes no excuses about the difficulty of the task ahead – for disciples then and now.

We do not need to examine earnest books of history to find people who have taken this Christian calling seriously. In our own life and times, there are courageous lay and ordained people who have suffered because they refused to compromise their following in Jesus' footsteps.

Bishop Gerardi Condera's brutal murder in Guatemala, April 1998, highlights the difficulty of true discipleship. He was killed because he would not stay silent. He was killed two days after making public a report on the civil war in Guatemala in which the military were blamed for about ninety per cent of the 150,000 deaths and 50,000 'disappearances'. He must have been aware of the risks of publishing the report, but that would have taken him into the zone of personal safety – from which Jesus constantly calls us!

In our daily living, wherever we are, our mission is to be faithful to the life and teaching of Jesus – or 'Do you also wish to go away?' (verse 67).

✳ *God of challenge, give us the strength to stand*
and be faithful to you in our meetings and daily living.
May our faithfulness be a gift to you in the new Millennium.

Wednesday January 19   John 10.1-10
Authority
How important it is to listen to the voices of those we trust. Of course, they don't always tell us what we want to hear; but people we can really trust will invariably tell us what we need to listen to. Like Jesus.

I was reading recently about a passenger in a small aircraft who had no experience of flying a plane. Then the pilot had a heart attack and, at a moment's notice, he was in the position of trying to land the aircraft safely. Establishing radio contact with an air traffic controller, he got expert help to talk him through all the necessary manoeuvres – in today's terms a steep learning curve! Against all the odds, he managed to land the plane safely in a field, but only by listening carefully to the voice in his headset and carrying out every instruction exactly.

Having heard the voice of God, do we always pay attention?

✳ *God of authority, help us to hear your voice in our busy days.*
Curb our arrogance when we act only in our own strength.
May this humility be a gift we bring to the new Millennium.

Thursday January 20   Mark 10.17-31
Stewardship
We are called to be disciples, followers of the Master. We are not independent, but in communion.

The biggest problem with possessions and riches is the tendency they have to encourage thoughts of independence. 'We have enough, so we can do things on our own'. Jesus here responds to that false self-sufficiency – and exposes it.

It is not just individuals who believe they can be self-sufficient: nations can also have the same ideas. In denying the needs of others, we impoverish ourselves by not allowing others to share in our own lives. Do we really want to live in communities where others are disabled from sharing with us the different gifts that they have?

Wealth is morally neutral. It can be used in a variety of ways and Jesus endorses giving to the poor as well as buying expensive perfume (John 12.1-8). As Christians there is a real need to pray carefully about our use of riches, to ensure that our stewardship of God's resources is in line with his will.

✳ *God of all that we possess, help us to pray carefully*
and discern your Holy Spirit
in how we use the wealth that you have entrusted to us.
May this wealth be a gift we bring to the new Millennium.

Friday January 21   Mark 10.35-45

Service

It happens in all walks of life – people want to be noticed! Many are the meetings that I have attended where, on looking around the assembled company, I have been surprised to see people there who had previously told me about their lack of interest in the subject matter. So why were they attending? To be seen, to be heard, hopefully by someone who could 'help' them later on in life – a promotion at work, a position on a Committee, political power, etc.

Jesus must have wondered about James and John! Had they misunderstood three years of teaching and living, if they could ask such questions about positions of authority in the Kingdom? Like any other country, the United Kingdom does not always get the leaders it deserves or needs! There is, however, a daily reminder to those who are elected to the highest offices that they are Ministers of State (servants). The 'first among equals' is the Prime Minister, the first servant of all. We may not have such titles, but we still serve – and follow – the Master.

✳ *God who encourages our loyalty,*
help us to seek ways to serve you and our fellow creatures.
May this surrender of the positions we hold
and the things that we are
be gifts we bring to the new Millennium.

26

Choices

I was merrily driving down the motorway when suddenly an alarming noise came from the back wheels. As I was close to the next service station I decided to get to the car parking area and phone for help from there. Somehow, I missed the breakdown van, and the first I heard was a vehicle blowing its horn in the middle of the car park, attracting attention. Looking up, I realized that the van driver was looking for me – just as eagerly as I was waiting for him! Once we were united, the car clearly required further repairs and I was towed into a nearby garage. I was in need; I was called; I followed gladly. I had no choice, actually!

Like Bartimaeus, we know we are in need; we know God alone can fill the need. Hopefully, we all know that God calls us, each one, by name, and desires that we should answer his call. So what do we choose? Do we follow, in gratitude, as though tied to the back of Jesus? If the tow-rope is fixed, Jesus will have let us tie it – it will be our choice.

Bartimaeus immediately 'fixed his rope' to Jesus. To what, or to whom, do we fix our own lives?

✳ *God of choice, thank you that you go on calling us.*
Thank you for rescuing us and supplying all that we need.
May our willingness to be led into the unknown
be our gift to the new Millennium.

FOR REFLECTION – alone or with a group

- Is it more important for us to know the final destination or to trust the person leading us?
- If we are to take the ongoing call of Jesus seriously, what things will we have to consider surrendering to his authority?

FOR ACTION

As individuals or as a group, work out where you could best serve those in need in your own community. Could this be where Jesus is leading you? If it is (like the early disciples) you will need to consider what time will need to be given, as an ongoing commitment; what resources you will need; what you will need to give up in order to divert energy to this new initiative. Then draw up an Action Plan'!

THE MILLENNIUM DAWNS
4. Proclaiming good news

Notes based on the New Revised Standard Version by
Simon Oxley

Simon Oxley leads the Education and Ecumenical Formation staff team of the World Council of Churches, based in Geneva, Switzerland. His work brings him into contact with Churches in many different parts of the world. He is a Baptist and was formerly General Secretary of IBRA.

Proclaiming good news used to summon up pictures of the preacher in the pulpit, the missionary teaching people in another country or an evangelist at a rally. We have come to recognize that we need to have more images than these. People relating to their neighbours, working for justice and peace, or reaching out to sufferers, can equally be proclaiming good news by their style of life and what they do as well as the words they speak.

3rd Sunday after Epiphany, January 23   *Mark 1.14-20**
The right time

It's never the right time. Those who want to delay can always find a reason why now is not the right time to do something. At a celebration of the 50th Anniversary of the World Council of Churches in 1998, Archbishop Desmond Tutu paid tribute to the organization's role in the movement which led to the end of apartheid. Yet when the WCC's Programme to Combat Racism was launched, many said that the time was not right. They claimed that the churches were not ready to fight racism in their structures and society. Although much remains to be done to fight racism, we can see the results of change of attitude, behaviour and policies – good news for many.

In Mark's Gospel, Jesus arrives on the scene saying that 'now' is the right time for proclaiming the good news of the Kingdom and he goes ahead to put it into action. When people are in need, there is no excuse for delay. Now is always the right time for good news of any kind.

✳ *Lord, when we are inclined to delay,*
   remind us that you love us now.

God alone

It is claimed that television has changed the nature of politics in many countries. Instead of concentrating on the issues and policies, the focus is redirected on the individual leaders. Politicians build their election campaigns around themselves – put your trust in me and I will run things well. As well as building up leaders, however, the media also ruthlessly exposes their personal and professional weaknesses. The problem is that presidents and prime ministers are only human.

This is not anything new. The Psalmist, writing two or three millennia before television, recognized the problem. There can be no hope if it is only placed in yourself or other people. Reading through Psalm 62, we see the writer keep returning to God as the only sure location of hope.

This is the heart of the good news we are called to proclaim. God is the one who is ultimately trustworthy in life. There is another aspect to this good news. Having a trustworthy God sets us all free to be human, without the need to pretend to be anything else.

✴ *When others make promises they cannot keep;*
when they offer more than they can give;
when we believe that we can save the world ourselves,
Lord, help us to know that you are God.

Proclaim release, sight and freedom

The slave dock at Salvador, Bahia, Brazil is not a remarkable place in some ways. The quay is like many quays, the church and other buildings like many of those of the same period. It is only as you learn and feel what happened there that the place does become extraordinary – the incredible numbers of those who were landed still alive after their terrible voyage from Africa and the awful future that waited for them. You can stand on the steps of the church where each wretched human cargo was seated and baptized all together. Christian slaves were more valuable. Baptism, a sign of liberation in Christ, became a sign of repression.

Jesus did not choose and claim the passage from Isaiah by accident. This is a fundamental statement about the good news – release from whatever holds people in slavery, clear sight so that we can see what oppresses us and others. Both the slaves and the slave traders need to be set free. The poor and those who are rich at their expense need to experience the good news.

✳ *We confess*
   that we have confused talking about the good news
   with acting to make the good news an experience for all.

Wednesday January 26   *Mark 6.7-13*
Travelling light

An airport is a fascinating place for studying human nature. Queuing at the check-in desk, you can see some people who have several large suitcases whilst others have just one small bag. Very often it's nothing to do with how long they are going to be away from home. Perhaps some people find it psychologically important to carry so many of their clothes and possessions with them on their travels. Foreign places may not feel as strange or threatening if they are surrounded by what is familiar.

This may give us a clue to why Jesus gave these instructions to the disciples about what to take on their journey. There was no possibility of drawing comfort from what they carried with them when things became difficult. They had to live with what happened on the journey and to depend on the one who sent them out. Jesus was helping them to discover that it is not possible to proclaim the good news from a position of comfort and safety. It is as we learn to become vulnerable that the good news becomes believable.

✳ *Lord, give us the faith to travel light,*
   to put our trust not in what we carry with us but in you.

Thursday January 27   *Romans 1.1-17*
Encouraged to proclaim

One of the most powerful aspects of the recently ended Ecumenical Decade of the Churches in Solidarity with Women was the team visits paid to many churches. A group of women and men from other churches in different parts of the world would spend time visiting a church and experiencing its worship and its work in relation to women. It was not just a fact-finding activity to discover whether women were playing a full and creative role in church and society. It was also an exercise in mutual encourage-ment to witness to the liberating power of Christ for women and men.

In the World Church we do need to learn from one another across continents, but even more we need to encourage each other to be faithful in our life and witness. Paul's letters are often critical of the churches to whom he wrote. Sometimes they are helpful in explaining the meaning or implications of Christian teaching. Occasionally they are defensive about his work. However, the thread running through all of them is that of encouragement to believe and live out the gospel.

✳ *Think of one or two people who have encouraged you in your Christian discipleship and thank God for them.*

Friday January 28   Romans 10.5-17
It does not just happen

For babies, being fed and changed just happens. It is part of growing up to realize that food on the table or clean clothes are there because someone has worked to provide them. Nor, of course, does it just happen that too many children and adults are deprived of the basics of decent human life. It is because other people are unwilling or unable to share and to fight with them for justice.

Paul reminds his readers that proclaiming the good news does not just happen. Someone has to act. He does not, however, leave it only to the individual conscience to respond. In verse 15 Paul talks about the one spreading good news being sent. Whatever form the spreading of the good news takes – evangelism, human care, working for justice – the Church has a responsibility to equip, commission and send people to act. Sometimes we may be sent to distant places but mostly we will be sent back into our families, neighbourhoods and places of work and leisure.

✳ *Lord, show me where I should be sent to spread good news.*

Saturday January 29   Acts 14.8-18
The message of the messenger

It is not always the best actors and actresses who become stars. Very often it is a matter of getting the right part in the right play or film that makes someone a household name. As audiences have found, being a star is not a guarantee of future good performances. At the same time, it is possible to visit the theatre and see a fine production acted by a cast whose names you have never heard of before. It is the coming together of acting skill, script and direction which makes for good theatre or film.

The crowds in Lystra, who witnessed the healing of a physically disabled man, wanted to make stars of Paul and Barnabas. They failed to recognize that the power of the gospel drama they had seen did not come from the actors. It is to the credit of Paul and Barnabas that they did not get carried along with the personal adulation. Unfortunately, many preachers and evangelists have not been as wise and have allowed the spotlight to stay on them rather than on the good news they proclaim. It is right to witness to what Christ has done for us but not to what we do for Christ.

✳ *May my living glorify you, Lord, and not myself.*

FOR REFLECTION – alone or with a group

- Think of some people in the news – locally, nationally and elsewhere in the world. What would be good news for each of them?
- Why is it not enough just to speak about our faith?

FOR ACTION

Do something which will be good news for someone close to you.

THE MILLENNIUM DAWNS
5. Opposing evil

Notes based on the Revised Standard Version by
Lesley G Anderson

Lesley Anderson, a Panamanian, is President of the Belize/Honduras District Conference of the Methodist Church in the Caribbean and the Americas (MCCA), Chair of the Presidium of the Caribbean Conference of Churches, and Vice-President of the Board of Governors of the United Theological College of the West Indies (UTCWI).

The New Testament word for 'evil', *diabolos*, is often translated 'the devil', or 'Satan' (Revelation 20.2) and means 'adversary' or one who slanders or falsely accuses another. In biblical thought, 'evil spirits' are the servants, principalities and powers of the Devil (Ephesians 6.12).

What forms of evil do you see in the world today, and how easily do we become ensnared by its power? What connection do you see between the New Testament concept of evil and those who today are engaged in devil worship, black magic, witchcraft, demonic practices and hellish behaviour?

Jesus Christ calls on us to resist all evil from whatever source in his powerful name. His victory over evil on the cross is already our victory, and it is that victory we must live. It is in this light that we must understand this week's Bible study.

4th Sunday after Epiphany, January 30   Deuteronomy 18.14-20*
God requires our commitment
In this passage there is a strong condemnation of those who meddle in occult, superstitious and magical practices. In the verses which precede today's reading, they are named as:

1. those who use **divination,** e.g. casting lots (Ezekiel 21.21);
2. **enchanters** who observe omens and signs in the sky, or **witches** and **sorcerers** who practise magic, using drugs and spells (Exodus 22.18);
3. **charmers** who tie knots, weaving magic spells and curses, or **wizards** who communicate with ghosts or spirits of the dead;
4. **necromancers** who consult with the dead (Leviticus 19.31; 20.27).

There is no need, says the book of Deuteronomy, for us to get involved in these practices. God communicates with us through his prophets. We are not to listen to those who appeal to a superficial and material curiosity to delve into the paranormal. God's prophets are those who make a stand for the truth. The gift of prophecy is what makes the Jewish and Christian faiths distinctive in the world, and calls society and nations to establish God's justice and peace.

And in New Testament terms, God reveals himself to us in Jesus Christ, through whom we have direct access to God. We do not need to meddle in the occult, voodoo, and other superstitious practices. God requires of us faithfulness and commitment in Christ.

✳ *Almighty God, help us to shake off*
all that distracts us from seeking the higher life in Christ.

Monday January 31   *1 Kings 22.1-14*
Seek first the Word of the Lord
Hostility between Judah and Israel had given way to friendship. The marriage between the two royal families gave strength to this relationship. Unfortunately, both Judah and Israel had been influenced by Baal worship – introduced by Ahab a few years before – and the people virtually abandoned the worship of the Lord for calf worship. Jehoshaphat, King of Judah, sought divine guidance before going on his journey, and was encouraged by the four hundred prophets who sympathized with and tolerated calf-worship to avoid persecution. But Micaiah, who was a genuine prophet of God, said, 'As the LORD lives, what the Lord says to me, that I will speak' (verse 14).

In many parts of the Caribbean and the Americas, people who live in poverty seek a day of liberation. Some, in doing so, have abandoned the things of God that last for the material things of life which perish. Sometimes we take God for granted. In my ministry I have met many people who were faithful to God when they were young and then turned from him when life began to go well for them. Now they are aged and weak and unable to serve God.

God calls us, often through prophets, in our best years to seek first his Word that we may be empowered to live for him, and be enriched by his presence always.

✳ *Pierce our hearts, O God, that we may seek you*
and your Word above all things
that we may receive the graciousness
and fullness of your love.

Tuesday February 1   1 Kings 22.15-28

Hold on to the truth of God's Word

'Go up and triumph...' (verse 15). The king recognized mockery in
the words of Micaiah, who was repeating the words of the four
hundred prophets (verse 6) who supported him. The king always
felt that Micaiah would 'not prophesy good' concerning him, but
'evil' (verse 18). In his vision, Micaiah saw the Lord and the 'host
of heaven' – the **angelic spirits** who constituted heaven. In verse
21, reference is made to a **spirit** from the Lord, whose personal
nature is not clearly known. Similarly, the **lying spirit** is
recognized as one of God's ministers, coaxing the evil Ahab to
his death. He does not merely damage, he causes lasting harm,
but always in subordination to the will of God. The concept of an
evil spirit opposing God was not yet developed in Old Testament
thought.

Zedekiah later challenged Micaiah to explain how they could
both speak for God, but prophesy differently. The difference is
verified in the truth of Micaiah's words, when news arrived of
Israel's defeat.

How do we verify true and false prophecy today? Have you
noticed the difference between Christians who speak out against
national corruption, racism, ethnic cleansing and other evils and
those who give lip service to God and remain silent about evil in
society?

Sometimes too, when things go wrong for us personally, do
we only listen to the words of friends who seek to comfort and
placate rather than to those who also challenge us to face the
realism of our situation and to look to the future? Let us
remember that God is always there for us – often speaking
through the voices of others – when, in times of sorrow or
difficulty, we call out to him.

✳ *Help us, O God,*
that we may be faithful to our high calling in Christ Jesus
to be instruments for good and not for evil.

God has chosen you

In this reading, the words 'to know' mean to have intimate knowledge, to care about the one who is chosen. God had chosen Israel to be his people. But being God's people is a call to responsibility, and so Israel is accountable for that trust.

But the nation has betrayed God's trust. Political instability, Amos sees, is a result of corruption and exploitation. The prophet's warnings must be taken as seriously as a lion's roar, for the time will come when God's people will be caught like a bird in a trap. Evil will befall the city (verse 6), and this will be a sign of God's judgement.

God warns every generation, through his prophets, to resist those who oppress the poor, social and political violence, the misuse of drugs and alcohol, irresponsible sexual relationships and all that destroys both mind and body. Warning signs surround us in abundance. Do we heed them?

✴ *We trust only you, O God.*
Grant us the blessedness of strength
to overcome and resist all evil.

Stay clear of evil

King Herod was one of four tetrarchs who ruled Palestine during the lifetime of John the Baptist. John the Baptist had denounced Herod's relationship with Herodias, his brother's wife, and her deep grudge at his words and hatred of John led to his death. Herod on the other hand was in a continuous state of perplexity and fear, for John was a holy man.

When Herod heard about Jesus and his dynamic miracles, he feared that John the Baptist had risen from the dead, and that the unseen powers of the spirit world were terrorizing him. There is no doubt that Herod's awareness of the evil he did in beheading John the Baptist became a nightmare. Verse 14 suggests that Herod feared Jesus because he believed that his 'miracles' were performed out of supernatural power.

But miracles are more than this. Miracles happen wherever God is present. The birth of a baby is a miracle. Like Jesus, we must be committed to using the power of God for good and to stay clear of evil. When we are tempted to do evil, let us pray for strength and courage to resist, so that the true power of God's presence may be seen in us.

✳ *Lord, help us to pray your prayer,*
  'Deliver us from evil',
  and give us courage to live by it.

Friday February 4   *Mark 9.42-49*

Choose a life that is worthwhile

The consequences of sin are serious. It brings unhappiness and even death. There must be times in our lives when we reflect and examine our thoughts and actions, times when we need to be prepared to exercise self-discipline for the sake of others and for our own eternal good.

By the 'fire' of discipline and the 'salt' of purification we can live a holy life. Salt is the divine grace – an emblem of friendship. But sometimes 'jealousy' has led people to create stumbling blocks against family, friends and colleagues. Jesus condemns such behaviour. It is degrading and offensive. The Greek word used here is *skandalizo* - 'to put a stumbling-block in the way to cause another to fall'. Innocent people are made to suffer. Think of examples.

We have to learn how to restrain ourselves, says Jesus, from putting obstacles in the way of others. It is better to be maimed or crippled, to have no eye, hand or leg, than to lose the life God offers.

The Greek word for 'hell' is *geena* from which comes the word Gehenna – the valley outside Jerusalem where people burnt their rubbish. It has become a symbol of everlasting punishment.

✳ *Help us, O Lord our God, to choose life.*

Saturday February 5   *Hebrews 4.12-13*

God's Word is living and active

When the Word of God is faithfully and powerfully proclaimed, it lives on and has power to change. It does not die.

We can proclaim God's Word with our lips as in our lives. Like a sharp sword it can penetrate insincerity, lack of trust and faith. The Greek words used here say that it literally cuts into our being, piercing through both soul and spirit. It becomes the 'discerner', laying us bare and open, analyzing, sifting out and bringing judgement on evil thoughts and intentions. We cannot hide from God, nor escape his living Word.

37

From the genesis of time, as the story of the garden of Eden symbolizes, individuals, communities, nations and the whole earth have experienced the suffering which human sin causes. We see the brutality and savagery of war; we hear the cry of the homeless, the hungry, naked and helpless. Let us respond positively to God's Word to reach out, touch and transform lives.

✳ *O God, grant us courage to go forth into the world*
to proclaim your Word,
and to live in the power of the Holy Spirit. Amen

FOR REFLECTION – alone or with a group

● Read again Deuteronomy 18.14-20. What do you know about the occult, voodoo and witchcraft? Why did the prophets condemn them?
● Describe your feelings when you know that evil is happening around you. How do you cope? How can you help others who are gripped by the power of evil?
● How can your faith be strengthened to resist evil?

THE MILLENNIUM DAWNS
6. Renewal

Notes based on the Revised English Bible by
Janet Nightingale

Janet Nightingale belongs to both Methodist and Anglican traditions in which she is a lay preacher/reader. She trained in education and has also worked for Christian Aid and Age Concern. She lives with cancer, but has been enjoying life to the full, travelling around the world, mainly to visit family and friends. A major interest is meeting fellow cancer survivors on the Internet where they share information and support one another.

The theme for this week's readings is about different ways of taking a fresh look at areas of our lives and mapping out suggestions for renewing various aspects of our faith – an appropriate task in the millennium year.

5th Sunday after Epiphany, February 6   *Isaiah 40.21-31**
Renewed strength

When energy is lacking, when things are getting out of proportion, it is uplifting to remember that God, like a mother caring for her children, never wearies or grows faint, but puts them first, especially the most vulnerable.

At this moment I am glad of it; I have just received an e-mail message from Madeleine in a hospital in the United States; she is about to undergo unique surgery to remove a kidney with a local anaesthetic because she is too weak to take a total one. I thrill at reading that, with God's help, people like this friend, whom I have never seen, will win new strength and soar on wings as eagles, whether in this life or the next. As a song based on Psalm 91 puts it, 'And God will hold you up on eagles' wings, bear you on the breath of dawn, make you rise like the sun and hold you in the palm of his hand.'

On a larger canvas, when we think that our country's or the world's future is bleak, we can take heart that by working with others we can make a difference and will be given the strength to do it.

∗ *God, we ask you not to lift us out of this life,*
but to prove your power within it;
not for tasks more suited to our strength,
but for strength more suited to our tasks.   Source unknown

Monday February 7   Psalm 30
Renewed faith
In recent years I have been brought face to face with the paradox of faith, which the psalmist expresses very clearly and which the poet Blake echoes: 'Joy and woe are woven fine, a clothing for the soul divine.' The psalmist expresses the mood-swings which may affect us all, from tears of despair at night, to seeing things in a different light when morning comes. This is the amazing capacity of God to renew faith even in times of distress. In the Psalm there is also a hint of arrogant certainty, which was soon undermined by an absence of God. But faithfulness to God brought an answer, and laments turned to dancing once again.

Hildegaard of Bingen put it in this way: 'The Creator has given us two wines to drink from: the white wine of bliss, harmony and ecstasy and the red wine of pain, suffering and loss. Fully to live, to live spiritually, is to drink from both wines in our lifetime.' It is in the midst of the hurricanes of life that we find out how little faith we have and how much, when in calmer waters, we need to sustain it and help it grow.

∗ *God, you lead us by ways we do not know, through joy and*
sorrow, through victory and defeat, beyond our under-
standing. Give us faith to see your guiding hand in all things;
that being neither lifted up by seeming success, nor cast
down by seeming failure, we may press forward wherever
you lead, to the glory of your name.
        Eric Milner White (1884-1963, and GW Briggs (1875-1959)
                Book of a Thousand Prayers (Marshall Pickering)

Tuesday February 8   Psalm 147.1-11*
Renewed vision
I am not sure that I agree with the psalmist when he says that God does not take pleasure in 'the strength of a horse' or in 'a runner's fleetness', but I think I know what these words are meant to convey! And that is that God's vision is unique. When we look at things with a broader vision, what had seemed impossible has become possible. To the Jews in exile it had seemed impossible

that they would ever return to the land of their ancestors, to Jerusalem, the city which expressed their aspirations. Yet these things had happened, and the people had been renewed. When they looked back they saw lessons in an experience which had seemed so devastatingly conclusive at the time.

Some of us who live with cancer, and know that our days are numbered, look upon that experience as a gift. It may seem strange to say, but it is true. It is a gift to be able to appreciate every day more fully, to concentrate on the things that really matter and disregard the trivial aspects of life. It changes one's vision.

✳ *Day by day, dear God,*
 of thee three things I pray:
 to see thee more clearly,
 love thee more dearly
 and follow thee more nearly,
 day by day.

Adapted from St Richard of Chichester (1197-1253)

Wednesday February 9   *Mark 1.29-39**

Renewed mission

This passage marks the beginning of Jesus' ministry, from home, outwards to other towns and into the whole region.

'Let us move on' is not a message which every Christian community is happy to hear. In my experience there are times when churches very definitely indicate 'Let's stay put', or even 'Let us go back'! What are your experiences of making changes in your church?

From the example of Jesus we take the message that renewal begins with local concerns, reflection and prayer, followed by a willingness to move on. Being a Christian is more like travelling than sitting; we must always be ready to move on, to make a fresh start. Static churches can become rather like stagnant ponds; they need a good stir to come to life and a good flow to sustain them. Is there a message here for you, for your church, for your community, as we begin a new millennium? What seeds are we sowing which someone will reap in the future?

✳ *God of every generation,*
 send again refining fire;
 fill us with your inspiration,
 with the warmth of your desire.

May we seek your priceless treasure,
make your love and justice known,
that our children, in full measure,
reap with joy what we have sown.   © Janet Nightingale

Renewed love

The woman with the box of expensive ointment was evidently giving to Jesus the best thing she could – her love. She was on the outside; she appreciated that Jesus had included her and this was her way of saying, 'Thank you'. Jesus' response indicated that he was profoundly moved by her unexpected generosity, and renewed by her love. There were times when Jesus was helped by surprising people – a child with bread and fish, the Samaritan woman, Joseph of Arimathaea. Many of us also will have been surprised by love from unexpected sources, which brings healing and hope.

I have experienced this myself from complete strangers whom I have met through the Internet cancer-support group I joined this year. When I decided to meet some of them on a Cancer Awareness March in Washington DC, I was astonished at their generosity, which meant that all I had to provide was my airline ticket. Strangers became friends through shared experience and convinced me (if I needed convincing) that love is one of the greatest treatments for disease of body, mind or spirit.

We have a choice to make: like the disciples on this occasion, we can reject the giver; or, like Jesus, we can be renewed by love.

✳ *O love that wilt not let me go,*
   I rest my weary soul in thee:
I give thee back the life I owe,
That in thine ocean depths its flow
   May richer, fuller be.   George Matheson (1842-1906)

Renewed wisdom

Spiritual gifts are not the same as the human gifts with which we were born. The kind of wisdom and knowledge to which this passage refers are quite evidently not to do with those abilities which count highly in a worldly sense; they are to do with seeing clearly that our value rests on our relationship with God and grows by taking time to be with God. With that wisdom all kinds of opportunities and resources become available, through the resurrection of Jesus Christ.

When I was a student teacher, I went once to a small Quaker Meeting in Liverpool. After a long silence, an elderly man, wearing rough clothes and with hands that showed the signs of years of manual labour, stood and recited the Lord's Prayer. He said it with such clarity and depth of meaning that the moment has influenced me ever since. He was probably not a man of great knowledge and wisdom as the world understands it, but in terms of spiritual wisdom he taught me more than all the lectures at my college forty years ago.

✳ *Spend a moment thinking of people who have influenced you because of their spiritual wisdom. Give thanks for them and pray for them. Pray that you may grow in this kind of wisdom.*

Saturday February 12   *Hebrews 13.5-16*

Renewed commitment

Jeremy Taylor, an English 'divine', once described the Christian life as a voyage and ended by saying that many people 'did not make the voyage, though they were long at sea'. They were 'swept off course' by all the trappings and encumbrances of the journey, moving aside from the aim and ending up where they started from. Many of our lives may be like that: money, possessions, a yearning for security, worry about future health, about our children, our job – these can take up so much energy that we forget the true purpose of our lives.

'It is good that we should gain inner strength from the grace of God,' says the writer to the Hebrews (verse 9). At times when we find ourselves wandering from the goal of the voyage, it is good that we should make a fresh commitment, point the compass once again away from where we have no lasting city, and towards the city which is to come. When we do that, all the encumbrances of the journey fall into the right place and do not occupy the centre of our minds.

✳ *Give some thought to the things which occupy you most. Are these moving you on towards the city of God? Make a renewed commitment to keep your compass pointing to God.*

FOR REFLECTION – alone or with a group

In recent years two things have renewed my faith: one was the gift of experiencing God through working with Christian Aid; the other was to be diagnosed with cancer of the lymph system and given only a few years to live.

- What are the experiences of renewal which you want to share?
- What might help to give your faith fresh impetus?
- Are you being called to a new kind of service in church or community?
- Is it time to change your lifestyle, your commitment, or even your job?

FOR ACTION

Find out about something new to you, for example: Christian Aid, a training course, a prayer group, or a Bible study group... something which might give your Christian life fresh impetus.

KEY WORDS OF FAITH
1. You are called

Notes based on the Revised English Bible by
Israel Selvanayagam

Israel Selvanayagam, a presbyter of the Church of South India who taught Religions, Mission and Inter-faith Dialogue at Tamilnadu Theological Seminary, Madurai, came to Britain in 1996 as a mission partner through the Methodist World Church in Britain Partnership. He now teaches at Wesley College, Bristol and Queen's College, Birmingham (UK). He has written several books and articles both in English and Tamil.

The most distinctive feature of the biblical faith is the call of a community to be 'partners in mission' with God. There is no job description but a challenge to be ready for unpredictable 'calls within the call'. There are moments of uncertainty and even despair, but there is no situation from which God isolates himself. We cannot expect success but we can rely on God's faithfulness. Even when there are overwhelming achievements we can only say, 'We have done our duty'. Whether we fall or stand, die or live, nothing is of greater worth than the assurance that we belong to God in a special way.

Sunday February 13   *2 Kings 5.1-14**
Called to be a witness

Think of the unnamed slave in Naaman's house: a young captive, Israelite girl. Her future looks grim, but she has not forgotten her roots. She remembers that her community is called to be a blessing to the world. She knows that her improved status in Naaman's household does not justify the ruthlessness of taking innocent people captive. Yet when the situation arises, her compassion crosses boundaries of age, gender and social standing. She introduces a prophet of her homeland who can heal her master. A slave girl's insignificant act moves courts and connects kings. Naaman is directed to wash seven times in the Jordan, the little river associated with the exodus of Israel.

The most authentic bearers of the gospel are not those in authority, but the powerless. Christian mission which was carried out purely for commercial, colonial interests met with little or no success. Today there is a new understanding: those who have suffered oppression and untouchability, and who have come to know God as One who is in solidarity with them, have come forward to proclaim the gospel of repentance and forgiveness. They call the Naamans of today to come down to the level of Jordan where they can meet the victims of injustice and the Son of Man who is in solidarity with them.

＊ *Compassionate God, who is in solidarity with us,*
let our present situation not deter us from extending
compassion
to those in authority over us. Give us courage
to tell them that their healing lies in their coming down
to the level of the weak and the vulnerable. Amen

Monday February 14   *Jeremiah 1.4-19*

Called to transform

Do vision and wisdom only come when we are old? Jeremiah seems to challenge conventional thinking. While he was still a young man God called him to be a prophet. The touch of God's word makes someone prophetic. God makes him or her 'a fortified city, an iron pillar...', and gives authority over nations and kingdoms 'to uproot and to pull down...to build and to plant'. The task is enormous but God's abiding presence will not fail.

There were times when Jeremiah doubted this (Jeremiah 15.18). But Jeremiah's political involvement never stopped. He reminds us that we have a right to question God's presence only when we are actively involved in fulfilling God's will.

God is calling us today to participate in his transforming mission. As we read in the Hebrew Scripture, Yahweh, at first understood as a tribal deity, was gradually perceived to be God of all. There is nothing wrong with this, but it is misleading to think of God as an abstract category with universal significance. The God who appeared on Mount Sinai has to be seen on our own mountains and hills. This universal God needs to be 'localized': as he called prophets like Jeremiah he calls each of us to a special task. Where oppression and injustice continue, where political systems manipulate people's emotion, where bureaucracy is corrupt and indifferent, and where people lock themselves behind closed doors – the process of destroying and building, uprooting and planting, needs to continue.

✳ *Eternal Father and loving Mother,*
create in us a new heart and mind to discern your will.
Prevent us from opting out of your mission
from lack of strength and other reasons.
Let us see you as the eternal 'I AM' in our own context,
and may every heart-beat become a living offering. Amen

Tuesday February 15   *Isaiah 43.1-7**

Called to move

People in exile are to return. They had struggled to settle down in a strange place, and now feel more familiar with the local culture; local contacts and relationships are well established. To stay in Babylon looks more attractive than the ruined city of Jerusalem. But there is a new call, a new opportunity. The people must get ready to return home and rebuild their community. There are rumours of many threats and hurdles on the way: attacks from enemies and dread of a tedious journey fill their minds. At this significant moment come God's comforting words. As their Creator, he tells them how precious they are. As long as God is with them there is nothing to fear.

After a spell of despair God appears to be a comforting Mother. She embraces us, and nurtures new life and courage within us. God's promise to be with us is not for living a comfortable and complacent life. The words 'have no fear' always come with power when we face a new challenge. These are not magical words to be recited irrespective of call and commitment. God's word is 'a lamp to (our) feet, light on (our) path' (Psalm 119.105). Its power and meaning are realized when we venture out in new ways as individuals and together in community.

✳ *Gracious God, let your words comfort and strengthen us*
so that we may prepare ourselves to make new beginnings.

Wednesday February 16   *Acts 26.4-18*

Called to tell our story

On trial before a king, Paul tells his story. He was a devout Jew and a Pharisee. Intense religiosity had made him a fanatic. It was so fulfilling to be authorized to arrest Christians and send them to prison. On his way to Damascus he was struck by a brilliant light. The voice he heard was penetrating, and he realized that the risen One was suffering in solidarity with his followers. It was not a startling message for a learned Jew, for in his own tradition was the vision of God identifying with a suffering, vulnerable community, and leading them to a new life. What is new, however, is the opening up of a way through faith in Christ for Gentiles to join the commonwealth of the people of God.

Each of us has a story to tell. It may not be dramatic, but it has meaning and significance, and particular turning points. There may even be a conversion of a distinctive nature. Paul's conversion was not so much from one religion to another as from a limited understanding of God to a more inclusive one. Our story may be from denominationalism to ecumenism; from an experience of untouchabilty to human dignity; or from an individualistic notion of salvation to a holistic vision. It is important to tell our stories.

✳ *Loving God, where we need to be silent make us silent and when we need to speak let us speak.*
Let our words spring from the depth of our being with honesty and integrity. Amen

Thursday February 17   *1 Timothy 1.12-19*
Called to celebrate

Paul gives thanks for what Christ had done for him and the grace lavished upon him. Hence the saying which merits full acceptance: 'Christ Jesus came into the world to save sinners'. The extraordinary humility of the saint makes him say that Christ comes first. If such a sinner as Paul could be saved, no one can be disqualified from new life in Christ. He addresses Timothy, a young Christian, asking him to 'fight the good fight with faith and a clear conscience'.

One of the tendencies in religious life is to measure everything by our own standard. We cannot love the most unlovable, and we think God stipulates the conditions on which people may enjoy his presence. So in persistent prayer we try to attract God's attention, like those Hindus who burst fire-crackers to wake up their deity, or like Christians shouting in the name of revival who appear to Hindus as nothing more than verbal crackers to wake up our Lord! Lifting up our 'begging bowls' becomes the major element of our prayer and worship, not realizing that this in fact undermines the grace of God that has been lavished upon us through Christ. In Christ God has accepted all human beings in spite of their 'unacceptability'. The most authentic Christian worship is to celebrate this grace and then to go out and call others to realize it.

Lord God, in Christ you call our name,
  And then receive us as your own,
Not through some merit, right or claim,
  But by your gracious love alone;
We strain to glimpse your mercy-seat,
And find you kneeling at our feet.

Brian Wren
© Stainer & Bell

Friday February 18   Hebrews 11.7-16

Called to act in faith

The author of Hebrews speaks of those in whom he recognized faith, rather like Jesus who recognized faith in the extraordinary qualities he found in certain individuals, within his own religious tradition as well as outside. Faith is the ability to transcend existing norms and ideas, daring to do something extraordinary, like the four men who opened the roof of a house to bring a paralysed man to Jesus, the woman who touched his garment in a crowd, the centurion who expressed his unworthiness to receive him in his house, the Samaritan who returned to thank him for healing him of leprosy... Jesus spoke of the minute 'mustard-seed' measure of faith which can move mountains.

Adherence to a set of beliefs and attachment to a particular denomination should not be confused with faith. They can either help or hinder faith according to whether they can transcend the status quo to change the present situation. It is by faith that we cross over caste structures and denounce untouchability. It is by faith that we struggle for equal rights for women and for the rights of children. It is by faith that we disturb the complacency of those who have no regard for the earth's limited resources. It is by faith that we challenge the lifestyle and attitude of the class-conscious and racially prejudiced. It is by faith that we speak out when others remain silent.

Eternal God, increase our faith so that, in the face of injustice,
we may distinguish tolerance from passiveness.
Strengthen our inner being so that we may not fear the threats
of those who expect uncritical loyalty and humble submission.
Make the Church a community of faith,
always ready to take radical steps forward
on our journey with you to heal your creation. Amen

Called to run and win

To engage, by faith, in God's mission, requires ongoing training and discipline as it does for those who run the Olympics. For Paul, discipline included conscious control of the body which can be carried away by unhealthy attractions. Paul was careful about this. Otherwise, as he rightly feared, his preaching would have been less effective.

The race we run is more like a relay race and every member of the World Church takes part. The problem is that some Christians seek popularity by using the manipulative techniques of secular commerce. This results in the development of sectarian groups which seriously damage Christian witness.

Sport is often exploited for commercial gain, but it is a gift of God. In this context, the Church is called to set a different model, a new quality of participation, not pushing co-runners aside but, with personal and collective discipline, having our minds fixed on the unfading prize promised by our eternal God.

✴ *Living God, give us love in our hearts,*
patience in our hearing and discernment of mind.
And let us reserve a smile and our teardrops
to offer to you at the end of the day.
Whether we win or fail, let us share together
and show the world that we are your children,
through Jesus Christ who has already run the race
and is waiting to share the prize with us. Amen

FOR REFLECTION – alone or with a group

● Every local congregation is called to witness to the gospel.
  To be effective, what kind of changes do you think are needed in the structure and life of your local congregation?
● Identify local community issues which your church needs to take seriously. Consider ways in which you can address them as individuals and church groups.

FOR ACTION

Prepare a tract describing things that have to be uprooted and things to be planted, things that have to be destroyed and things which need to be constructed. Consider the possibility of publishing it and of contacting those who may be able to work with you for change.

KEY WORDS OF FAITH
2. You are forgiven

Notes based on the Revised English Bible by
Salvador T Martinez

Salvador T Martinez teaches theology and ethics at McGilvary Faculty of Theology, Payap University in Chiang Mai, Thailand. He is a minister of the United Church of Christ in the Philippines, an international associate of the Common Global Ministries Board and director of the Programme for Theology and Cultures in Asia (PTCA).

The Swedish statesman, Dag Hammarskjöld (in *Markings, Night is Drawing Nigh, 1963),* wrote, '"To forgive oneself?" No, that doesn't work: we have to be forgiven. But we can only believe this is possible if we ourselves can forgive.' There is nothing harder for a human being than to forgive others. Only God can forgive completely, and the grace to forgive is a divine gift.

If we receive God's forgiveness with genuine thanksgiving, then we will respond by forgiving and showing mercy to others. So we can be sure that we are forgiven when we forgive those who have wronged us. In the parable of the unforgiving servant (Matthew 18.23-35), our Lord spoke of the master who said in anger, 'You scoundrel! I cancelled the whole of your debt when you appealed to me; ought you not to have shown mercy to your fellow servant just as I showed mercy to you?'

Sunday February 20   *Isaiah 43.18-25**
The meaning of forgiveness
After the sufferings of exile in the sixth century BC, God was about to do something new. Through the prophet, he points to the people's failure to call upon God, to bring whole-offerings to God, or to honour God with sacrifices and aromatic cane. God was burdened with their sin and wearied with their crimes. It was not really that Israel did not offer sacrifices and worship to God, but that their worship and sacrifices were unacceptable, because God's ethical demands were never met (cf. Amos 5.21-24). Yet after 40 years of exile in Babylon, God is ready to act with justice and mercy toward Israel. The 'I am God' (REB) – the only true God (verse 12) – out of his own initiative and unmerited grace, wipes out Israel's transgression and remembers its sins no more.

There is no limit to God's forgiveness. Even the unforgivable sin of which Jesus spoke in Mark 3.29, is only unforgivable to the extent that the sinner prevents God from reaching him.

Are you able to forgive and forget? True forgiveness harbours no resentment or bitterness.

✳ *O God, grant me the willingness to forgive
and the grace to forget.*

The effect of forgiveness

The psalmist prays for healing from a serious illness which has caused much comment from his friends. As he sees it, the sins which cause sickness are endemic in the world and society as a whole. The power of evil over human life is considerable.

There are still many who believe that sin and sickness are interrelated. This is true among the people who live with HIV-AIDS in Chiang Mai. For those who suffer, this results in low self-esteem and in being rejected by their families. In situations like this self-acceptance, family concern and community under-standing are the most effective ways of coping, and are channels of healing.

The psalmist expresses acceptance: 'I know that you delight in me', and 'I am upheld by you because of my innocence you keep me for ever in your presence.' He asks for God's forgiveness (verse 10) that he might be fully restored. Holistic healing comes through both human and divine forgiveness. As doctors acknowledge today, complete and true healing is the healing of the whole person.

✳ *O great God, forgive me all my guilt
that I may be whole again.*

The power of forgiveness

With which of the characters in the story of the healing of the paralysed man do you identify? Do you identify with the crowd who blocked the way to Jesus; the four friends of the paralytic who carried him and lowered him to Jesus; the scribes who cast doubt on the power of Jesus to forgive sin; or the paralysed man himself? One wonders what this man thought before and after Jesus healed him. Jesus saw his friends' faith. Most surely the paralytic also had faith. Like the Psalmist in the previous reading, he was healed because he found peace with God.

The theologian Paul Tillich, in a sermon, spoke of times when one is in pain and deep despair and hears a voice saying, 'You are accepted. You are accepted, accepted by that which is greater than you, and the name of which you do not know... Simply accept the fact that you are accepted.' At that very moment, transformation occurs. Tillich did not talk specifically about 'forgiveness' in that sermon, but surely this must be what happens at the moment of forgiveness!

✴ *O Redeemer God, help me to accept the fact that I am accepted.*

Wednesday February 23   *2 Corinthians 5.11-21*
The witness of forgiveness
There is a ceremony performed by the people of Thailand called *sukwan. Kwan* is the spirit or principle of life that dwells in all living things, especially the human being. It is believed that, as long as a person is well and healthy, the *kwan* remains in him, but it could be lost, or may flee, when a person is sick or in deep trouble. Hence the elaborate ceremony of *sukwan* is performed to bring the spirit back. It is also performed to bring people into unity with the community and the cosmos.

Some Thai Christians advocate the use of this ritual in pastoral counselling. There may be a huge leap from belief in *sukwan* to faith in Christ, but the idea that a person has been alienated from something, and needs to be reunited with it, has much in common with the Christian understanding of reconciliation. In the context of *sukwan,* one may better understand one's need to 'be reconciled with God'.

As a person who emerges from the *sukwan* is believed to be whole again, one who is reconciled to God in Christ is a new creation and becomes a witness of reconciliation (verses 17-19).

✴ *O great Reconciler,*
help me to be a worthy witness to your forgiveness.

Thursday February 24   *Romans 4.1-12*
The gift of forgiveness
Circumcision was fundamental to the faith of Abraham. Nevertheless, we are successors to Abraham not on the basis of the ritual but on the strength of his faith. Though he fulfilled the

rite, the quality of his relationship with God rested on his faith, 'and that faith was counted to him as righteousness' (verse 3b). This means a complete writing off of former sin to 'justify', to attribute innocence to those who put their faith in Christ. Justification comes not from evaluation of human merit but by forgiveness. A person is justified 'whose lawless deeds are forgiven' and 'whose sins are blotted out'.

Circumcision for Abraham was a seal of his faith. All who are truly regenerated and justified have such a seal. 'Faith,' Ernst Käsemann wrote in *New Testament Theology,* 'is the living out of the word which bears witness to his Lordship, nothing more, nothing less.'

✷ *O merciful God, help me to live a life worthy of your Lordship.*

Friday February 25   *2 Corinthians 1.18-22**
The seal of forgiveness
There are several words in the Thai language compounded with *jy,* the word for 'heart'. *Jydii* means to be kind-hearted. To be *jydiaw* is to be faithful (especially in love), and to be *jyboon* is to be pious or generous. Some words express negative characteristics, such as *jysaam,* to be vile or immoral; *jydam* is to be unscrupulous or mean, and *jykhod* to be crooked or dishonest. There are also neutral words, like *khawjy* which means to understand, *congjy* to deliberate and *diijy* to be happy. *Klabjy,* forgiveness, literally means 'to return heart'. Hence to repent and be forgiven is to purify and renew the heart.

Paul, in today's reading, wrote 'it is God who has set his seal upon us and, as a pledge of what is to come, has given the Spirit to dwell in our hearts.' The Thai *klabjy* – 'to return heart' or 'have a change of heart' expresses so beautifully what Paul is trying to convey.

✷ *Creator God,*
create in me a new heart where your Spirit may dwell.

Saturday February 26   *John 8.1-11*
The life of forgiveness
The story of the adulterous woman, although it is not found in the oldest and best Johannine manuscripts, is a very moving illustration of the teaching of Jesus that no one is qualified on the basis of his own righteousness to condemn another (cf. Matthew

7.3-5). If judged by God's standard, all are guilty and in need of God's forgiveness (Matthew 5.27-28).

The story is also a poignant illustration of how women were oppressed and discriminated against in Jewish society in the time of our Lord. For the crime for which this woman is being tried, the law requires that the man involved must also be tried and stoned to death if found guilty (cf. Deuteronomy 22.22; Leviticus 20.10). So what the scribes and Pharisees were doing here was a misapplication of the law.

There are countless cases of inhuman treatment of women today. In Asia, especially, women are exploited, abused, ostracized, oppressed and discriminated against. Jesus, on the other hand, respected the dignity and value of every person, regardless of gender.

'Where are they? Has no one condemned you?' She answered, 'No one, sir.' 'Neither do I condemn you.' And with forgiveness came a new beginning. After the woman was set free, Jesus said, 'Go; do not sin again.'

✳ *O God of all, show me how to make new beginnings.*

FOR REFLECTION – alone or in a group

● Think of all the people who have wronged you. Are you able to forgive and forget? What are the difficulties, and how can they be overcome?

● In our global village, many poor nations owe large debts to rich countries and the high rates of interest are crippling their economies. How do you respond to the campaigning of *Jubilee 2000* for the cancellation of the debts of the poorest countries of the world?

FOR ACTION

If you have not already done so, write to the leaders of the rich nations to express support for the remitting of the debts of the poorest countries. Encourage others to do so as well.

KEY WORDS OF FAITH
3. You are loved

Notes based on the New Revised Standard Version by
Pauline Webb

Pauline Webb grew up in a Methodist manse. From her early childhood she learned how to adapt to many different environments and yet to feel secure in the circle of a stable and loving family. In her adult life she has travelled widely in the service of the Methodist Church, of the World Council of Churches and of the BBC World Service. In retirement she lives alone in North London and looks on her local, multi-racial Methodist church as a constantly supportive family.

'Love' is one of the most difficult words to define. Most of us first experience it in the life of the family where, if we are fortunate, we are surrounded by the unconditional love of good parents. As our circle widens, we learn to value the love of friends as well as family. In our most intimate relationships we discover that love demands costly commitment. The Bible uses all these experiences of human love as mirrors of God's love for us.

Sunday February 27   *Hosea 2.14-20**
God's marriage vow

Even an unhappy marriage becomes for the prophet Hosea a lesson in what true love can mean. The unfaithfulness of Hosea's wife and his desire to punish her had been the theme of the first part of chapter 2. There he had compared his own anger to God's judgement against his unfaithful people. But here at verse 14 he sounds a new note, his longing for reconciliation. He recalls the Exodus when God had led his people in love out through a wilderness to the promised land. On the way there, even the place of their secret sinfulness (the valley of Achor, where some had tried to conceal the booty they had secreted away from Egypt) had become a place which opened up the new possibility of a restored relationship. God's love, expressed in his covenant with his people, is as close a bond as the marriage vow, a steadfast love which not only judges infidelity but also comes to the rescue of the unfaithful beloved. 'For better for worse, for richer for poorer, in sickness and in health', God's covenant love for us remains constant.

* *Lord, teach us the constancy of your love,
that we might be as generous in forgiving others
as you are in forgiving our unfaithfulness to you.*

Monday February 28　　　　　　　　　　　　　　*Hosea 11.1-9*

God's parental love

One of the most memorable television advertisements showed a small boy learning to ride a bike. 'Don't let go, Daddy!' he shouted as his father pushed him off down the path. Then came the magic moment when he realized he was riding alone, whilst his father watched proudly on, arms outstretched, still ready to catch him if he fell. That's something like the picture Hosea draws here of God's care for us being like that of a proud and protective parent.

The father knows the dangers that lie ahead. The children are so often wayward and head off in the wrong direction refusing to turn back into the safe embrace of the father's love. But, unlike some human fathers, God cannot give up on his children. They may have to experience his judgement against them by suffering the effects of their own wrongdoing, but there is always the promise that the father's love is waiting and willing for them to return. 'Return to God: rejoice in hope!' was the theme of the World Council of Churches' Assembly at the end of 1998. God loves us and lets us go; but when we fall, he is there to pick us up again.

* *Lord, we thank you for the cords of human kindness
that controlled us when we were small.
Help us now that we are grown
to trust in the love that still binds us to you
however far we have wandered. Amen*

Tuesday February 29　　　　　　　　　　　　　*Psalm 103.1-13, 22**

A list of love

'Count your blessings', ran the old gospel song. Here the psalmist seems to be doing just that. He recalls how God's love has surrounded him through all the days of his life, the bad days as well as the good ones. But he is not thinking only of the personal blessings that have been bestowed upon him. He recalls how God has blessed the whole nation and particularly has taken up the cause of the oppressed. God's love for the world is as undiscriminating as a father's love for a large and growing family. His love never depends upon our worth but upon the fact that we are his children, all of us, good and bad, strong and frail. As you read through the whole psalm it seems to swell into a great chorus of praise, as though the whole orchestra of creation joins in, but it ends again on the deeply personal note, 'Bless the Lord, O my soul!' In one of her most moving poems, Elizabeth Jennings writes:

'I count the moments of my mercies up,
I make a list of love and find it full.
I do all this before I fall asleep.'

✳ *Read verses 3-6 again, and match each of them with some memory from your own experience for which you can give thanks to God.*

Wednesday March 1   *Mark 2.13-22**
Choosing friends to love
'Friends are the family we choose for ourselves', wrote the journalist Jill Tweedie. In today's passage we see how Jesus chose his friends. Levi may have become one of the twelve disciples, known here by another name, but it seems more likely that he is one of many more than the twelve who heard Christ's call and followed him. The test of discipleship was obviously not one of worth or of respectability in human eyes. Jesus deliberately sought out and enjoyed the hospitality of those who were regarded by others as outsiders. It would have been easier to have stayed within the circle of people whose upbringing and outlook were the same as his own, but Jesus was always ready to make new ventures in friendship and to share a lifestyle which could include feasting as well as fasting.

How many of our friends come from circles or cultures different from our own, and how often do we share their hospitality? There is nothing like enjoying a good meal together that crosses cultural boundaries for strengthening a sense of fellowship. We who live in multi-racial communities discover this to our great enrichment!

✳ *Holding the fingers of your left hand, name five friends for whom today you want to pray. Then, holding the fingers of your right hand, name five people beyond your immediate circle of friends whose needs you can also make the subject of your prayers.*

Thursday March 2   *Mark 5.21-34*
Love in the crowd
Those of us who live alone know how, paradoxically, one feels most alone when surrounded by a crowd of people. In today's

reading, two people push themselves through the crowd in order to get as close as they can to Jesus, knowing that love radiates from his very presence. Both of them are rewarded by an immediate response from Jesus. It makes no difference to him that one of them is an important religious leader and the other an anonymous woman. All that matters to him is that they are both in urgent need of his love at that moment. So their need takes priority over every other concern.

We rarely know when we are in a crowd what needs there are around us. But how heart-warming it is to see a person who pauses to help another with heavy luggage, or to give clear directions to a stranger. Jesus was so sensitive to human need that even the slightest touch on his robe stirred his compassion.

Let us pray that we might never allow the press of daily business to crowd out of our lives our concern for others.

✳ *Where cross the crowded ways of life,*
    Where sound the cries of race and clan,
Above the noise of selfish strife,
    We hear Thy voice, O Son of man.

                         Frank Mason North (1850-1935)

Women's World Day of Prayer, March 3   *Mark 5.35-43*

Talitha cumi! Little lamb, get up!

Today, these two simple Aramaic words will be resounding round the world. They are the theme of the **Women's World Day of Prayer.** This year the women of Indonesia, by choosing this passage, are reminding us that the love of Jesus reached out in compassion to heal the grief of parents who thought they had lost a child. In a world where such loss is all too common, we are bidden to pray with and for all parents who are anxious about their youngsters. The use of the simple Aramaic words brings added immediacy and intimacy to the story. We all need to hear in our own language the assurance of Christ's power, not only to heal, but to raise up even those whom we have regarded as dead.

Let us join our prayers today with women as they gather in churches and cathedrals in all five continents to hear again the good news of the love of Jesus, who can heal the sick and raise the dead. With them let us rejoice that today:

✳ *As o'er each continent and island*
    The dawn leads on another day,
The voice of prayer is never silent,
    Nor dies the strain of praise away. *John Ellerton (1826-93)*

Living letters

Living Letters is the title of a book published by the World Council of Churches at the end of the Churches Decade in Solidarity with Women. It tells the story of the visits made during the decade by teams of women and men to churches across the world. Their concern was to find out more about the role and work of women. They uncovered some shocking instances of violence and abuse, both domestic and public. Their main aim, however, was not just exposure of evil, but to give assurance to women across the world of the love God has given us for one another, a love best expressed through our lives. So the visitors were not only 'living letters'. They were 'love letters' too.

Letter-writing is going out of fashion. The speed of e-mail and the immediacy of faxes means that many of us rarely put pen to paper these days. But we can all be 'love letters'. God has entrusted his message of love to us. We must not fail to deliver it.

✳ *God of the covenant,*
who has written your law of love in our hearts,
may it be so engraven upon our lives
that we shall become living letters
of that love for all with whom we come into contact.
For the sake of Jesus Christ our Lord. Amen

FOR REFLECTION – alone or with a group

● How would you define the word 'love'? The Greeks had three words for it – distinguishing between divine love, filial affection and sexual desire. How many words would you equate with love?

● What would be your criteria for choosing friends? How did you come to know those friends who are closest to you now?

● 'The opposite of love is not hate but fear'. How far can love cast out fear and how can hate be turned into love?

KEY WORDS OF FAITH
4. You are changed

Notes based on the Revised English Bible by
Edmund Banyard

Edmund Banyard is a minister and former Moderator of the General Assembly of the United Reformed Church. He is a committed ecumenist and currently edits 'All Year Round' for the Council of Churches for Britain and Ireland.

It is possible for us to fill all our waking hours with activity and give little thought to anything beyond the immediate requirements of everyday living. This can go on for years, in some cases for a whole lifetime. Each of our readings this week, however, probes deeper into what life is all about. In different ways they remind us that life is a drama played on a world stage, and that we are not spectators but actors with significant parts to play.

Sunday March 5   *Joel 2.1-2, 12-17**
Facing up to evil in the community
Ordinary, decent people may well know that there are things badly wrong in the life of their nation and yet fail to face the fact that they ought to get involved in trying to put those wrongs to rights. To some of these who were all too liable to say, 'God will put it right when the Day of the Lord comes,' Joel cries out (in verses 11-13), that 'the day of the Lord' will be a terrible day for them...unless they repent. And he adds, 'Rend your hearts and not your garments.'

Ezra tore his robes (Ezra 9.3) when he learned of certain practices. The High Priest tore his robes (Mark 14.63) when Jesus was convicted of blasphemy. In each case they were deploring the actions of others with a certain smug self-righteousness. But the image of rending the heart means acknowledging some responsibility for what is happening and an awareness of the need for penitence.

✻ *Lord, do not allow us to forget*
   that we share the blame
   for evils in the life of our community
   however much we deplore them.
   Help us so to live out our faith

in the everyday world
that we are involved in striving for what is good
and contending with what is evil,
for your name's sake.

Monday March 6   *Psalm 51.1-17**

Facing up to our own faults

This is an intensely personal cry of one whose very closeness to God makes him all the more aware of his failures. Centuries later Paul was to write, 'The good which I want to do, I fail to do; but what I do is the wrong which is against my will' (Romans 7.19). We all fall far short even of the good we recognize. The wonder is that God does not abandon us. John Newton, when very near the end of his life, is reputed to have said to a visitor, 'My memory is almost gone, but I remember two things, that I am a great sinner and that Christ is a great Saviour.'

This facing up to how far we fall is not meant to inhibit or in any way cripple us. With the plea for forgiveness goes the cry, 'Lord, open my lips, that my mouth may proclaim your praise' (verse 15). We acknowledge our need in the confidence that God will welcome us as the Father welcomed back his lost son (Luke 15.11-32). We rise from confession freed from the burden, that we may go out and live to the full the life to which God calls us.

✴ *God, be gracious to me.*
Blot out my misdeeds
and give me a new and steadfast spirit.
Lord, open my lips,
that my mouth may proclaim your praise.

Tuesday March 7   *Matthew 23.23-28*

Keeping within the law is not enough

In the everyday world the law is our safeguard. It provides a framework for a great variety of people to live peaceably together. It is to the law we can appeal if we believe that we have been wronged. Of course the law isn't perfect and it is constantly being amended to meet new situations or correct abuses, not least because there are always those who will seek ways of keeping within the letter of the law whilst avoiding its intentions.

In this passage Jesus roundly condemns those who use God's law in this way; who manage to hold to the letter and ignore the spirit. What God requires is not a fine legal argument, but true justice, mercy, and good faith. Living by certain rules – imagining that this is all that is required of us – is not good enough, and it is a danger of which Christians must always be aware.

✳ *Lord, never allow us to forget the law which is above all others,*
the law that requires of us that we should strive to love you
and the people around about us
with all our heart and soul and mind and strength.

Ash Wednesday, March 8   *Isaiah 58.1-12**
The offering of worship is not enough
Yesterday we were thinking of the things Jesus had to say about hypocrisy; about people who scrupulously lived by a set of rules which they claimed were given by God, whilst completely ignoring the intention behind those rules. Today we find Isaiah declaring that God takes no delight in worship unless the worshippers are also doing the work of the Almighty in the world beyond the church.

Instead of organizing special services and fast days, he cries: stand out against injustice, feed the hungry, provide shelter for the homeless, find clothing for the impoverished. Isaiah goes on to say, 'If you satisfy the needs of the wretched, then light will rise for you out of darkness.' That is, if we seriously attend to the needs of those who have in one way or another missed out in life, they will not be the only ones to benefit: the lives of all of us will be the richer.

✳ *Lord, help us to see more clearly*
what should be the priorities in our living.
We pray that as we worship
you will renew our vitality,
strengthen our sense of commitment,
and give us grace to follow wherever you may lead.

Thursday March 9   *2 Corinthians 5.20b-6.10**
Not burdens, but joy
What a catalogue of sufferings Paul sets out here and yet what a triumphant note he strikes. Verse 9 in particular is magnificent: 'In

our sorrows we have always cause for joy... penniless, we own the world!' How are we to understand this apparently impossible claim? There are some who 'own' great estates yet hardly ever see them; who 'own' great wealth yet get very little joy from it. Paul on the other hand speaks as one who sees everything as belonging to God and so to be enjoyed; every day as a gift of God to be offered back to him with delight.

If I can enjoy a walk in the countryside, or the riches of an art gallery, those experiences are mine and cannot be taken from me. 'Ownership' as generally understood only adds burdens of worry. The key to it all, Paul declares, is being reconciled to God and seeing life both as his gift and as a great opportunity to share in his work.

✳ *Lord, help us to value the riches that are ours,*
to realize how many and great are our blessings;
above all help us to value that greatest blessing,
your love to hold us
and your work to give our lives meaning and purpose.

Friday March 10   *Philippians 3.1-11*

The joyous hope

Paul had it made for him from the beginning. Being born a Roman citizen gave him considerable privileges, and in addition he had been born into the elite of his own nation. As he grew to manhood, his knowledge of and his zeal for his faith soon marked him out as one who would go far. Yet, as he cries out in this passage, he gladly forfeited everything to follow Christ. These were no empty words. His life as a Christian was one of appalling hardships yet he brushes them aside; they are nothing compared with 'gaining Christ'. And whilst he speaks here of the great future hope of sharing in the resurrection of the dead, we must not separate this from the exhilaration expressed in yesterday's passage where he declared that we always have cause for joy – that the world is ours!

✳ *Beyond the ups and downs of daily life,*
help us, Lord, to see
and to grasp
the joyful hope which flows
from the life you give
and which nothing can destroy.

The ultimate experience

This week our title has been 'You are changed', yet here we are finishing on an appeal to be changed. In John Bunyan's great book, *The Pilgrim's Progress,* Pilgrim is a changed man from the time he sets out on his journey, yet all along the way there are battles to be fought, times of failure as well as times of triumph. Changed as he is, the process will not be complete until he crosses the final river and enters the celestial city. So it is for us all. We are fallible pilgrims needing again and again to be reminded of our purpose and recalled to the path when we stray. Yet we are already changed if we have set our feet in the way, if our hope is in our Lord and we see as our goal the ultimate experience of knowing Christ as all in all.

✻ *Lord Jesus Christ, we thank you*
  that you meet us and accept us just as we are.
  In the security of the knowledge that we are already yours,
  help us to grow ever closer to you
  and give us grace to walk more surely in your ways.

FOR REFLECTION – alone or with a group

● Thinking back over what you have read this week how do you resolve the strange tensions in the gospel message? We are called, yet still need to be on our toes, listening for the call that is to come. We are forgiven, yet we know that we still need to seek forgiveness. We are changed, yet need to be ready for further changes.

● Can you identify with Paul's cry, 'Penniless, we own the world'?

LENT – READINGS FROM JOHN
1. Love, light and darkness

Notes based on the New Revised Standard Version by
Clare Amos

Clare Amos, an Anglican, is editor of the ecumenical publication 'Partners in Learning' which provides resources for all-age worship and for Christian education. She has lived and worked in the Middle East.

'Little children, love one another.' There is a beautiful story told about John, the disciple of Jesus. He had been a bit of a fire-brand. Remember how, with his brother James, he wanted to 'call down fire' upon a Samaritan village that had turned its back on Jesus! Yet he had mellowed. He had moved to Ephesus, and was surrounded by the affection and respect of the Christian community there. He had discovered for himself that only one thing really mattered, and that was love. So day by day, he would murmur, 'Little children love one another, love one another...' It was as though his whole being had been consumed and turned into a beacon of God's love.

We cannot be completely sure who was the author of 'The Gospel of John', but there seems to be a connection between the person referred to as 'the disciple whom Jesus loved' (13.23, 19.26, 20.2, 21.20) and the writer of this Gospel. It may be that they were one and the same. More likely, the writer was a younger friend or close companion of the 'disciple whom Jesus loved'. Tradition has long held that this beloved disciple was John the apostle. So in these notes we suggest that, even if the apostle John did not actually hold the pen that wrote the words, his is the vision that permeates this Gospel.

I also believe, however, that this Gospel was one of the last of the New Testament books to be written: perhaps at the very end of the first century AD. Its writer (to whom we will refer for the sake of convenience as John) was looking back at the ministry of Jesus. From his viewpoint, perhaps almost seventy years after Jesus' earthly life, John could realize more clearly the eternal significance of Jesus. He gives us a portrait of Jesus that takes us behind and beyond the other Gospels.

Tom Wright in his exquisite little book *Following Jesus* comments that John's Gospel 'takes us up (a)...mountain and says

to us, "Look – from here, on a clear day, you can see for ever.'"
During Lent we are joining John on his 'high mountain' and looking
at the story of Jesus through his eyes and in his own words.

1st Sunday of Lent, March 12   *John 1.1-18*

In the beginning...light

It took me a long time to understand. Jesus was my beloved
friend. He had chosen me, with my brother James, to journey with
him, even though I was young at the time. And when you are so
close to something or someone it *is* difficult to see things clearly.
Of course we always knew there was something special about
Jesus. We would be joking with him, or arguing among ourselves,
or trudging along weary or afraid. And then Jesus would do or say
something, and there would be a moment, a flash – you could call
it inspiration – and I would find myself looking at my friend
through new eyes, and wondering just who he really was.

You might have thought that his death would have settled it,
once and for all. But of course it didn't. And even after we saw
him again, we, his disciples, still couldn't agree: was he our
Messiah, was he a prophet, was he simply God's servant?

But for me it was that moment in the Upper Room when he
breathed upon us, and I suddenly felt alive as I had never done
before. There came into my mind the story of how our world
began, how God breathed upon the formless chaos, and gave life
and light to the world and its creatures. And I saw. I saw then the
true light that had burned first at creation's dawning. Dimmed
though it had been through the centuries since, it now shone out
again more brightly than ever, as it surrounded my friend and lit
up the room in which we were gathered.

They always said that no one could see God and live. Not
even Moses was able to see God's face clearly, though he caught
a glimpse. But when I saw the face of Jesus that day I saw God –
and I was given life that even death will not be able to take away.

✳ *Christ of God, Light of Lights,*
  who shone first in creation's dawning,
  shine in our hearts.

Monday March 13   *John 1.19-34*

Brighter than a shining lamp

Do you want to know how I first met Jesus? Some of the others
thought that it was by the Sea of Galilee, when he tugged at me

68

and my brother James so strongly that we instantly left the nets we were mending to join him. But I had met him before. I was one of those who followed John the Baptizer when he journeyed down from Galilee to the Jordan, preaching and telling people that they needed to make a new start in their lives. The Baptizer was a great man – a hero for a young enthusiast as I was then. He could see things so clearly. Everything was light or darkness for him; there were no shades of grey. He didn't have much time for social niceties, but then he was harder on himself than on the rest of us. He kept on saying that he wasn't the One we should be looking for and follow. There would be another who would come.

But I think that even he was taken aback when he first met Jesus. It was as though heaven itself was suddenly split open and a flash of light struck the earth, hiding Jesus from our eyes, and yet revealing him at the same time. I couldn't quite see whether John actually baptized Jesus or not – there has been so much debate about that ever since. But I knew then, as John himself did too, that in this man who stood before us radiated a light brighter than any lamp.

✳ *Christ of God, Sun of Righteousness,*
help us to realize your importance in our daily lives.

Tuesday March 14   *John 3.1-21*

The visitor in the night

Thomas and Simon and some of the others never really trusted Nicodemus. They wondered where his loyalties lay. Was he a spy for the High Priest? Why was it that he came to Jesus by night? If he really wanted to be a follower, surely he would have approached him openly by day? But I understood. It must have taken a great deal of courage for Nicodemus to visit Jesus – even at night. After all, it was just after Jesus had created that uproar in Jerusalem by turning the Temple upside down, and at Passover time. Jesus certainly wasn't the most popular person among Nicodemus' fellow members of the Jewish Council.

Jesus didn't go out of his way to set him at ease either. It was as though he was teasing Nicodemus, almost playing with words to discomfort him. I think Jesus probably enjoyed the fact that this great teacher of Israel was stumbling around in a kind of fog with so much still to learn. But I knew that deep down Jesus respected him and wanted Nicodemus to see things in a new light for himself. After all, if you think about it, when Jesus told him that people who do the truth come to the light, he actually included

Nicodemus among the truth-doers, because what had he done –
but seek out the light, Jesus himself! Nicodemus never saw
things in the same way again.

✽ *Christ of God, Teacher of your people,*
be gentle to those who approach you in the shadows of fear.

Wednesday March 15   *John 5.1-18*

Life to be lived

Sometimes these days the people that Jesus helped begin to blur
together in my imagination. There were so many of them, like this
man who had been lying for years by the great reservoirs in
Jerusalem, hoping to be cured. What I remember most clearly is
why Jesus healed people.

Yes, he was sorry for them, but it was more than that. He
wanted to show that God was God of life, of creativity, enabling
people to live their lives to their fullest potential. He wanted them
to be able to join in the excitement and struggle of real living. How
he annoyed the religious leaders by healing men and women,
and children too, on the Sabbath! But, as he said, the Sabbath
was the crown of God's creation, of God's gift of life to the world:
what better day than the Sabbath to expand the scope of the lives
of these human beings!

Of course he puzzled and annoyed people at the same time –
even some of those he healed. They didn't like being told to 'sin
no more'. Surely Jesus couldn't be suggesting that their sickness
was caused by sin? But Jesus knew that living life the way it
should be lived was a difficult business. When you have been ill
for years and years, and used to others doing things for you, it *is*
hard sometimes to take responsibility for yourself in the future
that you have been given.

✽ *Christ of God, Sabbath Breaker,*
do not cease from your work of creation in our lives.

Thursday March 16   *John 5.19-29*

Life through Jesus

Jesus feels so much a part of me that there are moments when
I'm not sure whether I am remembering his exact words or
hearing my own reflections on what he said. Quite often when he
had healed someone, he took us aside and tried to explain what it
meant. It was as though the miracle was an outer shell that

70

everyone could see and witness, but what was really important was on the inner layer.

When he healed the paralyzed man in Jerusalem, as you can imagine, the fact that it took place on the Sabbath was bad enough, but then he went on to defend what he had done by reminding people that God was still active in creation even on the Sabbath. It took people's breath away. What was he really saying? He talked to us his friends about it in private. In effect he was saying that he was like God, perhaps even *was* God himself – and that his actions mirrored those of the Almighty. That was the first time he dared say anything like that, and even some of us, his friends, were scandalized. If he had said it so directly in public he might have been lynched there and then. Living near Jesus was living rather close to the heat, and yet we also knew that if we turned our backs on him we would be turning away from life itself.

✳ *Christ of God, Son of the Father,*
   enable us to see through to your eternal truth.

Friday March 17   *John 7.1-13*

The city set on a hill

I always wondered what Jesus' brothers really thought about him. He couldn't have been the easiest person to have around when you were growing up. Of course they were proud of him. Who wouldn't have been? But we, Jesus' friends, weren't sure that they really understood him. And though James, Jesus' brother, later became leader of the Church in Jerusalem, I still sometimes doubt that he fully realized that Jesus was the One around whom history revolved and life itself depended. James always wanted to prove what a good Jew Jesus was, and he longed for the name of Jesus to be respected by the Jewish religious leaders. Somehow he couldn't see beyond that.

There was that time when the brothers wanted Jesus to travel up to Jerusalem for the Feast of Tabernacles. I suppose they thought that by staying in Galilee he was hiding his light under a bushel. Jerusalem was where the crowds were, and Jesus could make more of a stir there. After all, everyone went up to Jerusalem for the festival. It was the place where God's Temple was. It drew people from all over the world. It was a city set on a hill whose light couldn't be hidden. What the brothers didn't realize – and would have been horrified even to think of – was that when he finally came to Jerusalem Jesus actually replaced it in God's scheme of things. From then on it was the incarnate

Jesus, rather than Jerusalem the city, that was the point on our earth where the light of God shone strongest.

✳ *Christ of God, Divine Presence on earth,*
grant us grace to welcome you whenever you choose to
come.

Saturday March 18   *John 7.14-39*
Streams of living water

As a small boy I loved the Feast of Tabernacles – building our shelter out of branches, and all the fun of eating in it for the eight days of the feast. And I remember praying for rain – after the long dry months of summer when we were almost panting for water. In the Temple in Jerusalem on the last day of the Feast, they brought water from the Gihon spring at the foot of the hill, and poured it into the great bowl just outside the Temple building. It was a way of asking God to send rain, and a powerful reminder that life itself depended upon God, his presence and his power.

Some people thought Jesus was mad when he stood up and spoke of living water springing out of him. He was the spring on which life depended! But we who had travelled with Jesus knew something of what he meant. There was that woman we met in Samaria by a well and whose life Jesus turned upside down. She already knew the refreshment of soul and body that Jesus was offering to all. But a gift like that was costly to the giver: I don't think I fully understood the meaning of what Jesus was saying at the Feast of Tabernacles until that awful day, some months later, when I watched the soldier pierce Jesus' side with his spear and saw blood and water flow freely from his dying body.

✳ *Christ of God, Spring of living water,*
give us refreshment and peace.

FOR REFLECTION – alone or with a group

Imagine that you are one of the other people included in this week's readings. How would you describe your encounter with Jesus to your friends? In a group, share your reflections.

2nd Sunday of Lent, March 19   *John 8.12-30*
The light of the world

Jesus could really pierce you with that glance of his. Sometimes it was too painful to bear. I was with Peter that night at the High

Priest's house, when he said over and over again that he didn't know Jesus. And then the cock crew and Jesus looked straight at Peter. You felt that all the tears Peter shed then, and later, would never quite be able to extinguish the searing heat of Jesus' gaze.

Jesus often talked about light. But the time it made the most impact on me was one night in Jerusalem when the Feast of Tabernacles was coming to its close. The priests had lit all the immense golden candlesticks in the Temple courtyard, and the light from them seemed to be reflected through the whole of Jerusalem. It was a wonderful sight. But for those of us gathered round Jesus, an inner light that was brighter still seemed to shine from within him. You know, with those lamps in the Temple courtyard, people had to climb up ladders and kindle them. They couldn't set themselves alight! But with Jesus, you knew that the light came from within – it was as though he had created it himself. He *was* the light of the world. People really did judge themselves by their reaction to him. Were they willing to come and stand in the pool of light that surrounded Jesus, or did they want to scurry away to hide in the darkest corner?

✶ *Christ of God, luminous in the brightness of our night,*
   help us to reflect your face in our actions and our lives.

Monday March 20   *John 8.31-47*

The truth will set you free

Lots of stories are told about the strange circumstances of Jesus' birth – how he was born before Mary's marriage to Joseph; how he wasn't Joseph's son at all; how he wasn't born at the family home in Nazareth but in Bethlehem, the birthplace of ancient kings. Sometimes people got the details tangled, and couldn't see clearly what really mattered. Of course Jesus himself knew of the stories, and on more than one occasion the word 'bastard' was thrown at him. But he responded by pointing away from himself and his own personal circumstances towards God. He talked over and over again about God being his Father. And yet he also told us that we too could dare to call God 'Father', 'Abba', in that prayer that he taught us so long ago in Galilee, but which I still say every day of my life. Did he mean that God was his Father, his alone, in a unique and special way, or could we all claim to be sons and daughters of God? One thing I am sure of is that Jesus wanted us all to be free: free to be in relationship with God, to be like children of God's household of love, rather than being slaves to an arbitrary emperor.

When I think of how that war between the Jews and the Romans a few years ago brought slavery rather than freedom to the descendants of those to whom Jesus spoke, I weep still with frustration.

✳ *Christ of God, Seed of Abraham,*
welcome us into your Father's house.

Tuesday March 21   John 8.48-59

Before Abraham was, I am!

I am very old now. I hope the day will not be long delayed when I see Jesus again face to face. I know the stories they tell about me – how Jesus himself once said to me, when we met by the lakeside after his resurrection, that I would not die. But Jesus didn't say that – not exactly. He was teasing Peter at the time – Peter, who always wanted to get things organized, to keep tabs upon all of us. Peter was just a bit jealous of me, and of how close I was to Jesus.

But I can remember the day when Jesus did say that those who kept his word would not see death. It was in the Temple, during the Feast of Tabernacles. It was the day that they tried to stone Jesus. He had been talking about Abraham and asked the crowd whether they were really children of Abraham, believing in God's promises as Abraham had done. The crowd mocked Jesus, saying that Abraham had died, in spite of his faithfulness. Then Jesus stunned them by talking about how he, Jesus, had existed before Abraham was born. For an instant, there was silence and then the crowd raged threateningly. For Jesus had just claimed to be God, the 'I Am' of our Scriptures. At that moment he said it more clearly than he had ever done before.

I think that is what he meant when he talked about people not seeing death. God is eternal. God enfolds past, present and future in his arms. God is also the source of life and love. Those who place themselves close to the Father's heart are held in God's extravagant love that shatters the boundaries of time.

✳ *Christ of God, the 'I am who I am',*
grant us a spirit of wonder at your eternity.

Wednesday March 22   John 9.1-17

As long as day lasts

When Jesus gave sight to the blind man that day near the Pool of Siloam, I think he already knew the end of his life on earth was approaching. He had survived one attempt to stone him. There would surely be others. He talked about his time on earth as though it was 'day'. When he was finally put to death it would be night, the power of darkness. Perhaps that was why he healed the man on the Sabbath. Time was running out for the One who was bringing light to the world; he had to do his work whenever and wherever he could.

I was puzzled by the way in which Jesus chose to heal the man. He could have given him sight just by a simple word or a gesture – he did that at other times. Instead he used his own spittle, and moistened mud which he put on the man's eyes, and then told him to go and wash it off. Perhaps he was trying to show that his ministry of giving sight involved his whole self, and that those who wished to receive sight from him had also to play their part. Being able to see Jesus for who he really was, wasn't easy: so many people failed to do so during Jesus' life on earth: perhaps only those who knew the depth of their blindness cared enough to seek for sight.

✳ *Christ of God, Light-giver,*
remain with us throughout our days.

Thursday March 23   *John 9.18-41*
I was blind, but now I see
I reckon the man who was given sight by Jesus that day in Jerusalem was truly brave, certainly braver than many of us who called ourselves his friends. He had been blind all his life: yet the moment he could see, there he was proclaiming Jesus as a prophet and more before the Jewish Council. His parents didn't dare to do so: they were afraid of what the religious leaders might do to them. But there was no stopping the man: the more he was criticized and challenged for his views, the more openly he proclaimed Jesus. When they tried to get him to say that Jesus was a sinner, he really got annoyed. He wasn't having it! He knew what he owed to Jesus. I still remember and savour that moment when he asked them if they wanted to become disciples of Jesus as well. I thought the leader of the Pharisees would explode!

Afterwards Jesus said something rather odd – about those who didn't see now seeing, and those who thought they saw being blind. When he first spoke it, I think he had the Pharisees and others in mind: they were too sure of themselves to realize that they needed the gift of sight. But it is a word of Jesus that I have never forgotten; for we who are his friends must never be so blinkered that we cannot see new truths that God may be opening before our eyes.

✳ *Christ of God, Courage of the faithful,*
   grant us the strength to witness for you wherever we may be.

Friday March 24   *John 10.7-21*

That they may have life

It seemed strange to hear Jesus speaking about sheep and shepherds there in the Temple in Jerusalem. The only sheep around were the ones being prepared for sacrifice. Though perhaps it wasn't so strange after all: for it was only a few months afterwards that Jesus himself died in Jerusalem at the very moment that the Passover lambs were being slain.

But when he spoke about shepherds, wolves and sheep, I could see that in his mind's eye he was remembering the paths he had trudged with us around the hillsides of Galilee. Several times we came upon the mauled carcasses of sheep that shepherds had not managed to protect from marauding wolves. And then there was a shepherd who died trying to save his sheep when a pack of wolves suddenly came from nowhere in the middle of the night. I remember how quiet Jesus was when the villagers told us about that shepherd.

Yet we too were quiet when he spoke about shepherds in Jerusalem. I suppose, looking back, he had given us hints before about the fate that was likely to await him. But that day – it was so cold, in the middle of winter – was the first time he spoke to us clearly about his death. I shivered, and wondered if I would ever get warm again.

✳ *Christ of God, Lamb and Shepherd,*
   we give you thanks for your gift of abundant life.

Saturday March 25   *John 10.22-42*

The Father and I are one

It was as though a candle was burning down until there was only a tiny piece left. When it was extinguished we would be in darkness once more. I somehow knew there wasn't much more left for Jesus to do. He had healed the paralyzed, fed the hungry, given sight to the blind. Surely people could see – plainly – what had been done before their very eyes. Couldn't they perceive that only someone who intimately shared God's own creative power

76

would be able to work signs like these? What more did they expect him to do? Raise the dead?

Perhaps they were right. Jesus did talk in riddles – riddles that didn't make sense unless you stood close enough to him to be warmed by his love. You might have thought that when he started telling the religious leaders they too were gods, they would have felt flattered. I wondered what he was on about. Only afterwards, when I went back to the Scriptures, I realized Jesus had quoted from Psalm 82. And then I read these lines:

'They have neither knowledge nor understanding,
they walk around in darkness;
all the foundations of the earth are shaken' (Psalm 82.5).

Was Jesus trying to say that the light and love focused in him were like threads that wove creation itself together? If we choose to walk in darkness rather than seek the light of life, it is as though creation itself is beginning to unravel all around us.

✳ *Christ of God, Expression of the Father's love,*
weave your threads of light into our lives.

FOR REFLECTION and ACTION – alone or with a group

Begin to compile a list of images used in John's Gospel, and add to it in the next four weeks of Lent and Passiontide. Are there any images from contemporary life that Jesus might use? Reflect on the richness of meaning in each image.

LENT – READINGS FROM JOHN
2. Rejection and hope

Notes based on the Revised English Bible by
Jan S Pickard

Jan Sutch Pickard is a writer who worked for 15 years for the Methodist Church as editor of the magazines NOW and Connect, and then moved to the Isle of Iona as Deputy Warden of the Iona Community's work there.

The readings for the next two weeks are packed with the powerful imagery and themes of John's Gospel, such as light and darkness. The notes do not attempt to 'unpack' every passage, but to read it in the light of people's lives. During the first week, we focus on the people around Jesus, relating in different ways to what happened to Lazarus. During the second week the people are not biblical characters. All bar one lived in the 20th century – most died for their faith – all lived for what they believed in. All were motivated by love and a sense of justice. All experienced rejection – often violent – but held on to hope. They are worthy companions to Jesus on the Way of the Cross.

3rd Sunday of Lent, March 26   *John 11.1-16*
The doubts of the disciples
When a crisis happened to a group of people whom Jesus loved (Lazarus and family), he was too far away to respond quickly. We see the disciples, who had become part of his extended family, react in ways that show the complexity of the situation.

When he talks about going back across the Jordan into Judaea, they are anxious (verse 8). Political and religious controversy mean physical danger. When he gives, as a reason, the illness and death of Lazarus, they do not understand – they avoid the painful truth. When he puts it more plainly, and is clearly determined to go, Thomas is fatalistic (verse 16) – this can only end in their death too.

How do we respond to crisis? If, like the disciples, we show anxiety, a confusion that avoids the truth or a resignation that falls short of hope, then we are just behaving like most of our fellow human beings most of the time. Jesus came to show us a different way (verses 4,9,15). What are the key words here?

* *Living Lord, when the light fails, we stumble:*
  help us to overcome our doubt and fear,
  loving Lord. Amen

Monday March 27   *John 11.17-27*

The faith of Martha

If you were writing a card to someone recently bereaved, what would you say in it? Would you feel able to share your faith? What helps when words fail? Have you ever been encouraged, in a time of distress, by a gift of flowers, or by someone saying, I will light a candle'?

Martha and Mary had been waiting for Jesus. Instead, death came to their house; then the mourners. Four days later, the house was still full of folk. Martha refused to be a victim of this family tragedy. Her waiting was not passive. She went out to meet Jesus. She spoke with strong conviction: 'If you had been here my brother would not have died.' Do we hear this as a reproach, or simply a statement of what she believed with all her heart?

Read again verses 21-27. Mark the four strong statements that Martha makes, and the four strong statements with which Jesus responds, by reading them aloud, underlining or writing them down, by lighting candles or by putting flowers in a vase one by one.

* *Lord, in fear and hope, because we are human,*
  we wait for you.
  In our love and care for our sisters and brothers
  we meet you.
  In your promise, 'I am the resurrection and the life',
  we believe. Amen

Tuesday March 28   *John 11.28-37*

The tears of Mary

Draw the shape of a tear-drop. Write in it something or someone about which you feel anxious or sad.

Remember that – even when you feel helpless – that person, that situation, is in God's hands. Re-read verses 32-37.

Mary's words to Jesus are the same as Martha's first words (verse 21). This time they sound more hopeless. This time we are told that they are accompanied by tears. Who weeps?

Mary, the other mourners – and Jesus.

Why do you think Jesus wept? Look at verses 33 and 36. What emotions do people see in Jesus? Does this surprise you?

Some of the onlookers were surprised, because they remembered at least one miracle (verse 37) and thought that this time Jesus could have fended off mortality. But what they were now seeing was equally wonderful – the one who helped the blind to see is blinded by the tears of humanity. Jesus is moved by Lazarus' death and Mary's distress. He shares her tears, because he shares fully in what it means to be human.

✻ *In deep gratitude, offer to God what you have written, read and learned today.*

Wednesday March 29   *John 11.38-44*

The loosing of Lazarus

While these notes were being written, the news was full of distressing stories, of the discovery of mass graves in Kosovo, and then the aftermath of a hurricane in Central America. Television reports showed families who were being asked to identify the bodies of their loved ones. We pray that this will never happen to us. We shrink from the ugly physical realities of death. But in these verses Jesus brings into the open the thing we most fear. He tells the people gathered at the tomb to 'take away the stone' with which we hide our eyes from death.

Martha is grimly realistic – after four days the body will stink. How out-of-place it seems here for Jesus to speak of God's glory. When the stone is moved, he gives thanks to a God who is present even – or maybe most of all – at the graveside: present and listening to the fears and hopes of humanity.

And, from the other side of death, Lazarus hears his name called and returns to the land of the living. God still has work for him to do. Jesus sets him free to do it.

✻ *God with us, when we need you most,*
  you are near, listening to our questions,
  understanding our fear.
  Your glory breaks out on the brink of the grave;
  your word brings us life and hope. Amen

Thursday March 30   *John 11.45-57*

The challenge to the onlookers

So far the story has focused on Jesus and his friends, on the distress and renewed hope of one family. Now others are drawn in. Read verses 45 and 55-56.

Here are ordinary folk – who came to the wake for Lazarus, and became witnesses when he was set free from the tomb. Now they put their faith in Jesus. They are joined by others, gathering in Jerusalem for the Passover. All are now on the look-out for Jesus, wondering what he might do next. What they saw in Bethany took them by surprise. Now they are expectant.

The people in power are also on the alert. The Council of chief priests and Pharisees is convened to discuss what Jesus is doing, and how they might respond. For them it is not awe, but anger and anxiety at the threat to their authority. Yet Caiaphas' words (verses 49-50) are not about 'taking out' or 'terminating' Jesus (in the crude language of gangsters) but about Jesus *taking on* the sentence of death under which they all live – under which we live too, as mortal men and women. The 'onlookers' include ourselves, not passive bystanders but part of the action.

✳ *Pray that the Holy Spirit may open our eyes to God's presence and that, when we have seen where God is at work, we may become witnesses to others.*

Friday March 31   *John 12.12-19*

The hope of the pilgrims

Have you ever been part of a large crowd? Where? Was it exciting? Frightening? How does it feel when everyone does something together: cheering, clapping, a standing ovation, a Mexican wave – or the mourners throwing flowers at the funeral cortege of Princess Diana?

Siegfried Sassoon wrote:
'Everyone suddenly burst out singing;
And I was filled with such delight
As prisoned birds must find in freedom,
Winging wildly across the white
Orchards and dark-green fields; on – on – and out of sight.'

In large crowds, at points of celebration, we can experience great liberation.

The crowds in Jerusalem were shouting about liberation. *Hosanna* means 'Come, free us now!' They were full of excitement and expectation – arising from the significance of Jerusalem in their history, the promise of the coming Messiah in their faith, and the eyewitness accounts of some of their fellow pilgrims, the folk who had been present when Lazarus came out of the tomb (verses 17-18). The Pharisees reacted with anger and frustration (verse 19) and the disciples with faithfulness but some confusion (verse 16), but the ordinary people demonstrated their joyful hope (verses 12-13) – that in the face of political oppression and personal suffering and failure, they might be set free – just as Lazarus had been.

✳ *Hosanna, Jesus, come into our lives,*
as our loving Saviour, here and now,
as the One who can change everything.
Help us to understand your way, and to respond with joy.
Amen

Saturday April 1   John 12.20-26
The curiosity of the Gentiles
Today is April Fool's Day. Foolishness takes many forms. Our reading reminds us of the 'folly of God' which, Paul says (1 Corinthians 1.25), is 'wiser than human wisdom'.

Human wisdom says, 'Ask a silly question and you'll get a silly answer.' In today's reading it is rather that a simple question receives a profound answer.

The crowds in Jerusalem during the Passover festival include pilgrims from further afield. Though not Jews they have still come to worship. Wondering why the people are shouting 'Hosanna', they ask to see Jesus.

When Philip and Andrew find Jesus and tell him this, he responds in a way that may help his disciples – and others – to 'see' in a different way who he is and what he is doing – if they use their imaginations. Jesus uses a vivid image, one that has taken root in the imaginations of Christians ever since (verse 24). What happens to the grain of wheat is that it is 'thrown away' by the sower, apparently rejected, left to die. So this is a story about loss. When have you had to 'let go' of something you cherished, or to abandon plans on which much turned? When have you felt rejected? When have you done a foolish thing because it felt that was where your faith was leading you? Offer these experiences to God in prayer.

The story of the grain of wheat is also a story of hope. When it is 'let go' then it can grow. From its death (a symbol for the death of Christ on the cross) comes new life – many times over.

This parable is the profound answer to the people who asked to see Jesus.

✶ *God of wisdom,*
thank you for those with the courage to ask questions.
God of surprises,
thank you that out of loss comes new life. Amen

FOR REFLECTION – alone or with a group

● With which characters in the story told this week do you most closely identify?
● Explain to each other what that person or group might have valued in Jesus and why.

4th Sunday of Lent, April 2   *John 12.27-36a*

Children of the light

'Trust to the light while you have it, so that you may become children of light' (verse 36). 'Children of light' are those who see the world in God's way, follow the light of God's guiding, and whose lives are a light to others.

In July 1998 ten new statues representing 20th century Christian martyrs from every continent were unveiled on the West Front of Westminster Abbey in London. One was Dietrich Bonhoeffer, Lutheran pastor and theologian, executed by the Nazis in 1945. In *Life Together,* one of his many challenging and inspiring books, he wrote, 'For Christians the beginning of the day should not be burdened and oppressed with besetting concerns for the day's work. At the threshold of the new day stands the Lord who made it. All the darkness and distractions of the dreams of night retreat before the clear light of Jesus Christ and his wakening word. All unrest, all impurity, all care and anxiety flee before him. Therefore, at the beginning of the day, let all distraction and empty talk be silenced and let the first thought and the first word belong to him to whom our whole life belongs. "Awake thou that sleepest, and arise from the dead and Christ shall give thee light."'

Imagine Jesus with his 'soul in turmoil' (verse 27) facing the certainty of his own death, and remember his disciple Bonhoeffer, nearly 2000 years later. Slowly read aloud Jesus' words in verses 35-36a, and reflect on your own discipleship.

✶ *God, to whom our whole life belongs,*
we have seen your love in the clear light of Jesus.
Help us to become children of the light. Amen

Glimpses of glory

The statues of 20th century martyrs also include Martin Luther King, Baptist preacher and civil rights leader from the USA, who was assassinated on 4 April 1968. The day before he died he said, 'I've been to the mountaintop. And I don't mind. Like anybody, I would like to live a long life... But I'm not concerned about that now. I just want to do God's will. And He's allowed me to go up to the mountain. And I've looked over. And I've seen the promised land' *(Speech in Memphis: 3 April 1968)*.

Martin Luther King saw both God's glory and the – still far off – 'promised land' for his people, though at a point when his own death was imminent. Many are afraid to go 'up the mountain', to take a wider view, or to trust the vision. The Gospel writer remembered what the prophet Isaiah said of such people (verses 38-40).

In John's Gospel the 'signs' of Jesus are pointers to the promised land. Jesus challenges the values of this world; he came to bring hope, as well as judgement. Do we act as though we believe this?

✳ ***God of hope, help us to share the vision***
of those who have gone to the mountain top.
Help us to glimpse your glory
in the world of our every day. Amen

Becoming like a servant

Read again the words of Martin Luther King, who died on 4 April 1968. 700 years before, there lived a saint remembered on 3 April: Richard of Chichester. His memory is cherished because he served his fellow men and women. Born into a prosperous family, he was orphaned when young and, though a relative helped him to go to Oxford to study, he could not afford a fire in his lodgings or even a cloak. The story is that he lived with two other poor students; they had one tunic and one cloak between them and took it in turns to go out!

He became a small-town parson, much sought as a counsellor. Against the wishes of King Henry III, he was consecrated Bishop of Chichester. The king denied him access to the cathedral and the Bishop's palace, so Richard spent two years wandering barefoot through his diocese, living on the charity of his flock. When the quarrel was settled and Richard moved into the palace, he lived there very simply, fasting often and sleeping on the floor. Yet he entertained the poor with great generosity and, when he died, left everything to hospitals, widows and orphans.

What connections do you see between this story and the description of Jesus washing the disciples' feet?

What can we in today's Church learn from Jesus' action, and from the life of disciples like St Richard of Chichester?

✳ *O most merciful Redeemer, friend and brother,*
may we know thee more clearly,
love thee more dearly,
and follow thee more nearly;
for thine own sake. Amen

St Richard of Chichester (1197-1253)

Wednesday April 5   *John 13.21-30*

Challenging the darkness

It was night. Under cover of darkness evil can flourish. Darkness is not itself evil; it can wrap us gently in God's gift of sleep. It can reveal to us the mystery of the night sky. But it can also hide what should be seen, confronted, challenged. Judas went out to betray Jesus, to prepare for his death, by night.

On 20 November 1998, Galina Starovoitova was gunned down in a dark doorway in St Petersburg. She was an MP, representing the party called Democratic Russia. In a country where political murder was becoming more and more common, she was known for her courage and for speaking out – against corruption, extremism and, just days before she died, anti-Semitism.

She knew too much about the dark doorways of her own society. She was also a woman who loved life, caring for people, seeing where doors of hope could open.

Think about both kinds of doorway – of despair and hope – in the world where we live now, and in the story of Jesus.

A friend of Galina, writing in the *Guardian* when her death was announced, remembered her saying, 'I think I know what the best thing in life is. It is when you know that you are loved.'

Remember that Jesus experienced both light and darkness, hatred and love: and in this Gospel passage we glimpse both.

* *Goodness is stronger than evil;*
  love is stronger than hate;
  light is stronger than darkness;
  life is stronger than death.
  Victory is ours through Him who loved us.

  Archbishop Desmond Tutu – An African Prayer Book
  (Doubleday)

Thursday April 6   *John 13.31-38*

Knowing no limits

The 20th century martyrs carved on the West Front of Westminster Abbey include Saint Maximilian Kolbe, a Franciscan Friar and Catholic Priest, who died in Auschwitz in 1941. He was a gifted scientist and mathematician. He had worked as a religious journalist – that was what led to his arrest. But in the concentration camp he communicated God's love through actions as well as words. He comforted his fellow prisoners – with both a sense of humour and the sacraments. He reminded them that even sufferings come to an end, that God had not abandoned them, that the way to glory was through the cross.

In verses 31-32 notice how many times the word 'glorify' is used. We often associate the word with beauty and power. How can God be glorified through humiliation and suffering?

One day a prisoner escaped from Auschwitz. In reprisal the guards chose ten men to be starved to death. One was a young Polish soldier, recently married. Maximilian Kolbe begged to be allowed to take the young man's place. In the narrow cell, he comforted each of the others as, one by one, they died. He was the last to die – his death hastened by his torturers.

Read verses 34-35, noticing how many times the word 'love' is used. In Maximilian Kolbe's last letter to his mother he wrote, 'Pray that my love will be without limits.'

* *Pray that your love and care for others may also give glory to God, who gave you the capacity to love.*

Friday April 7   *John 14.1-14*

'Follow me'

Read again John 12.36-38. Simon Peter wanted to share in what his friend, leader and Lord was doing. Jesus warned him that he would find it too hard. Did he? Read John 18.16-17, 25-27.

When it came to the crunch, would you or I have courage to admit that we were followers of someone seen as a rebel, heretic, enemy of the state? If we did, what price might we have to pay?

Among the 20th century martyrs depicted at Westminster Abbey are:

- Manche Masemola, a young South African Christian convert killed in 1928 at only 16 by her animist parents;
- Lucian Tapiedi of Papua New Guinea, a layman murdered in 1942 during the Japanese occupation of his island;
- Esther John of Pakistan, a Protestant evangelist who died in 1960 because of her witness in a Muslim country;
- Wang Zhiming, a Chinese pastor killed in 1972, during the Cultural Revolution;
- Janani Luwum of Uganda, the Anglican Archbishop who was assassinated in 1977, during the dictatorship of Idi Amin.

They are women and men of different cultures and age groups, who died in different and terrible ways – because of their faith. What they have in common is that they wanted to follow Jesus (as Peter did) and though they may have been very afraid, they stood the test. Jesus said, 'Set your troubled hearts at rest. Trust in God always; trust also in me. There are many dwelling places in my Father's house...'

And what about Simon Peter? Read John 21.15-19.

✻ *Find an atlas, and in it identify all the places mentioned above. With your finger resting on each in turn repeat verse 6.*

Saturday April 8   *John 14.15-31*

'If you love me'

Jesus said, 'If you love me you will obey my commands'.

'No soldier is obliged to obey an order contrary to the law of God. It is time that you come to your senses and obey your conscience rather than follow sinful commands.' These words are from a sermon by Archbishop Oscar Romero in the cathedral in San Salvador on 23 March 1980. The next day he was shot dead at the altar, while celebrating mass. In the country of El Salvador, where power lay in the hands of a few people – the landlords and military rulers – the poor went hungry and lived in fear. It was important that someone should speak out for justice.

To the government and their death squads Oscar Romero was not a safe 'religious' figurehead but a dangerously 'political' person. Even the Church found him too political – although his courage and his martyrdom are acclaimed he has not yet been declared a saint. Jon Sobrino, a liberation theologian, says, Romero became a saint within society...gave the people hope at 'a time when there was no hope...was a man who told the truth and loved the people. In Third World countries like El Salvador, telling the truth is absolutely explosive.'

Jesus spoke about the 'Spirit of truth' which the world cannot accept '...but you know him because he dwells with you.'

Imagine Jesus going courageously to his death, and give thanks for others over the years who have been prepared to make the same journey and the same sacrifice. They have been obedient to God. They have been moved and motivated by love. They have given others hope. Where do you find hope, now?

Jesus said, 'Peace is my parting gift to you, my own peace, such as the world cannot give.' Repeat and reflect on these words.

Read aloud verse 31, as encouragement for your own journey.

✳ *Go in the love of God,*
   the courage of Christ,
   the truth of the Holy Spirit.
   Go in peace. Amen

FOR REFLECTION – alone or with a group
● Where do you see hope now?
● Where do you see the 'dark doorways' and the doors of hope in our world?
● Do you know anyone – not famous – whose courage and love put them alongside those named this week?

FOR ACTION
● Find out more about the 20th century saints and martyrs mentioned this week.
● Learn about the work of Amnesty International today (99-119 Rosebery Avenue, London EC1R 4RE).

LENT – READINGS FROM JOHN
3. The way of the Cross

Notes based on the New International Version by
Norman Taggart

An Irish Methodist minister and author, Norman Taggart has served in Ireland, India, Britain and Sri Lanka. He was President of the Methodist Church in Ireland from 1997 to 1998, and is minister of Ballymoney and Coleraine Methodist churches.

John's Gospel is the most reflective of the four Gospels. Over the next two weeks we shall be privileged to see behind the scenes of Jesus' last hours on earth. It can be a deeply humbling and challenging experience, causing us to re-examine our values and beliefs and to consider a deeper commitment to Christ, his Church and the world. In some ways, Jesus' times were so different from our own, in other ways so similar. Now, as then, we have to reckon with an unhealthy mix of religion and politics in some parts of the world, and with various forms of opposition to Christ and the gospel.

5th Sunday of Lent, April 9   *John 15.1-10*
The believers' relationship with Christ
Personal relationships are often under strain nowadays, due to increased mobility, rapid social change, the erosion of traditional values and other reasons. Relationships are all-important in the Christian life: with Christ, with fellow-believers and with all with whom we come into contact. The Bible knows nothing of solitary religion, or of truths not expressed in attitudes and relationships. Faith in Christ is relevant to every aspect of life and every relationship.

Total dependence, love, obedience and fruitfulness are vital aspects of our life in Christ. Relationships need to be kept in good repair, ours with Christ being no exception. We are to remain in him (verses 4-7). We do this through the means of grace, including Bible reading, prayer and worship, and through service. People often grow closer as they do things together. We are to remain in his love, obeying his commands (verse 10).

✱ *Thou, O Christ, art all I want;*
   More than all in thee I find.   *Charles Wesley (1707-88)*

Monday April 10   *John 15.11-17*

The believers' relationships with one another

We are chosen by Christ to be his friends, called to a life characterized by joy, love and fruitfulness. He confides in us (verse 15). Our relationship is not only with him, but with one another in him. A hostile or indifferent world can cause hassle and hurt. Jesus therefore commands us to love each other (verses 12 and 17). He sets an example and gives us strength to live up to this 'eleventh commandment'.

Christian love has more to do with the will than the emotions. It is a determination always to do the right thing by others, to want only the best for others, friend and foe alike, irrespective of feelings. Within the Christian fellowship our aim is to love one another with a sacrificial love, as Jesus loved us (verse 12). We are unlikely to have to die for our brothers and sisters in Christ, but keeping in touch with them and loving them can make enormous demands upon us. We will have to listen to them, to share with them and to put them before ourselves.

✳ *Lord, I thank you for fellow-believers.*
Like members of my family,
they have been given to me, not chosen by me.
Help us to value and appreciate one another,
even when we differ. Keep us together in your love.

Tuesday April 11   *John 15.18 to 16.4*

When the going gets tough

We have been thinking primarily about our relationships with Christ and with other believers. Today we turn to our relationship with the world, here understood as a fallen universe hostile to God. In the world we encounter hate and alienation. This should not surprise us since we follow one who was 'despised and rejected by men, a man of sorrows, and familiar with suffering' (Isaiah 53.3). Our calling is to be with Jesus, to take the way of the cross. If we do not experience persecution, or at least rejection and ridicule in the world, is it because we have lost our cutting edge? Do we conform to the world's standards and values, and fail to present a challenge to the world?

When the going gets tough, we are strengthened by Christ's choice of us, by his example, by the example of fellow-Christians in this and earlier generations, and by the power of the Holy Spirit. The Spirit is God's gift to us, to enable us to face the world's hostility.

❋ *Teach us, O Lord, to hold fast to that which is good;*
to render to no one evil for evil;
help us to strengthen the faint-hearted,
to support the weak and to help the afflicted.
May we honour all people and love and serve you;
rejoicing in the power of the Holy Spirit.   Traditional

Wednesday April 12   *John 16.5-15*

Loss turned to gain

Jesus spoke to his followers in riddles; or, as with us, was it a case that they would not accept what ran counter to their own preferences? Understandably they did not want to part company with Jesus. True, Jesus baffled and disturbed them at times, but he also reassured and comforted them. It was surely much better to face the trials of life with him by their side.

Not so, says Jesus. It is for their good he is going, to make way for the Holy Spirit. The work of the Holy Spirit is indispensable to Jesus' ministry, extending it and bringing glory to Jesus. The Holy Spirit convicts the world of sin and unbelief, and convinces people of the need for righteousness and judgement. There is no personal renewal or social transformation without the Holy Spirit. 'Mission', wrote Lesslie Newbigin, 'is primarily a work of the Spirit, a spill-over from Pentecost'.

❋ *Spirit of truth, guide us into all truth*
so that we may see things more from your point of view,
for the good of the Kingdom, for our own good,
and to bring glory to Jesus.

Thursday April 13   *John 16.16-24*

Sorrow turned to joy

Is death the end? That was the challenging topic presented to me in a Lenten series in Colombo, Sri Lanka, where tragically death has been all too common. There is a real end in death, a painful parting that has to be acknowledged before inner healing can take place. Yet, for the Christian, death is never 'the end'. The last word does not lie with death, but with Christ who died and rose and robs death of its victory.

This passage is full of promises: that Jesus' followers will see him after death, because of the resurrection and through the power of the Holy Spirit; that those who ask in accordance with his will, receive; and that grief is turned to joy which is complete. Jesus strikingly likens his sufferings and death to the purposeful pain of a mother giving birth to a healthy child. In Jesus' death is our joy!

✳ *O let thy love my heart control,*
Thy love for every sinner free,
That every fallen human soul
May taste the grace that found out me;
That all mankind with me may prove
Thy sovereign, everlasting love!   Charles Wesley (1707-88)

Friday April 14   *John 16.25-33*
Peace beyond conflict
As the disciples' understanding of the awe-fulness of Jesus' words grows, he is able to become more direct in his teaching. He is leaving the world and returning to the Father. They themselves will be scattered. Yet, against all appearances, there are larger and more lasting realities. Their faith has grown; the Father loves them, and they can pray to him direct; above all they can take comfort from Christ's own victory.

Vision, claimed Jonathan Swift, is 'the art of seeing the invisible'. Faith is 'being...certain of what we do not see' (Hebrews 11.1). 'Take heart', are Jesus' astonishing words, 'I have over-come the world' (verse 33). Peace is both God's gift and our goal.

Such faith and vision are needed in many parts of the world today. As Desmond Tutu affirms:

'Goodness is stronger than evil,
Love is stronger than hate,
Light is stronger than darkness.
Life is stronger than death,
Victory is ours through him who loved us.'

✳ *Lord Jesus, show us the path of life,*
and give us the grace to take up our cross
and follow you.   The Pilgrim's Manual (adapted)

Saturday April 15   *John 17.1-5*
Jesus prays for himself
Jesus' prayer – for himself, for his disciples and for all believers – takes up the whole of chapter 17, which has been described as 'the holy of holies' in John's Gospel. As William Temple points

out, Jesus' glory is about to reach its full splendour in the cross. It is the glory or shining forth of love. The Father glorifies the Son by sustaining him in his perfect obedience, even unto death. The Son glorifies the Father by the perfection of the obedience which he offers. He completes the work of salvation committed to him. Eternal life is in knowing the Father, the only true God, and Jesus Christ whom the Father has sent (verse 3).

Prayer was central in Jesus' life, an expression of the unique and intimate relationship he enjoyed with the Father. He prayed at critical periods of his life – at his baptism, in choosing his disciples, as he approached the cross, and on the cross itself – and throughout his life. His 'prayers and petitions with loud cries and tears' (Hebrews 5.7), coupled with his compassionate response to every form of human need, challenge us to become involved in the 'politics of holiness'.

✳ *Father, fill us with your Spirit*
that our lives may glorify your Son
as we do the work you give us to do.

FOR REFLECTION – alone or with a group

● In what ways do you think Jesus expects us to be fruitful? How can we become more fruitful?
● Explore the priority of unity. Is there a difference between unity and uniformity?
● How can relationships be strengthened with Christ, with fellow Christians and within the community?

Palm Sunday, April 16   *John 17.6-19*
Jesus prays for his disciples
Jesus turns again to his disciples' relationship with a world estranged from God. As his disciples, they are clearly not 'of the world' (verse 16). Their values, aims and motivation, for example, will be different, shaped primarily by their commitment to Christ. Yet his disciples are not to withdraw from the world (verse 15). How could they, when they follow One whose revelation of God depended on his coming to earth from heaven?

Jesus indeed prays that, just as he was sent by the Father into the world, to redeem it, his disciples too are to immerse them-selves fully within the world (verse 18). The illustrations he uses elsewhere – light, yeast and salt – have no meaning unless they refer to a faith expressed in and for the world. He therefore prays for:

their unity (verse 11),
    their protection from the evil one (verse 15), and
    their distinctiveness (verse 17),
that they may be sustained in their life and mission by God's truth.

✳ *Lord God, we would not seek you,*
        if you had not found us in Christ.
    In this our earthly pilgrimage,
        enlarge our hearts,
        enlighten our understanding,
        that we may walk the ordinary road of life
        in freedom, hope, and joy,
        through Jesus Christ, our Lord. Amen

The Pilgrim's Manual

Monday April 17   *John 17.20-26*

Jesus prays for all believers

It is deeply moving to become aware that someone has been praying regularly for us, perhaps during an illness or in some other need. In my year as President of the Church, I was often humbled as people, including strangers, came up to me simply to say that they were remembering me in prayer. This is an encouraging example of good relationships within the body of Christ.

How much better to realize that Jesus himself prays for us (verse 20). His prayer is that we may be one, as he and the Father are one, that the world may believe. He prays too that we may see and share his glory, that we may know the Father's love, and that through the Spirit he may live in us. We should all try to contribute to the unity of Christ's body, so that we can reach out more effectively to the wider community in loving service and witness.

✳ *Gather and scatter us, O God,*
        according to your will.
    Build us into one church,
        a church with open doors and wide windows,
        a church which takes the world seriously,
        ready to work and to suffer
        and even to bleed for it.

Eastern Europe

Tuesday April 18   *John 18.1-18**

Betrayal, arrest and denial

Jesus leaves the place of prayer. He is now ready to face his enemies. Do we tend to be overwhelmed by life's pressures due to our neglect of prayer and reflection?

Jesus' calm courage and strength are impressive. He is well aware of the danger he is in, yet is unafraid (verse 4). Indeed his thoughts are much more of his disciples than of himself. The search party is looking for him, so his followers should be allowed to go free (verse 8). Above all, his imperative is to do the will of his Father (verse 11). Nothing else matters.

Peter, by contrast, misreads the situation, though he remains by the scene after the others have fled. It has been suggested that, in trying to defend Jesus, Peter used the wrong weapon, had the wrong motive, acted under the wrong orders, and accomplished the wrong result (18.10-11). At times we are tempted to take things out of God's hands into our own, working to our own agenda. Had Peter had his way, Jesus would not have gone to the cross. God's plan of salvation could have been thwarted.

✳ *O God, whom to follow*
   is to risk our whole lives;
   may we abandon the ways of the past,
   hold to one another,
   and travel together wherever you will lead us,
   through Jesus Christ our Lord.   Adapted from a prayer
                              by Janet Morley, All Desires Known (SPCK)

Wednesday April 19   *John 18.19-40**
Denials and trial

It is easy to sit in judgement on the disciples for deserting and denying Jesus, and on the Jewish authorities for building a case against Jesus using false witnesses (Mark 14.55-59). Have we never closed our eyes to the truth? Have we too not been guilty of denying the Lordship of Jesus in vital areas of our life, or concealing our identity as Christians in certain company or circumstances? The Jewish leaders observed the ceremonial requirements of their religion (verse 28), while harbouring murder in their hearts. Have we ever been guilty of such hypocrisy?

The contrast between Peter and Jesus is striking. Peter is free, yet becomes caught in a web of denial. Jesus, on the other hand, is bound in the garden, before Annas and before Caiaphas (verses 12, 13 and 24). At a deeper level, however, Jesus is free. He speaks 'openly to the world' and says 'nothing in secret' (verse 20). He stands by and for the truth, whatever the circumstances (verse 23). In time he chooses to forgive Peter, refusing to become a prisoner to past disappointments and hurts.

‑ *O dearest Lord, thy sacred heart*
    With spear was pierced for me;
 O pour thy spirit in my heart,
    That I may live for thee.   *Father Andrew (1868-1946)*

Thursday April 20   *John 19.1-16**

'He suffered under Pontius Pilate'

Yesterday we noted the contrast between Peter and Jesus. Today we turn to the contrast between Jesus and Pilate. To all appearances, Pilate is in charge. The reality, however, is much different. Though in a position of authority, Pilate is unsure and fearful (verse 8). He claims to have power, yet is impotent (verses 10, 12 and 16). Jesus, on the other hand, though abused and humiliated, conveys strength and authority in his silence and in what he says (verses 9 and 11).

Pilate vacillates over what to do with Jesus. He makes four attempts to handle him, without success:

he tries to put the responsibility on to someone else (18.31);
he attempts to find a way of escape (18.39);
he tries to compromise, having Jesus flogged (19.1-3); and
he appeals to the sympathy of Jesus' accusers (verse 15).

If we are tried or ridiculed on account of our faith, we should recall that it is really our accusers who are on trial before God.

‑ *Help us, O God, to refuse to be embittered*
    against those who handle us with harshness...
 Save us from hatred of those who oppress us.
 May we follow the spirit of thy Son Jesus Christ.   *South Africa*

Good Friday, April 21   *John 19.17-37**

'Was crucified, died...'

The brutalizing effect of violence is seen in the casual indifference of the soldiers beneath Jesus' cross. By contrast, Jesus shows a deep concern for his mother. Even the most extreme circumstances do not excuse us from family obligations. Jesus' honesty (verse 28) and confidence (verse 30) also inspire.

The words 'I am thirsty' are the only ones spoken from the cross which hint at his physical suffering. All four Gospel writers play down the physical side of his agony in his last hours on earth. Nothing must be allowed to detract from the eternal spiritual significance of his death.

Matthew, Mark and Luke refer to Jesus calling out in a loud voice. It is only John who supplies his words, 'It is finished' (verse 30). This is not a cry of defeat but a shout of victory. What the prophets had foretold, the task his Father had sent him to do, has been accomplished!

✳ *Rock of Ages, cleft for me,*
  Let me hide myself in thee;
  Let the water and the blood,
  From thy riven side which flowed,
  Be of sin the double cure,
  Cleanse me from its guilt and power.

William Williams (1717-91)

Saturday April 22   *John 19.38-42**

'...and was buried'

Joseph of Arimathea and Nicodemus were members of the Jewish council and were secret followers of Jesus. Had they been open followers, they probably would have been prevented by the council from caring for Jesus' body. Nicodemus provided clothes and spices sufficient for a king. Joseph placed Jesus' body in a newly-prepared tomb.

It was Jesus' death which gave Joseph and Nicodemus courage to 'come out', in terms of their Christian discipleship. Their actions were loving and respectful, in line with Jewish practice. Their courage lights up an otherwise sombre scene, providing a promise that darkness has not finally triumphed. Here, already, are glimmers of hope and light, pointing to the transforming power of the cross.

Those who find it difficult to make a public declaration of faith are sometimes harshly criticized. They may have been silenced by well-founded fear of ridicule or persecution, or by the feeling that they may let Jesus down. We need to encourage, not criticize, one another. With the help of the Holy Spirit, all can be enabled to witness sensitively by word and life for Jesus.

✳ *Lord Jesus,*
  we thank you that you died to save us from our sin
  and to redeem the whole world.
  Give us courage to share your life-changing love with others.

FOR REFLECTION – alone or with a group

- What difference does the Holy Spirit make to living the Christian life?
- Can we learn from Jesus how to respond to insults and abuse?
- What should be our mission priorities?

FOR ACTION

Think of a variety of situations known to you, in which relationships are far from ideal. They may, for example, be under strain, or misunderstandings may have arisen, or perhaps people are simply blind or indifferent towards one another. Work out ways to try to improve matters, and act on them.

EASTER – RESURRECTION
1. The victory of love

Notes based on the New International Version by
Burchel K Taylor

Burchel K Taylor – who has been pastor of Bethel Baptist Church, Kingston, Jamaica, for over twenty-five years – is internationally recognized as a leading Caribbean biblical scholar and theologian.

Jesus Christ is risen. He is risen indeed! Yet this is not something that rushed judgement, immediate common-sense or conventional wisdom will grasp or consider possible. Through our encounter with him, the risen Christ leads us step by step to discover the reality of his Resurrection for ourselves, and then brings about a complete transformation of our lives – both as individuals and in community – as the indestructibility of God's love becomes clear to us.

Easter Day, April 23   *John 20.1-18**
Surprised by joy

For Mary, a key figure in the appearance stories, Resurrection was not the first thing that came to mind, even with the pile-up of indications that something had happened.

If we are always controlled by presuppositions and close our minds to insights and indicators that there might be more in it than we think, we rob ourselves of the opportunity to be surprised by joy. We learn from Mary's experience that knowing the risen Lord is a gift of his own self-revelation. It is not a matter of discovery so much as disclosure. It is a matter of being lovingly affirmed and having renewed and joyful knowledge of the presence of the living Lord. There is no voice like his. She did not only see him but also heard her name on his lips. He owned her. He calls his own by name and his own knows his voice (John 10.4).

This is a cause of joy unspeakable and leads to an irresistible urge to share it. Indeed the risen Lord defies any gesture that might get in the way of sharing this joy. It is the joy of renewed vision, a renewed sense of meaning, purpose and significance of life. We miss out on this if we allow presuppositions or limited judgement to close our lives to the revelation of God in Christ.

✳ *Lord, thank you for the gift of your self-revelation in Christ.*
Teach us not to settle with our own rushed judgement
on that for which you alone hold the key.

Monday April 24   *Luke 24.13-35**

Hope reborn

Only the Gospel of Luke reports the story of the two unknown disciples whom Jesus met on the Emmaus Road. It is characteristic of this writer to focus attention from time to time on people who are not of high profile, and who do not seem to belong to the centre but who for a brief moment in the spotlight make an unforgettable and lasting impact.

The Resurrection has significance not only for those of the inner circle; it is for the greatest and the least. For these two disciples life was at its lowest ebb. 'But we had hoped that he was the one who was going to redeem Israel,' they said (verse 21). The pathos and disillusionment of dashed hope are evident. But encounter with the risen Christ changed it all. In a moment of re-awakening, hope was reborn. It was restored and re-established. It was hope now built on the revealed reality of the fulfilment of God's purpose that was thought no longer possible. It was hope re-energized to face new challenges in a new way.

The Resurrection is not just something we talk about, but something we meditate upon with openness and expectancy. The written word of Scripture assumes real significance when we become aware of the living Word to which it witnesses. The real blessings of the Resurrection are not experienced in a casual acquaintance with Jesus, but in a new relationship of intimacy and fellowship initiated by him.

✳ *Lord, in a world in which so much seems to deny real hope*
and at the best create only false hope,
grant us the undying hope inspired by you the risen Lord.

Tuesday April 25   *Luke 24.36-49**

Blessed assurance

The two disciples, fresh from their Emmaus Road experience of hope reborn, headed back to Jerusalem to share their story with the other disciples. They knew that the tomb had been found empty but it had not convinced them of the Resurrection. But now they knew that it meant one thing, and one thing only: Jesus had risen from the dead. They had met him and nothing was the same again for them.

Meeting and knowing the risen and living Christ is not meant to make us a privileged elite, savouring and nurturing the experience, cherishing it as giving us an edge of superiority over others. What God gives us of his grace for the qualitative transformation of our humanity, is to be shared. This is what we see again and again in the appearance stories.

While the two disciples were telling their story, Jesus himself appeared in the midst of the group. This should have been a powerful confirmation of the witness of the two disciples, but the group was frightened and nonplussed. They started to imagine that it was unreal. Jesus gave them the assurance they needed, and it made all the difference. What they saw of him gave the evidence that settled their questions. The important thing is for us to be open to this, and respond by grasping it for what it is – the reality is the living Christ, raised from the dead. Our assurance is found in this. The Spirit continues to make this possible and available.

This is reinforced and maintained by the witness of the Word and participation in a common life of fellowship forged by the living Christ himself. Peace and love are gifts that are manifested, celebrated and shared in a way that would be impossible apart from the Resurrection and the blessed assurance of its reality, given by the risen Lord himself.

✷ *Lord, thank you for giving us the assurance we need*
of your living presence
that inspires and sustains fellowship in your name.

Wednesday April 26   *John 20.19-23**

Breakthrough

The disciples are seen huddled together behind locked doors, bound by and united in anxiety. The crucifixion of Jesus had not only left them in confusion and doubt, but the prospects of facing the authorities and public at large struck them with terror. For the moment they could only lock themselves away with their fear. A breakthrough came when Jesus, the risen Lord, breached the barrier behind which they sought security. But it was more than a breakthrough of physical barriers. It was profoundly spiritual. The appearance of Jesus, his action and spoken words, transformed the whole situation.

When the mystery of Christ's living presence breaches barriers – behind which we often search for a security and peace which cannot last – everything changes. Crippling fear is replaced by unrestrained joy. People torn by anxiety, estranged from any

101

sense of purpose and united by common threat, are given a new sense of wholeness and unity of vision that only God in Christ can give. People withdrawn and in hiding are empowered and liberated to reach out and to exercise authority in the service of grace, mercy and truth. When the living Christ breaks through into our lives all things become new. To God be the glory.

✳ *Lord, it is an open door that you offer to our lives.*
   Come in, we pray,
   and make the influence of your presence truly felt.

Thursday April 27   *John 20.24-31**

Belief and blessing

Evidence that Jesus previously gave to the disciples, reassuring them of the continuity of his identity and the reality of his presence, was now given to Thomas. Thomas had already indicated that he would consider such evidence as viable and irrefutable. Thomas' remarkable confession expressed the meaning and significance of the Resurrection for him. It was truly a moment of life-transforming disclosure and acclamation.

Jesus in his response spoke a word that was liberating, encouraging and challenging. Believers who do not have Thomas' opportunity are not at a disadvantage. They too can share the wonderful privilege of knowing the risen Lord by faith, itself a God-given gift by which we see the invisible. Faith, with the help of the Spirit, grasps the self-disclosure of the risen Lord. It produces a confession and commitment that witnesses to our own experience of the Resurrection-life itself. Paul sums it up succinctly and profoundly: 'If you confess with your mouth, "Jesus is Lord," and believe in your heart that God raised him from the dead, you will be saved' (Romans 10.9).

When faith opens the door to an experience of the risen Christ as Lord, there is a liberating power that releases us for worship and witness, fellowship and discipleship. At the same time, there is now no excuse, based on lack of evidence of the Resurrection, for not opening ourselves to a life of commitment to Jesus as Lord. We are not restricted to or limited by Thomas' requirement for belief. The Lord himself has set us free to know and receive him by faith. Now we walk by faith and not by sight with no less assurance and confidence. *Hallelujah!*

✳ *Lord, we thank you for the gift of faith*
   and its wonder-working influence in our lives,
   so that we may know you truly as our Lord and our God.

True testimony

The life-transforming experience, which results from an encounter and response in faith to the living Christ, is both the basis and the inspiration of faithful Christian testimony. This testimony is not an option but an essential expression of the transformed life. Here we are given valuable insights concerning this most important but undervalued and often misunderstood aspect of Christian commitment.

Christian testimony is backed by first-hand experience of the living Lord Jesus Christ who is none other than the same Jesus, the Word that became flesh and dwelt in our midst. The conviction and earnestness of personal testimony are certainly significant. Yet the testimony is also the expression of a corporate experience which adds to its power and effectiveness. The writer speaks not as an isolated individual with a private and exclusive experience, but as a member of a community with shared first-hand experience of Christ and shared commitment to make it known to others. The aim is also to widen the embrace of the fellowship through the testimony. Isn't this a serious challenge to the rugged individualism and self-centredness of our times, not unknown in Christian circles?

Christian testimony is not only of words but also of a transparent life. This is a life of fidelity and honesty. This life is assured of the renewing grace of forgiveness and benefits from interceding advocacy by the One most worthy of all, the living exalted Lord. Living with this knowledge gives our testimony integrity, trustworthiness, confidence and humility.

✳ *Dear God, give us grace and courage*
to witness faithfully in the name of the Lord Jesus Christ,
who has made us one with himself and with one another in
him.

Praise the Lord!

Here is an unrestrained thanksgiving and a celebration of God's goodness as an expression of his abiding and unflinching love, experienced by the community of God's people. Love that is discovered by one is a cause for joy by all. Such is the experience of the community that God graciously wills to make his own.

It is love recognized as undeserved, patient and kind. Yet it is not indulgent or doting. It chastens and disciplines when necessary but never deserts or abandons. It extends itself in defence of life, ensures victory and offers protection in the face of the powers that threaten, victimize and seek to destroy. Yet triumphalism and arrogance are not part of the thanksgiving and praise it evokes. Instead there is the call to the unbelieving and doubting to behold and to open themselves to the love of God.

It is clear that in the midst of life with all its questions and contradictions, God gives reasons for praise and thanksgiving. His love overcomes and outlasts the enemies and the struggles. Isn't this what the event and experience of Easter exemplify to the full? The praise and joy, thanksgiving and celebration that this evokes must be brought to the attention of the world that all may taste and see that the Lord is good.

✳ *Lord, your praise is on our lips.*
Help us to utter this with sincerity and truth.

FOR REFLECTION and ACTION – alone or with a group

● Read John 1.1-14. How does the experience of Easter bring out the significance of the prologue of John's Gospel?
● Having celebrated Easter Day, think realistically about a) how we are helped to face personal and communal difficulties, and b) how we respond to the suffering and conflict which are everyday realities in many parts of the world.

EASTER – RESURRECTION
2. Community of love

Notes based on the New Revised Standard Version by
Kate Hughes

Kate Hughes was an Anglican nun for 20 years and then spent 14 years working with the Church in Southern Africa. Today, she works from her home in an Urban Priority Area council estate, editing books and writing and editing distance learning courses in theology. Currently she edits 'Light for our Path' and the Preachers' Handbook for the IBRA.

When did the Church begin? The obvious answer is 'at Pentecost', but many of the writings of the New Testament show the disciples and followers of Jesus learning to be the Church from the moment of the Resurrection. From a group of bickering, doubting, often selfish individuals, they gradually learnt to become the 'community of love', which is still a description of the Church at its best. Most of our readings this week come from the writings of John and his circle, with their particular interest in the nature and effects of love.

2nd Sunday of Easter, April 30   *John 21.1-14*
Supporting each other

John 21 is generally considered to be a later addition to the Fourth Gospel, which may have been written by the original author or one of his followers. The chapter provides an additional resurrection appearance not recorded by any of the other Gospel writers; it also provides an explanation of how Peter, who denied Jesus, was still accepted as leader of the Church.

After three years of squabbling and rivalry, and the traumatic events of Good Friday and Easter, the disciples have begun to be a community. Seven of them return to their familiar tasks and go fishing together. It is in this familiar communal activity that they meet Jesus. 'The disciple whom Jesus loved' recognizes him first – but, typically, it is Peter who impulsively jumps into the sea to get to Jesus on the beach. The other disciples quietly support his action by continuing the work of landing the catch, just as, later in the chapter, they hang back so that Peter and Jesus have privacy to sort out their relationship.

Love of God is not a matter of fine words and big promises. It is shown in practical love, support and care of those nearest to us – our brothers and sisters in the Christian community.

✳ *Lord, help us to show that we love you*
by our support and care to those nearest to us –
our brothers and sisters in Christ.

Monday May 1   *John 21.15-19*

Commitment to each other

This passage clearly harks back to Peter's denial of Jesus in John 18. There, Peter rejected his role in the community of the disciples; he denied any connection with them and thereby weakened the community. Our sins and failures not only harm ourselves and other individuals – they also damage the witness of the whole Christian community. How often have you heard someone say, 'Christians are no better than anyone else, so their God obviously makes no difference'?

So Jesus makes commitment to the Christian community the condition for Peter's renewed relationship with himself. Jesus does not water down the cost of this commitment: Peter will lose control over his own life and death. But if Peter wants Jesus to believe that he loves him, he is going to have to show it in action – by caring for his brothers and sisters, the sheep and lambs, in the Christian community.

✳ *'See these Christians, how they love one another';*
deepen our commitment so that people may say this
of all Christian communities.

Tuesday May 2   *John 21.20-25*

Minding your own business

Peter, perhaps typically, is not content simply to put his own relationship with Jesus straight. What about the other disciples? Is Jesus going to make the same demands on them? And, in particular, what about the disciple who had a specially close relationship with Jesus? Is there a touch of jealousy here? Is John going to do better than Peter?

The response of Jesus is, in effect, 'Mind your own business!' Much teaching about community today stresses sharing and openness. But any community also needs to respect individuality and privacy. God also deals with us as individuals, and he often deals with us in secrecy. We need to respect that in others. How God is leading someone else is not our business, unless he asks us to help them. We have plenty to occupy us in our own relationship with him, and in what he has called us to do.

✳ *Teach us to be sensitive to the needs of others,*
and to give them the space to love God
in their own time and in their own way.

Wednesday May 3 Acts 4.32-37*

Of one heart and soul

When I worked in South Africa in the 1970s, we had parish weekends which measured today's Christian community against this description of the first Christian community in Jerusalem. But the life of a parish in Kimberley under apartheid was very different from that of first-century Palestine. Can we compare the two? Is this picture in Acts so idealized as to be unrealistic? Or can we learn from it characteristics of community which can help and inspire us today?

Even if the Jerusalem community did not always live up to this ideal, they were obviously aiming for four things:

- **Unity** Elsewhere in the New Testament, we read of arguments and conflicts in the Church. Unity does not mean never arguing, but having a basic oneness which is prepared to compromise, forgive, heal hurts and work through disagreements.
- **Generous sharing** No one in the community should be in need.
- **Support for the leaders** In the first Christian community they were those who witnessed publicly to the resurrection.
- **Receiving God's grace** Without this it would be impossible to be a 'community of love'.

✳ *'Of one heart and soul':*
may this be characteristic of all our community life.

Thursday May 4 1 John 2.7-17

Darkness and light

This is a familiar theme in the Johannine writings, and there is no compromise: if you love, you are in the light; if you hate, you are in darkness. This is not a vague general principle. It is about loving or hating 'a brother or sister' – members of the Christian community. The test of your love for God is to love the harassed mother and screaming child who disrupt the Eucharist, the smelly old man who sits next to you, the old ladies who talk all through the service, the bossy woman who is always telling everybody what to do, the teenagers who giggle at the wrong moments – all of them our brothers and sisters in the family of believers.

The first letter of John is addressed (verses 12-14) to the old and young in faith, whose experience of God makes them well-equipped to love their brothers and sisters and so live in the light. It is those who love the world, human society organized without reference to God, who find it impossible to love and therefore live in darkness. In the Prologue to the Fourth Gospel (John 1.5), Jesus is described as 'the light (that) shines in the darkness, and the darkness did not overcome it'. The scattered communities of love, the little groups of Christians in a pagan world, are also called to be such lights in the surrounding darkness.

✻ *Help us to shine as lights in the darkness,*
so that others may be drawn to your light.

Friday May 5   1 John 3.11-18

Giving and receiving

Here, the image is no longer light and darkness but life and death. Those who love are truly alive; those who hate a brother or sister are murderers and cannot have true eternal life within them. But the message is the same: we prove our love for God by the love we show to others. It is not a matter of word or speech but of truth and action (verse 18). This love imitates the love of Christ. It means laying down our lives, a total commitment in which, like Peter in John 21, we give up control over our own life and death.

There is no jealousy in this love, like Cain's envy of his brother Abel. It is a matter of recognizing needs and doing our best to meet them. But we have to discover the needs before we can meet them and this is not always easy. Pride and reticence make people reluctant to reveal their weakness. But part of love is being willing to let others love us, to receive their love graciously, even when it is expressed as financial or practical help which hurts our pride. A community of love is a real sharing – generous accepting as well as generous giving.

✻ *Give us grace to share our needs as well as our strengths,*
so that others have opportunities to show love to us.

Loved, we can love

In our final reading for this week, we reach the core of Christian love: 'We love because he first loved us' (verse 19). It is God's love which gives us the confidence and sense of self-worth to reach out to others in love. It is our confidence in God's love which enables us to put aside our fear of rejection and offer his love to others. It is God's unshakeable love for us which makes us love and value ourselves.

The proof of God's love for us is that he sent his Son to free us from the prison of sin and draw us into the life of the Trinity. The proof of our love for God is our love for our brothers and sisters in Christ. We and other people cannot see God; but he will be revealed through our love for others. If we do not love one another, those outside the Christian community will not be able to see and 'believe the love that God has for us' – and for them.

✳ *Thank you for loving us, so that we have love to give to you, to others, and to ourselves.*

FOR REFLECTION – alone or with a group

● From this week's readings, draw a picture of what the Christian community should be like.

● How realistic do you think this picture is? How can it be put into action today?

● Our readings seem to limit love to the members of the Christian community. Why do you think they do this? Do you think they are right?

FOR ACTION

How far is your local church a community of love? How could it become more so? Decide on ONE practical thing which you could do, as a group or an individual, to show your love for your brothers and sisters in Christ.

EASTER – RESURRECTION
3. People of faith

Notes based on the Revised English Bible by

Joy Mead

Joy Mead is a poet and writer who is involved in justice and peace work.

All the readings this week are about the interweaving of the old and the new. They involve standing firm in what is known and responding to the immediacy of the moment. People of faith – like Peter – carry within them the poetry, stories and shared memories of the faith and culture into which they were born. They are also open to what is before their eyes; prepared to take the risk of a new way of seeing and being; alert and alive to the freshness, hope and challenge of each God-given moment.

3rd Sunday of Easter, May 7   *Acts 3.1-10*

Giving attention

Peter had learnt a lot during those healing days in Galilee when sick and broken bodies – hot, sweaty, dusty, smelling of suffering – had sought out the one whose looking was love, whose touch could liberate body and mind. He had followed Jesus into unknown places where his imagination ran riot. Sometimes he knew the holiness of an ordinary moment; another time not knowing was like a fever in him.

Now, at the gate called Beautiful, Peter looks with love into the eyes of one man and sees himself reflected there. He knows that all are in need of healing. Peter gives the beggar his attention: that rarest and purest form of generosity. The results are startling – miraculous. The man finds hope and a reason to live – someone has really noticed him, looked into his eyes, touched him, seen his worth. Peter's faith is active; it empowers and enables. The man is not dismissed with a money handout. He is given back his self-esteem. He stands on his own two feet and walks tall.

✳ *God our healer,*
    may we value risk and give ourselves to make miracles.

Monday May 8   *Acts 3.11-19**

Awakening!

People are astonished! They are awakened, surprised into life – all of them: the healed man, and the people who see, hear and come running. Peter speaks to them of the Servant Lord and the God of Israel, encouraging understanding of the new Christian community as a continuation of Israel. He carefully balances tradition and continuity with a sense of new life, of awakening and surprise. There is no turning back; for the first Christians or for us. Once we know – as Peter knew – that's it! This knowing is faith and it's not about dogma or creed; it's about letting be and letting live. It raises consciousness and confronts those who think they have a monopoly on thought, ideas and power. It raises previously unnoticed people – individuals and communities – to stand tall and be the subjects of their own lives; to refuse to be labelled as 'underdeveloped' or an 'underclass'. That's what food co-ops, credit unions and groups like the 'Movement of the Landless' in Brazil are all about. That's what will change the world: the activity of small groups of thoughtful, committed citizens: people of faith transforming situations and building new communities.

* *May the Spirit fill our praise,*
guide our thoughts and change our ways.
God in Christ has come to stay.
Live tomorrow's life today!   *Brian Wren*
                   Piece Together Praise (© Stainer & Bell)

Tuesday May 9   *Acts 4.1-12*

'There's a Spirit in the air'

The priestly leaders, the learned men, ask of Peter, 'By what power have you done this?' All their learning is of no help to them now. They are faced with something beyond the reach of rational argument. Peter has grown in self-knowledge. He has begun to understand the freedom of walking his way with love and wonder every day on the good earth – the element for which he was designed.

Peter is filled with fire-bright energy. He has the gift of looking with wonder on all life, knowing the mystery of each human being, connecting body and spirit, work and play, life and death. He is fired into encounters with beggars and leaders, calmed into moments of reflection, excited into moments of change. He understands basic human needs like love, faith, peace and a sense of wonder. He sees what is in front of him, sees into deep places. It all began with one whom the educated and powerful had rejected. Jesus came that we might have life in all its fullness – that is the resurrection story and Peter cannot stop telling it.

＊ *Spirit of Truth, may our faith enable us to see*
   ourselves and others as we really are,
   and tell what we see.

Wednesday May 10   Acts 4.13-22

A banning order!

Jewish rulers, elders and scribes – the learned men thrown into panic by two uneducated laymen: 'What are we to do with these men?' (verse 16). They are dangerous, these people who speak out when all else is silence. Those with power are threatened by people's dreams, worried by those who tell their stories of people's real experience of life with a sense of immediacy. These stories express truths – in what is often the only way possible – through ambiguity and paradox. Every one of us has a need to tell and to hear stories – 'We cannot possibly give up speaking about what we have seen and heard' (verse 20), particularly stories of healing and awakening, resurrection and hope, stories of people entering, challenging and enlarging the cultural traditions into which they are born. I think of a book I read recently called *Forging New Identities,* a collection of writings by refugee and minority children in Britain. It reflects the importance of speaking out – for we are no longer strangers once we have shared stories. Telling the story makes a difference: it turns 'me' into 'us' – it gives faith to act together. Each time a story is told it is born again for the listener and the story teller. The telling is an enactment of the resurrection.

＊ *Lose your shyness, find your tongue,*
   tell the world what God has done:
   God in Christ has come to stay.
   Live tomorrow's life today!   Brian Wren
                              Piece Together Praise (© Stainer & Bell)

Thursday May 11   Acts 4.23-31

Earth-moving togetherness!

Again in these verses, we are looking at the relationship between established thought and awakening consciousness. Peter and John return to their friends and tell their story. They have been silenced – banned. The little group raises 'their voices with one accord' using a recognized prayer formula and familiar words from the Psalms. They find comfort and support in tradition, a habit of faith and a community of prayer. There are reserves here to draw upon when energy is low: reserves built up from regular attention to prayer and meditation, health and well-being, work, pleasure, positive thinking and tolerance. It's all about more than words. It's about friendship. This earth-moving togetherness (see verse 31) gives them hope, faith in being themselves, in being the people of God. The words that the little group share reflect a deeper sharing – the solidarity of friendship and common under-standing and companionship. All accept responsibility for their own lives, refusing to let tradition lull them into accommodating themselves to the prevailing situation. The courage, compassion and love of a small group of companions renews faith, makes them bold to speak out.

✳ *God of Vision, may we be people of faith*
creating communities of transformation
where people believe in one another.

Friday May 12   1 Peter 1.13-25

Given moments

Call them epiphanies, spots of time, or moments of vision – they are all moments that make our hearts sing and take over our whole being. The Buddha was once asked, 'What makes a person holy?' He replied, 'Every hour is divided into a certain number of seconds and every second into a certain number of fractions. Anyone who is able to be totally present in each fraction of a second is holy.' There is nothing common about common life – it takes an awakened sense to see what is mysterious and ineffable in every ordinary moment. Listen to your life – see what a deep mystery it is – live each moment fully. 'Be holy in all your conduct,' Peter says (verse 15). Have faith in the moment – live it with joy. The Rev Jackie Treetops, part of the 'Faith in Elderly People' Project in Leeds, calls one of her booklets *Holy, Holy, Holy*. She tells of her ministry amongst those suffering from dementia, whose life is lived in the present – or in the distant past – but who do not know of the passing of time. Perhaps we can learn from these folk something about the holiness of the present moment in which there are glimpses of eternity.

✳ *God of today,*
help us to uncover the radiance of each given moment.

Looking slowly

Faith isn't static. It's dynamic: an active way of looking at things. It's about learning and endurance, growing and being obedient to who you are, developing those gifts without which you will be 'wilfully blind' (verse 9). Knowing who you are, seeing what is there – that's what matters.

Anthony de Mello tells this story: To the disciples who wanted to know what sort of meditation he practised each morning in the garden the Master said, 'When I look carefully, I see the rose bush in full bloom.' 'Why would one have to look carefully to see the rose bush?' they asked. 'Lest one see not the rose bush,' said the Master, 'but one's preconception of it' (from *One Minute Wisdom,* published by Doubleday, 1988). People of faith believe in something beyond their own preconception of things. They look at things slowly; feel the wonder of life. This is that deep understanding, that looking with wonder into the heart of things which Peter tells us leads to Christ-like knowledge and love (see verse 8).

✴ *God of joy, help us to let go of preconceptions,*
look with love and be ready for surprises.

FOR REFLECTION – alone or with a group

● What do you see as the link between faith and action?
● Think about the language you would use to tell your story. What is the language of faith?
● How would you express what you have seen and heard as near as you can in its original impact – not from the perspective of an existing theological interpretation?

FOR ACTION

Meet with others to tell your stories.

LIVING ENCOUNTERS
1. Encounter with Judaism

Notes based on the New International Version by
Jonathan Gorsky

Jonathan Gorsky is the Educational Consultant of the Council of Christians and Jews. He is an orthodox Jew who has worked for many years in Jewish adult education and small community ministry.

Jesus was a Jew and the earliest Church was made up of Jews who were steeped in the Jewish Scriptures. The commentary in this series is an attempt to offer an insight into the living world of the Jewish reader of Scripture today as reflected in contemporary observance and spirituality. We will encounter covenant, Sabbath, holiness and Messiah as parts of a living tradition, and share the spiritual yearnings that inspire the Jewish faithful. The comments seek to evoke the inner world of the Sabbath, the great festivals and practical Jewish observance.

4th Sunday of Easter, May 14   *Psalm 23**
The Lord is my Shepherd

Psalm 23 is one of the best known of all the psalms. It is most natural to understand it as a testimony of a personal experience of our relationship with God. The psalm is attributed to King David and there is an underlying sense of his turbulent life in several of the verses. The image of God as Shepherd perhaps recalls David's early life. He knew precisely what it was to be responsible for sheep in a parched and difficult landscape where water was scarce and pasture in short supply.

Whatever the travails of his material circumstance, the Psalmist lives in constant awareness of the Divine Presence, which is a source of infinite splendour and all-encompassing love. As we contemplate His holiness, we find the still waters that are the only true comfort for the restless yearning of the human soul, and we instinctively search out the righteous paths of life that God has chosen for us.

Our spiritual journey proceeds and the fearfulness of human existence gradually melts away, as we come to know that ultimate reality is not the shadow of death, but the knowledge of

God who grants us the vision of eternal truth. When God is with us, the reality of the Divine is the staff of our comfort, for evil is but a dark shadow lacking any real substance. Enemies from within and without cannot diminish the ultimate holiness of all life and, amidst the turbulence of this world, our innermost longing is to dwell in the house of God eternally and for ever.

✳ *Be with us, O Lord, in our times of darkness,*
and help us to find comfort in the shadow of Your presence.

Monday May 15   Genesis 17.1-21

The Covenant of Abraham

'Covenant' is a key word of the relationship of God and Israel. It should be seen against a background where humanity's relationship with supernatural powers was unpredictable, as the gods were seen as capricious and capable of appeasement only if rituals and magical acts were properly performed. Covenants are binding agreements made between rulers and vassals in the ancient near East, but the biblical usage of this device to provide a framework for Israel's relationship with God is a remarkable theological innovation.

Covenant implies a stable universe, where we can understand how God responds to us. The world is no longer capricious, and covenant becomes the basis of our spiritual development. When a child is brought up by parents whose responses are erratic and seem to lack rhyme or reason, her development will be very different from that of a child who has been nurtured in a stable and loving environment. This is the significance of the covenant for humanity as a whole.

As marriage implies infinitely more than the basic agreement between husband and wife, so covenant is the beginning of a relationship that transcends its legal origin. It becomes a profound personal engagement that survives even the blatant dereliction of its basic terms, for it is rooted in the love of God and His people Israel which endures for all eternity.

Abraham's circumcision is the symbol of his covenant. Even the most powerful of our human drives can be restrained and sanctified in marriage. Husband and wife bring into their own lives the covenant love that is at the heart of Israel's relationship with God, and bring new life into this world as they participate in the sacred privilege that is the act of procreation.

＊ *Help us, O Lord, to trust those for whom we care,*
and to share their burdens, even when we do not understand.
Teach us to love them, as You have loved Your people Israel,
and to be with them always,
wherever they are and whatever their need.

Tuesday May 16   *Exodus 31.12-18*

The Sabbath

The weekly Sabbath is at the heart of Jewish life. It commences about half an hour before sunset on Friday afternoon and concludes when the stars are visible in the night sky on Saturday.

Even in non-traditional homes, Friday night is the time when people come together to relax at the end of the working week. The dining table is covered with a white cloth and formally set. Two loaves, reminiscent of the double portion of biblical manna, are placed on the table with a bottle of wine and a goblet. The loaves are covered by a second cloth and candlesticks complete the setting. Candles are lit, usually by the woman of the house, just before the onset of the Sabbath. Candle-lighting is accompanied by a brief blessing and sometimes a quiet personal prayer.

Before the meal the family sanctify the Sabbath day verbally and everyone has a little wine, followed by the breaking of bread. The meal is a relaxed occasion and, in a traditional household, Sabbath songs are sung between courses.

For the whole of the Sabbath, orthodox Jews do no creative work. Cars, televisions, telephones and fax machines are forgotten for 25 hours of tranquillity. All cooking is done in advance and food left on a covered stove for the three meals that are taken on Friday night and the following day.

On *Shabbat* - the Sabbath – the world is seen as it was at the beginning of time, and it becomes a place of holiness, as at the first Sabbath, the seventh day of creation. The Sabbath is a moment of intimacy between God and Israel, a sign for ever of the Divine presence in this world, and a time when we realize that the sanctification of life is the ultimate purpose of all existence.

＊ *Thank you, O Lord, for the holiness of creation.*
May the spirit of the Sabbath be a part of all our lives
and may we learn once again the ways of Your simplicity.

117

You shall be holy

When something has been set aside for the service of God, it becomes holy and can no longer be used for any mundane purpose. In these passages, the term is applied to every aspect of the life of the people of Israel.

Israel is to be holy, as the Lord their God is holy. Inherent in this simple sentence is a remarkable vision of human possibility. With all of our fragile and apparently incorrigible physicality, we can nevertheless achieve a sanctification of our lives that allows us to participate in the Divine. Egoism can be transformed and the physical made sacred if we will but follow in the paths that God has set out for us in His commandments.

The first passage gives extraordinary prominence to treating parents with reverence, locating this injunction in the context of Israel's relationship with God. Parents have participated in the creation of humanity – it is as Creator that we first encounter God, at the beginning of the Bible – and in knowing them we encounter the miracles of love and selflessness that are at the heart of the religious life.

In society we encounter the temptation of purely self-centred behaviour and our innate egoism has to be redirected toward a life of righteousness and concern for the poor, the disadvantaged and the stranger. The creation of a holy community starts at ground level, in the most mundane aspects of daily existence. Only if we are aware of God in the fields and vineyards can we begin our journey to the realm of holiness.

✱ *Teach us, O Lord, to be ashamed of our callousness,*
and to lay aside our harshness of heart.
In a time of wealth, people are sleeping on the streets
and we walk past them when they ask for small change.
Help us, O God, to make our shame the beginning
of our redemption, for we are far from your vision of holiness.

Love thy neighbour

Hatred, vengefulness and bearing grudges are matters of the heart that cannot be disciplined by a judicial authority, but if we are to walk in the way of holiness, we must address feelings which become especially powerful when we have been hurt by others.

We are to cultivate mutual responsibility. If I see a person going astray, I must not respond with indifference. A rebuke might be in order, but it must be appropriate and sensitive, not an occasion for indulging in angry or vengeful feelings which would be both sinful and destructive.

Ultimately, the people of Israel are to love one another with the same depth of concern that they show for their own individual well-being. The exemplary person is one who develops an engagement with others that is the focal point of his or her purpose. Such a person gradually transforms egoistic feelings into the full maturity of relational love, and the ways of her life reveal the presence of the One who is her Creator.

This depth of concern is not to be confined to those who are members of the community, and the feelings that bind people to each other must not degenerate into tribalism, or discrimination against the stranger who does not share their faith or their culture. The people of Israel know the full weight of the prejudice of Egypt in the slavery that was their formative experience, and they must not permit such behaviour in their own society. Even the small matter of accurate weights and measures must be carefully observed, so that a sense of justice will permeate every aspect of social life.

✱ *Help us, O Lord, to love people who are not like us,*
and share the depth of their pain.
Be with those who seek asylum in their terror and distress,
for we have betrayed them, and they are utterly alone.

Friday May 19   *Leviticus 11.1-12, 41-45*

The dietary laws

Ideally, we should live without harming other creatures of the world, but eating meat and fish is, for most of us, an ingrained desire. The verses we have read today place limits on what can be eaten; only certain animals, fish and fowl are permitted for our food, while all other living things are forbidden. Such boundaries are the first stage in returning to the sensitivities of the Garden of Eden. We have not been put in this world to destroy all around us in order to satisfy our physical desires. We have to begin to discipline our response, for this is the beginning of our journey to holiness.

Observant Jews are guided by these dietary laws and carefully refrain from eating any of the forbidden creatures. Other biblical sources are interpreted traditionally to sanction only a particular form of animal slaughter, which is taken to minimize the inevitable cruelty of life-taking, and also to prohibit the consuming of milk and meat together. Milk is a vital source of life we have taken in order to eat meat. In separating the two, Jews recall their reverence for the living world, and begin to develop anew a sensitivity to all creation.

✳ *Lord, we have ransacked Your creation*
and wantonly destroyed the work of Your hands.
Help us to know the preciousness of all life,
and to turn away from the path of destruction.

Saturday May 20   *Deuteronomy 6.1-9*

Hear O Israel...

Over-familiar language falsifies the religious experience while reverence is indispensable to the spiritual life. Israel is instructed to focus on the Divine Oneness that transcends all human thought. In such engagement she discovers that the love of God is an all-consuming passion that embraces every aspect of our being.

The ultimate task of the Jew is to bring this sense of God into the everyday world, by teaching and understanding the words of the tradition, and applying them in all the situations of life. Such teaching is the first and most vital responsibility of parents to their children.

We are physical as well as intellectual beings; in binding the words of the Torah in phylacteries upon our hands and forehead, we recall the inner task of bringing our most physical desires into the realm of the holy and seek to restore our minds to the tasks of study and devotion.

Every observant Jewish home has a small receptacle affixed to its doorpost, containing a scroll upon which are written the verses of Deuteronomy 6.4-9, and an additional passage, which also enjoins this practice. By nailing the scroll firmly to the doorpost, Jews seek to bring the transcendent love of God into the everyday realities of their families. The scroll comes down from its heavenly origin, and sanctifies the bricks and mortar of the earthly life. This is the great purpose of Jewish observance.

✳ *Help us, O Lord, to recover our reverence for Your holiness.*
May the language of prayer be at one with our deepest
yearning, and may our words not be dimmed
or spoken in haste before You.

FOR REFLECTION – alone or with a group

Reflect again on this week's studies from the perspective of your own faith, and continue to do so next week as the theme develops.

5th Sunday of Easter, May 21   *Deuteronomy 16.1-8*

Passover

For Jews, the story of the Exodus is the most significant of all scriptural narratives. In the slavery of Egypt, they encountered a God who heard the anguished cry of the wretched, and shattered the forces that held them in bondage. God is moved by human suffering and injustice, and history becomes a place of Divine engagement where the forces of evil will never know ultimate triumph. The darkness of night is to be a time of redemption, rather than utter despair and, in the offering of the paschal lamb, physical fragility is transformed into redemptive holiness.

At the Passover table, and throughout the days of the Festival, Jews eat unleavened bread and leaven is not permitted. In the absence of yeast and fermentation, the bread remains wafer-like, flat and hard. It is the bread of affliction, the staple diet of poor people, but simultaneously it is the bread of redemption, recalling for ever that the unfathomable darkness we encounter in our lives can pass away so quickly that the dough will not have time to rise before the morning is upon us.

Passover is the springtime of the world and, in the simplicity of its celebration, Jews have found a source of hope and comfort even in the darkest hours of their tragic history.

The Exodus narratives have also inspired and sustained other people in their afflictions: in slavery and under apartheid. Oppressed people still find a source of hope in the story of God's redemption of Israel. They know that their suffering has not been forgotten, and the day will come when they also will hear joyous tidings of redemption and freedom.

✳ *Help us, O Lord, to remember your acts of redemption,*
to know that darkness will pass
and morning will soon be upon us.

Monday May 22   *Deuteronomy 16.9-12*

Pentecost

In Jewish tradition, Pentecost is identified as the anniversary of the revelation at Mount Sinai. The Exodus from Egypt, the end of the suffering that Jews endured in their bondage, was the beginning of a redemptive journey, which culminated with the giving of the *Torah* at Mount Sinai. *Torah* means 'teaching', and classically refers to the Five Books of Moses.

The *Torah* is the eternal link between God and Israel. In any synagogue, the focal point is a curtained alcove. When the curtain is drawn, and the doors behind it are opened, we see the hand-written scrolls of the *Torah,* wrapped in velvet mantles and adorned with silverware.

When a scroll is taken out to be read, it is paraded around the synagogue amidst solemn formalities, and the singing of appropriate psalms, as worshippers bow or come forward to kiss the mantle. When the reading is complete, the scroll is raised aloft and the congregation reminded of their link with the giving of the Torah at the first Pentecost.

Between Passover and Pentecost each day and week are counted formally, giving a sense of gradual ascent from bondage to the dawning of a new spiritual life.

In everything they do, Jews are to remember their suffering in Egypt; and especially in times of joy they must ensure that the poor, the lonely and the stranger are with them, for this is the essence of their life in the community of Israel.

✳ *Help us, O Lord, to share what we have*
with those who are in poverty and want.
Teach us to give with joyousness of heart
and restore among us the passion of Your righteousness
and the ways of Your holy community.

Tuesday May 23   *Deuteronomy 16.13-17*

Tabernacles

In biblical times, the feast of Tabernacles was celebrated at the end of the autumn harvests, to teach the people of Israel that, even in their time of prosperity, they should retain the simplicity of their lives and not forget the Divine presence that sustains all creation.

Today, Jews still celebrate this autumn festival a few days after the days of penitence at the opening of their New Year. Observant Jews construct a temporary dwelling outside their homes: the roof is made of leafy evergreen branches sufficient to provide a shelter, and the *Succah* – 'Tabernacle' – has to be able to withstand the winds of the autumnal season. Weather permitting, all meals are taken in the tabernacle, and in warm climates people sleep in the *Succah* every night.

It is the most basic of dwellings, offering a minimum of material comfort. It is fragile, and open to the elements, providing little by way of shelter. Living in the *Succah* is an act of trust and faithfulness, when Jews rekindle their relationship with the Divine and the spirituality of the High Holy Days becomes a living reality.

Amidst the enormous power of modern technical achievement, the *Succah* stands as an eternal challenge; like the voice of God in the Garden of Eden, it asks us where we are, and whether in the midst of all our fashionable possessions, we have really found a home or encountered the splendour of Divine creation which is the longing of our soul and our true and ultimate dwelling place.

✳ *Help us, O Lord, to live in faithfulness and trust.*
Spread over us the tabernacle of Your peace
and help us to know the holiness of Your simplicity,
in all the ways of our life.

Wednesday May 24   *Psalm 22.1-22**
Why hast Thou forsaken me?

Our sense of being forsaken in this world and bereft of the comfort of the Divine Presence is one of the most powerful and troubling experiences that we have to endure. When we encounter suffering that is wholly unwarranted and undeserved, or when the powers of evil seem transparent in the political realm, our faith is stretched to breaking point and can be utterly shattered by the darkness that is all around us.

The wonder of Psalm 22 is that the Psalmist's faith appears unbroken, despite the terrifying perplexity of his situation. Like the burning bush which was not consumed by the flames, it forces us to turn aside and seek understanding.

If faith is based on Divine intervention and, when we are in dire need, no help is forthcoming, then our grounds for believing are shattered beyond repair. But the source of the Psalmist's fidelity lies elsewhere. His first thought is the transcendent holiness that he encounters in the life of prayer, and he then recalls the miraculous wonder that accompanies the birth of children. Such signs of the Divine cannot be quenched even by overwhelming evil and, in their presence, we cannot conceive of a wholly meaningless universe. The sense of God is continual and intimate, and it is, paradoxically, the ground of the Psalmist's anguish. It is not the Divine absence, but the constancy of God's presence, that makes him confront the mystery of suffering.

✳ *Teach us, O Lord, to be with those bereft of Your comfort,*
for they are grief-stricken and alone.
In all the busyness of our lives, may Your presence remind us
of what is truly important, and may we be always
with each other, as You are with us.

Thursday May 25   *Psalm 22.23-31**

Universal redemption

The latter part of the psalm presents particular difficulty, for it appears that the Psalmist is offering the prospect of his praises as an inducement for Divine intervention. Furthermore, the consequences of such praises, including a reverbatory effect at the ends of the world, seem greatly exaggerated.

But it can be maintained that the Psalmist was overwhelmed by a redemptive vision that came upon him in the midst of his prayer. The latter part of the Psalm would then be classified as prophecy, rather than inducement. According to the rubric, the Psalm was recited at daybreak, as the darkness of the night was dispersed, and the Psalmist was moved to look beyond his own suffering and await the redemption of Israel, which would indeed be of consequence for the faith of the world.

The poor and afflicted of the earth would witness the destiny of Israel and be comforted, for they would know that their cries too were heard by God, and that they too would be redeemed from their sufferings. The Kingdom of God would replace the tyranny of the powerful, and even those who had previously waxed fat would be transformed by the Divine Presence. God's redemptive act would not only rescue this suffering people, but it would transform worldly perception and restore idealism to the life of the nations, for righteousness would have clearly triumphed over the forces of brutal tyranny and oppression.

✳ *May we pray before You for others as we pray for ourselves,*
and may their needs be as our own.
Help us, O Lord, to long for the redemption, for such longing
is a source of blessing for ourselves and all the world.

Friday May 26   *Isaiah 2.1-5*

The End of Days

Jewish hope is focused upon an age when our world will be transformed by the manifest presence of Divine holiness. For Jews, the end of war is a key feature of redemption. Particularly in the twentieth century, when European Jews were devastated by the Holocaust, a redeemed world in Jewish thought had to be a world freed from murderous hatred.

The text does not only envisage an absence of armed conflict; it speaks of the disappearance of bellicose impulses and the fearfulness which inspires even pacific countries to maintain massive military arsenals. Warlike values will be set aside, weaponry abandoned, and the pruning hook will replace the spear in the stock of national imagery. Human nature having been transformed, societies will no longer be moved by insecurity and aggression.

Jewish hope is rooted in the Exodus from Egypt, when God heard the cries of their ancestors and delivered them from brutality and abuse. As a small people, Jews have suffered throughout their history, at the hands of the great and the powerful, but their first collective encounter with God gave them an undying faith in the prospect of redemption which encompasses the wretched of all nations.

Only when our hatreds have been transformed can we learn once again to walk in the light of our Creator. This is the blessing that Abraham's descendants will share with all the families of the earth, and it is the ultimate longing of the people of Israel down the ages.

✳ *Help us, O Lord, not to be fearful of one another.*
Still the imaginings of our hearts
and teach us the ways of Your peace.

Saturday May 27   *Isaiah 19.19-25*
Saving the Egyptians
This remarkable passage indicates that God is concerned for Egypt and Assyria, as He is for Israel. The Jewish people have their eternal calling, but their way is not the only way, nor is their covenant an exclusive relationship with God, who is eternally present for all the peoples of the earth.

The text refers to historic national enemies of the people of Israel, but states clearly that their hostility will not last for ever. Even Assyria will be transformed, and the three peoples will live together in harmony and mutual blessing.

Historic conflicts are sustained because group hostility is passed from one generation to the next. Fear and hatred dehumanize each community in the eyes of the other and people are identified with the most negative aspects of their collective identity.

The text forestalls such development by emphasizing the transformative quality of penitence. Like Israel of old, Egypt will encounter oppression and physical deliverance from its suffering. It will turn away from the pursuit of power and discover a new way in the midst of its affliction. Like Israel, it will choose to live in the presence of the Divine, and know the blessedness and truth of the life of faith. In turning away from the pursuit of power it will find the beginning of national redemption.

✳ *Help us, O Lord, to pray for all the peoples of the earth,*
even those who have been a source of our affliction.
May our prayers dissolve our fearfulness and our anger,
and bring us closer to Your presence and Your peace.

FOR REFLECTION – alone or with a group

- How is our understanding of suffering and redemption broadened by Jewish experience and thought?
- Try to identify those strands which speak to peoples who suffer economic exploitation in the contemporary world and which have given rise to 'Liberation Theology'.
- What can we learn from the Torah about our treatment of strangers and ethnic minorities?

FOR ACTION

If you live in the UK, find out more about the witness of the Council of Christians and Jews (Drayton House, 30 Gordon Street, London WC1H 0AN).

LIVING ENCOUNTERS
2. Encounter with other Faiths

Notes based on the New Revised Standard Version
Elizabeth J Harris

Elizabeth Harris is Secretary for Inter-Faith Relations for the Methodist Church in Britain. Previous to this, she was a Research Fellow at Westminster College, Oxford. She has studied Buddhism and Christian-Buddhist encounter in Sri Lanka where she lived for over seven years. She has written extensively on Buddhist and inter-faith themes, including 'What Buddhists Believe' (Oneworld: Oxford, 1998), a book based on a series of radio programmes she wrote and presented for the BBC World Service.

We live in a religiously plural world. Few countries can boast religious homogeneity. Few cities do not have people of different religions living next door to one another. Christians react to this in different ways. Some are fearful, seeing conflict and competition ahead. Others are excited, hoping for reconciliation and mutual enrichment. Whichever stance is taken, two needs arise: a theological framework for encounter with people of other faiths, and practical guidance for the encounter itself. This study will look at the light which key biblical texts can shed on these needs.

6th Sunday of Easter, May 28   *Acts 10.1-16*
Breaking the barriers
What kind of action or statement would you consider to be a betrayal of your faith? Breaking one of the ten commandments? Denying the uniqueness of Jesus? Each one of us may give a different answer.

For Peter, dietary restrictions based on the rules given in Leviticus 11, were part of his religious identity. He would have been taught from childhood to detest the animals he saw in this vision. Each was impure, capable of contaminating humans. Absolute abhorrence must have arisen in Peter. That he refused what the voice asked three times is understandable. To have said 'yes' would have betrayed his identity.

It can be argued that what happens in this chapter is the most important event in the history of the early Church. At its heart is the breaking of rules and a crossing of fixed religious boundaries. Cornelius was a non-Jewish sympathizer with Judaism. He had no doubt been influenced, even nurtured, by the religion of Rome but he had chosen to travel into new spiritual territory. Peter has also travelled into new territory with Jesus but he is asked to go further. For neither is the journey easy.

The question thrown out across the centuries is: can that which we hold dear from the past actually prevent us from hearing what the Holy Spirit is saying in the present?

✻ *Lord, give us the discernment*
to know when you are calling us into what is new.

Monday May 29   Acts 10.17-33
Freed for encounter
By the time Peter reached Caesarea, the meaning of his vision had become clear to him. Certainty had replaced confusion. How did this change happen? Certainly the Holy Spirit had a hand in it. But the Holy Spirit works through our own experience and so perhaps Peter's experience was important also.

It was thirty miles from Joppa to Caesarea, a two-day journey. During this time, Peter travelled with people who had been brought up within another faith. What kind of experience did he have? Did he come face to face with a goodness which humbled and challenged him? We can only speculate. But by the time he reached his destination he was willing to be the guest of these people and therefore to break with his past.

Changes in theological understanding are often preceded by changes in experience. Christians who make friends with people of other faiths usually discover that their friends are filled with deep faith, sincere commitment and high moral sensitivity. The result is that condemnatory generalizations about other faiths cease to make sense.

✻ *In this new world where old beliefs collide*
Where faithful neighbours fall to narrow pride,
Help us to fling the Kingdom open wide.
               Hymn for a Multi-faith Society, Nick Sissons (1996)

Tuesday May 30   Acts 10.34-43
God has no favourites
Peter has been on a steep learning curve, to use modern terminology. His cultural and religious inheritance has been

challenged through both his dreams and his experience. When he then attempts to speak of Jesus, the result is a sermon which breathes inclusivity. No hint of religious or racial exclusivity enters.

The question he raises at the beginning has not lost its relevance: who is favoured and accepted by God? In a multi-faith society, it cannot be escaped. Can we know how God looks on Muslims, Sikhs or Hindus? Peter's words alone cannot give a definitive answer. We should not expect one: so different was Peter's context from our own. Yet, what he claims before those he might have considered outside God's purposes – only weeks before – can certainly help us create a relevant theological framework.

God shows no partiality. God accepts anyone who fears him and does what is right. This is what Peter proclaims. One helpful starting point for inter-faith relations is the maxim that wherever there is sincere religious faith and a concern for righteousness, there also is God.

✴ *O God of all truth, who ever seeks to lead humans into truth,*
we thank you that you have no favourites
but pour out your love to all.

Wednesday May 31   Acts 10.44-48*
The call to reassess
Would Peter have baptized these Gentiles if this had not happened? Theologically he had almost reached the point where he could not refuse. But emotionally and psychologically he might not have been ready. That God could be working to such an extent in those outside his family of faith might still have seemed incredible.

The unmistakable sign of God's presence proved to Peter that God certainly was working in this way. It also pointed to the need for radical reassessment within the early Christian community, for a new way of thinking about where evil and the impure were located.

Throughout Christian history, there have been Christians who have located evil in other religions. Even where touching points with Christianity were identified these have been seen as wiles of the devil to turn people away from the true faith. Kenneth Cracknell – in *Justice, Courtesy and Love: Theologians and Missionaries Encountering World Religions' (Epworth 1995)* – suggests that change came when some missionaries began to recognize the action of the Holy Spirit in the lives of people within other faith communities, and to realize that the fruits of faith within 'the other' could only be judged good. They found that evil could no longer be located 'out there' within other systems. It was present in all systems, Christianity included. Mission and witness then had to be reassessed.

✳ *O'er lands both near and far*
Thick darkness broodeth yet
Arise, O morning star,
Arise, and never set!   Lewis Hensley (1824-1905)
Adapted for Hymns and Psalms (Methodist Publishing House)

Ascension Day, June 1   Acts 1.1-11*
How large is our Christ?
This passage leaves a few questions tantalizingly unresolved. At the end of the Gospel of Luke, the Ascension occurs on the very day Jesus is seen to have risen from the dead. Here, it is suggested that Jesus taught the disciples for a considerable period after the resurrection and shared food with them. But little is said about what he taught.

The question the disciples ask (verse 6), however, shows that, whatever Jesus had been saying, their minds were still rooted in the immediate political situation. They are still convinced that if Jesus is the Messiah then his role must include the liberation of the Jews from foreign domination, in other words that his mission was an ethnocentric one.

Jesus' response forces the disciples beyond the ethnocentric to the whole world with a Great Commission different from that found at the end of Matthew. No mention is made of baptism. The emphasis is on witness to the love of God seen in the person of Jesus, rather than on the building of a Church. What implications does this have for Christian mission in a religiously plural society?

✳ *Christ reigns.*
He has triumphed over evil and death.
He is with us always, to the end of time.

Friday June 2   1 John 5.1-6, 9-13*
All who love are God's children
In the context of inter-faith relations, how should we deal with passages such as this which, when read literally, seem to condemn those outside the Christian faith to alienation from God?

For the writer, the Christ event is paramount. From the depth of conviction, he cries that it is only the one who believes that Jesus is the Son of God who can conquer the world. Yet, the chapter before has a far more inclusivist statement: 'Everyone who loves is born of God and knows God' (4.7). The first statement seems to exclude loving, God-fearing people of another faith whilst the second includes them. Which should be taken as the message of John, or can they both be held together?

There is no simple answer. One way forward is to parallel verse 5 of the reading with the kind of statement a woman might make about her husband: 'He is the finest man in the world'. This is not totally satisfactory but it makes the important point that language is used differently in different contexts. An outpouring of personal faith or love will be different from a reasoned argument. Another approach is to place the sentences within the total context of the New Testament, where more than one criterion is used to judge whether someone is in or out of the Kingdom of God, and to ask which is closest to what we know of the mind of Christ.

✳ *For the love of God is broader*
  Than the measures of man's mind...

But we make his love too narrow
  By false limits of our own;
And we magnify his strictness
  With a zeal he will not own.   *Frederick W Faber (1814-63)*
  Adapted for Hymns & Psalms (Methodist Publishing House)

Saturday June 3   *Genesis 1.26-31; Psalm 104.24-30*

Humanity is one

One way of finding theological aids for our encounter with other faiths is to ask of the stories which mould the Christian tradition what they say about the nature of God's relationship with creation. Do they present a picture of a God who purposely creates division and the potential for chaos? Do they show a God who separates what he creates into the blessed and the alienated, the despicable and the beloved? Or do they provide inspiration for asserting the oneness of humanity and of humanity's religious quest?

Taken together, today's passages stress that the world's rich variety is unthinkable without God's creative and sustaining activity. God is seen delighting in what has been made, blessing the fruits of his work. More than this, there is delight in the unity

131

given to men and women through the very fact that they are made in the image of God. Humanity is one.

This is worth pondering. What does it mean for us, now, in a multi-faith society? If God created humanity to be one and delighted in it, can we believe that God left himself without witnesses in parts of the world untouched by Christianity and Judaism? Should we be surprised when we find what is holy within other religions?

✳ *Let us praise God that there is but one human race, united by more than divides it.*

FOR REFLECTION – alone or with a group

● Should our understanding of God's Word remain static or should it be open to change?
● In a multi-faith situation is witnessing to Christ different from building a Church?
● What different criteria are used to judge people in the New Testament and can these help us develop theological aids for inter-faith encounter?

7th Sunday of Easter, June 4   *Genesis 9.8-17*

Generosity unlimited

Repeatedly this passage stresses, 'all living creatures'. The heartbeat of the story is again the inclusivity and generosity of God's relationship to the world. There has been a purge. There has been suffering. But the fundamental and profoundly precious insight here is that God's covenant to protect and sustain creation has no limits, however various, however sinful that creation becomes. It is not limited by time, nor space, nor condition. Apocalyptic scenes of judgement and destruction are utterly rejected. This is not how God is to work.

Some millennial predictions seem to ignore this. They present a picture of a God who will destroy the earth in order to save the elect few. What a betrayal of this vision from Genesis! If our environment on earth is destroyed it will not be because of God's action but because of humanity's greed and hatred. God's covenant as presented here is with all, not with an elect, nor with one race, nor with one religion. God's love is unlimited.

Throughout the centuries not only Christians but also people of other theistic faiths have attempted to express this conviction. Of God's love, Charles Wesley wrote, 'Its streams the whole creation reach, So plenteous is the store'. The Guru Granth

Sahib, the Holy Book and supreme teacher of the Sikhs, declares, 'Grace abounds beyond all reckoning' *(part of the morning prayer, Jap)*.

✳ *May we make both these lines our prayer of praise.*

Monday June 5   Mark 7.24-30
Testing and affirming faith in the other'
This is a story some avoid because it seems to show a hesitant Jesus, an ethnocentric Jesus unwilling to heal someone who is not a Jew. His words seem to contradict other parts of the Gospels and to come perilously close to the kind of attitudes present in such things as ethnic cleansing.

Yet, to stress Jesus' hesitation alone is too superficial a reading. It lacks imagination. That the woman responds so vigorously, even humorously, shows that the context was not one of confrontation. Eric Lott, Christian minister and scholar of Indian religions – in *Healing Wings: Acts of Jesus for Human Wholeness* (Asian Trading Corporation, India, 1998) – has suggested that Jesus could have used a well-known saying to test the woman's faith in the same way as some Indian teachers at first discourage the new inquirer in order to find out whether he or she is sincere. In other words, it was as though Jesus is saying, 'This is what Jews think. What do you say to it?' He is evidently delighted with the robustness of the answer.

Important here is that it is a non-Jew, a person of another faith, who recognizes the holy in Jesus. She could not have done it without possessing spiritual insight of her own, and it is this spiritual insight which is recognized and affirmed by Jesus.

✳ *Teach us to hear and heed the Spirit's call;*
   God present now with grace enough for all;
   Great is such faith, although its seeds be small.
                   Hymn for a Multi-faith Society, Nick Sissons, 1996

Tuesday June 6   Mark 9.38-41
Good found in unexpected places
The wish to be a member of one or several clearly defined groups based on family, nation, race, colour, culture, religion, age or gender almost seems to be part of human nature. It holds out security and identity. 'She or he is not one of us,' has rung through each century within families and nations. It undergirds

Mafia networks and religious sects. The response of the disciples is therefore understandable.

Jesus is shown making clear that he is not forming an exclusivist sect. He implies that neither his healing power, nor his message, is the possession of a small privileged group. So, if an outsider sincerely recognizes and seeks to use Jesus' healing power, this should be welcomed not condemned.

The God of Jesus Christ is one who affirms goodness wherever it is found, whether inside the Christian community or outside. The key question is whether actions bear positive fruit and are sincerely motivated, not whether a person or community is 'in' or 'out'. As we meet people of other faiths we should expect to come face to face with insights into the holy which touch our own. For goodness, love, compassion and healing power are not the sole possession of Christians.

✳ *Lord, may we never forget that you affirm*
goodness, love and compassion wherever it is found.

Wednesday June 7   Mark 12.28-34

Facing the touching points between faiths

There is more in this passage than meets the eye. The two commandments identified by Jesus were central to Jewish practice. The first, from Deuteronomy 6.4-5, formed part of daily Jewish devotion. The second came from Leviticus 19.18. Few Jews could quarrel with his response, for he could be heard as saying that these were the two from which all other laws followed.

It is not Jesus but someone else who suggests the more radical interpretation – that the two laws should in fact take priority over any other structure of faith or practice. This is what would have caused controversy among the Jews present, not Jesus' original statement.

It is passages such as these which suggest that there is no discontinuity between the basic principles taught by Christ and Judaism. To go further, if these two commandments are used as criteria with which to approach yet other faiths, the same thing can be discovered. Many faiths centre on love and devotion to God, and in almost every faith can be found the golden rule – do to others what you would want them to do to you – which is very similar to loving one's neighbour as oneself.

Can we any longer say that there is a radical discontinuity between Christianity and all other faiths? If the answer is 'no', what pattern of relationship should be encouraged?

Thursday June 8   *Acts 17.16-28*

Affirmation not demonization

This passage is frequently cited as an example of good practice in mission within a multi-religious context. For Paul does not decry what distresses him within the culture of Athens. On the contrary, he affirms what is good in it. He accepts that Greek sages had insight into truth and quotes from them. No doubt other Jews did the same when commending their beliefs within Greek culture.

Down the ages many have come to see that the Christian gospel is not helped if coupled with the demonization of the spiritual convictions of others. For instance, if the Buddha, a symbol of pure wisdom and compassion for Buddhists, is condemned, Buddhists are unlikely to see that Christians are speaking about a God of love. The injustice done to their own beliefs would prevent it.

So, how is the gospel communicated within a multi-faith society? A code of conduct based on respect for the other is the first step. Paul uses what has come to be known as the fulfilment theory – that Christianity is the fulfilment of all other spiritual searches. Yet, such an approach can appear arrogant to those who sincerely find all they need within another spiritual tradition. What alternatives are there?

* *Lord, may our witness to your love*
  be sensitive to the beliefs of others.
  May we never hinder your purposes
  through our short-sightedness.

Friday June 9   *Ruth 1.1-22*

Touching points and differences

It is probable that the book of Ruth was written in protest against the policies of people such as Ezra and Nehemiah who sought to build up the post-exilic Jewish community through racial and religious exclusivism. There is much in this passage intended to be abhorrent to apostles of racial purity, for the central theme is praise of a gentile woman, a foreigner, a person originally of another faith.

The author is answering two questions, Is it good that a gentile should be welcomed into Judaism? Is it good that the line of David should run through a non-Jew?' There is a resounding 'Yes' to both.

To speak of a pure lineage within any religion can be a product of self-deception. Religions and thought systems interact, intermingle. The religions of India owe much to each other. Christianity grew from Judaism but also became indebted to Greek thought. In turn, Christianity touched other traditions and influenced them. The religions of the world have not grown up totally in isolation from each other.

Many Christians this century have found that they have been strengthened in their own faith through encounter with other faiths and cultures. The faiths of the world are not the same. Those involved in such encounter discover heart-warming touching points but also differences. Differences can sometimes be difficult to sympathize with, but sometimes they can provide new and enriching insights.

✻ *In all our relationships and encounters, O God,*
   may we be guided by your Spirit
   and strengthened by your love.

Saturday June 10   *Jonah 4.1-11*

To be evangelized by the 'other'

The purpose of the book of Jonah echoes that of Ruth. Again, religious exclusivism is challenged. But the author goes further. Throughout the whole book, people of other faiths are shown in a better light than the Jews. The Ninevites who repent, relying on God's mercy, have a better understanding of God than Jonah, who is horrified at the thought of compassion being shown to a city of heathens. Even the sailors in chapter 1 are shown to be more humane than Jonah.

In his sermon, *On Faith,* John Wesley wrote of those he called 'Heathens, Mahometans and Jews': 'we may wish their lives did not shame many of us who are called Christians.' It is a radical statement but as true today as in Wesley's time. The non-violence of Gandhi put the aggression of the Christian British in India to shame. The self-immolation of some Buddhist monks in south-east Asia did the same for American military action later in the century.

No one religion has a monopoly over love and self-sacrifice. Similarly, no religion can claim that in practice its adherents are never guilty of bigotry and short-sightedness. This opens up the possibility of Christians being evangelized, being called back to their own roots, by people of other religions. 'No man is an island, entire of itself,' wrote the Elizabethan poet, John Donne. Could it be that no religion is an island, complete of itself?

✳ *Praise be to thee, Lord,*
for the cords that bind us into one humanity
and for all that we can receive from one another.

FOR REFLECTION – alone or with a group

- Are you fearful or hopeful about inter-faith relations? Why?
- Do you know a person of another faith? What were the difficulties? What did you learn?
- Are there aspects of faith in other religions that we can learn from and draw into ourselves?
- How can people of different faiths be witnesses to one another?

FOR ACTION

Choose a faith you do not know much about and read a book about it written by a person of that faith.

THE SPIRIT IN THE WORLD
Making us one

Meditations, based on the New Revised Standard Version, on
Pentecost 2000 in the Holy Land by

Harry Hagopian

*Harry Hagopian, an Armenian Christian in Jerusalem, is
Executive Director of the Jerusalem Liaison Office of the Middle
East Council of Churches (MECC). As an international lawyer, his
work has included human rights advocacy, interpretation and the
communication ministry. He is Middle East Consultant for
Bethlehem 2000 and Pax Christi International.*

Pentecost is a major Christian feast for all the churches in the
Holy Land. It is also a colourful and summery event. Christian
children can often be seen, in best Sunday costumes,
accompanying their parents to visit relatives and friends. I usually
celebrate Pentecost by praying at the Church of the Holy
Sepulchre in Jerusalem. And I suppose the history and setting of
this Church of the Resurrection (as it is known in Arabic) make
me question the real impact of Pentecost on the faithful
Palestinian Christians and on different churches that dot this
conflict-ridden land today. Pentecost in the Holy Land is not
solely a popular occasion for rejoicing. Rather, it represents both
a *kairos* and a *chronos* (Greek – 'an opportunity' and 'a time'),
allowing for the spirituality of the indigenous Christians to be
revived and to express itself anew.

The local Palestinian Christian community still witnesses to its
faith in the Holy Land today, and runs hospitals, homes for the
elderly, schools and other institutions as part of their service
ministry. Our faith is a Christ-centred one. Every church and
every cobbled stone in Israel and Palestine reminds us of this
truth. And, with the experience of Pentecost, the truth has been
'globalized'.

Pentecost, June 11   *Acts 2.1-21**

The coming of the Holy Spirit

Imagine for a moment that you are closeted in a shuttered house,
pretending that the outside world does not exist! The Acts of the
Apostles tells us how Jesus' followers were huddled in a house,

fearful for their own safety. Suddenly, a wind-like sound was heard and they saw what looked like tongues of fire spreading out and touching each of them. They all came out of the house and started talking in different tongues. Peter even felt the need to reassure the crowds that they were neither confused nor drunk!

Just as this motley group of early believers was led by the Holy Spirit to spread the good news 'in Jerusalem, in all Judaea and Samaria, and to the ends of the earth' (Acts 1.8), so it is with the Mother Church of Jerusalem today. The Churches here often speak different – and at times contradictory – languages. They might even look confused or bewildered. But when faced with political pressures, discrimination and harassment at every corner, is it any wonder that their faith is at times challenged and that they are apprehensive for their own safety and well-being?

✳ *Let us pray that the activity of the Holy Spirit which came with power upon the believers on the day of Pentecost will continue to guide, strengthen and inspirit the Church of Jerusalem and all its leaders.*

Monday June 12   *Ephesians 2.11-22*
One in Christ

The Holy Land is home for two peoples and three religions. Israelis and Palestinians share the same small parcel of land. Jews, Christians and Muslims can often be seen going to their synagogues, churches and mosques to attend regular services. It is here that a true manifestation of faith can be witnessed. But it is also here that tensions and divisions surface more visibly than in other parts of the world.

For local Palestinian Christians, historical Palestine witnessed the birth, crucifixion, resurrection and ascension of Jesus. It is here that the Word became flesh, and it is here that all the different Orthodox, Catholic and Evangelical Churches profess to that very faith. But it is also here that enormous differences abound. The ecumenical spirit is certainly not always evident in the hearts and minds of present-day followers of Jesus.

At Pentecost, we reflect on the letter to the Ephesians as it appeals to all to seek unity through oneness with Jesus Christ. God's promise of unity to his people is guaranteed by the Holy Spirit, and Christians in all parts of the world as well as here must strive to live in such a way that their oneness in Christ may become real in their daily lives.

* *Let us pray that the Holy Spirit will help the Christian communities in the Holy Land to overcome their divisions and focus on the larger goal of working together toward their unity within the diversity of their traditions. Only then can the Church truly liberate itself and seek the grace which transcends all earthly powers and interests. Only then will it be the worthy descendant of the First Church of Pentecost.*

Tuesday June 13   *Ephesians 3.1-13*

Inclusive faith

One of the neighbourhoods in Jerusalem that fully retains its Jewish orthodox traditions and practices is Mea She'arim. It can easily be viewed from my office and, on every Jewish Sabbath day, it is fascinating to see the roads being barricaded so that no cars can pass. Mea She'arim comes to a complete standstill as its residents diligently observe their religious – *haredi* – identity.

Such religious observance is very moving: it is not everywhere that one can perceive religion being practised with such attention to every minute detail. Yet, it is also disturbing since such rites are often observed to the detriment of men and women of other traditions or faiths. I often find myself struggling with this reality, since I believe that our own Christian faith is not an exclusive – or exclusivist – one. Rather, I believe that everyone is part of God's plan revealed by the Holy Spirit to those apostles to bring all creation, and everything on earth and in heaven together, with Christ as head.

Paul, in his letter to the Ephesians, reminds us that the gospel enables people of all nationalities and cultures to share with the Jews in God's blessings. He adds that they are members of the same body and share in the promise that God made through Christ Jesus. Yet, given the political divisions and human frailties in this land of the Resurrection, those of faith – Christians and non-Christians alike – do not always recognize how to be inclusive, or how to think of their neighbour as a fellow human being created in the likeness and image of God.

* *Let us pray that the Holy Spirit will help us to understand God's inclusive plan for his creation, and that all peoples will learn to overcome their fears, doubts and prejudices to rediscover their oneness in Christ.*

The love of Christ

Last year, my brother was married at St Stephen's Church in Jerusalem. Haig asked me to take one of the readings, and I chose this passage which speaks of the love of Christ. The message was as moving then as it is now.

Struggling under difficult circumstances, with their basic human rights being constantly violated and their lives often reduced to daily attempts at survival, is it any wonder that some local Christians in the Holy Land walk away from their faith? Being faithful has become too onerous an obligation. People here are weary enough as it is, and their prayers for a peace that comes with justice often appear to remain unanswered!

Reading this letter again, however, I can detect three distinct messages that encourage me. Paul reminds us first to be strong in our inner selves. Then he tells us that Christ will make his home in our hearts through faith. But most importantly, Paul's prayer reminds us to anchor our roots and foundation in love so that we may come to understand how broad and long, how high and deep, is Christ's love for all of us.

✳ *Let us pray that all those who become weary or cynical will rediscover the faith that is 'blown' into us like a wind at Pentecost, and which fills us completely with the very nature of God. Then, renewed strength will produce courage and endurance for those who live in this troubled land.*

The unity of the body

One of the most precious gifts I have ever been given can be found in my bedroom. It is the Good News Bible in Today's English Version, and the first page carries a hand-written inscription which says, 'With Love', bears a date and then the reference to Ephesians 3.14-21. This was a gift from my wife some eight years ago before we were married at St Sarkis' Armenian Apostolic Church in London.

And I suppose an epistle that speaks volumes to me can equally speak volumes to many other local Christians in this land who are willing to listen to its message. For it is true that the Christian communities here sometimes forget to be humble, gentle and patient. Faced with divisions within their own ranks, feeling vulnerable from the pressures of war, the occupation of their land and the discrimination that assails them almost daily, they either become jaundiced and drift away from their faith, or else become arrogant and try to protect themselves and survive.

But St Paul calls us to be tolerant with one another. He exhorts us to preserve the unity of the Spirit in the bonds of peace. Does this message not encourage us? Does it not help us overcome some of our doubts at moments of panic and despair? Does it not renew us to face a new day with fresh courage? Does it not also carry with it the message that unity and peace are not only external qualities, but should also become internal ones? How appropriate this is for a land where conflict and fear of the *other* reign unchecked, and where unity is a timorous hope.

✳ *Let us pray for all the peoples of the Holy Land that they may use their different God-given skills for the common good, and let us also pray for the one ecumenical fellowship as represented by the Middle East Council of Churches in Jerusalem.*

Friday June 16   *Ephesians 4.12-16*

A vision of unity

Last year, all the Churches of Jerusalem came together to celebrate the Week of Prayer for Christian Unity. One of the preachers chose this particular text to underline his belief that our Christian faith is anchored in service as much as in worship. Helping people in refugee camps on the outskirts of Bethlehem or Gaza, providing accommodation for those whose houses are demolished, rebuilding areas that have been shattered by wars and earthquakes, tending the oppressed or marginalized, healing those who are wounded in their souls and hearts – are all part of what distinguishes us as true Christians.

And in such caring, might we also not discover anew the indivisibility of the Body of Christ? Might we not work and mature together in order to reach to the very height of Christ's full stature? As we celebrate this year the 2000th anniversary of Christ, can we all not operate together as the different parts of the same body, so that when each separate part works, the whole body grows and builds itself up through love?

✳ *Let us pray for all Israelis and Palestinians that they may learn to speak and to apply the truth in a spirit of love. Then they can truly know a Pentecost-like experience in which the shackles of fear and doubt that bind them will be released.*

And what a gift it would be to embrace this conversion in a year when the world ushers in the Millennium with new hopes and experiences.

Saturday June 17   *Romans 8.22-27**

Anguish and glory

As a man, I cannot claim even to imagine the pain associated with childbirth! A friend of mine who had given birth to a child likened it once to the racking pain experienced with kidney stones. I took her word for it, not having experienced that either!

St Paul's letter to the Romans is a prime dissertation on the practical implications of the Christian faith in our lives. The apostle discusses the power of God's Spirit in the believer's life and wrestles with the question of how Jews and non-Jews fit together into God's plan for humankind. This theme also points me to the Gospel of Matthew as it refers to the new alliance that fulfils the old, but also ensures that justice prevails for all (Matthew 5.19).

But Paul's letter also highlights our weaknesses as Christians. In the Holy Land, Christians – as much as Jews and Muslims – have become professional 'groaners'. And I believe that part of this moaning and groaning results from a faith that forgets what happened at Pentecost. We have not yet fully taken on board the gift of the Spirit. The Spirit emboldens, encourages, refreshes and renews us in our daily lives. The hope that comes with our faith is also a practical ingredient which should encourage us to carry on despite all the hardships that confront us every day.

In our weaknesses, we need to rely more on the Holy Spirit which intercedes for us and helps us in our darkest moments. At Pentecost, tradition in Jerusalem has it that all church-goers light a candle and then share a message of hope with each other. This message should encourage Christians in their ecumenical journey together, confident that the Spirit will not abandon them, but rather render them more intrepid.

✳ *At Pentecost, then, let us pray that the Spirit will imbue the 'Living Stones of the Holy Land' with the hope that enables them to face the future with spirited determination. May the Spirit also draw the Churches together, strengthen their communities and become a wind that blows gently but never howls too loudly.*

143

FOR REFLECTION – alone or with others

- The Holy Land is where Jesus left his footprints on earth. It is where he walked and talked, and where he assumed our humanity in order to save us. As you visit this biblical land and meet its Living Stones – or as you read the daily news of what is happening here – how does Jesus become visible to you today? Do you begin to recognize him around you?
- Remember that Jerusalem, the City of Peace, is a divided city of suffering and strife for peoples of all faiths. Pray that it may truly live up to its calling, and that the tears of those local Christians who live within its walls may cease.
- In imagination – or in actuality if you are visiting the Holy Land – go to the Church of the Nativity in Bethlehem. Think about how undemanding our Christian faith has become, and then light a candle of hope as you express your solidarity with your fellow Christians of the Holy Land.
- Think about those early Christians gathered in the Upper Room, and then compare their faith with ours today. Has it changed, and how?

FOR ACTION

- When visiting the Holy Land, make a special effort to meet with some of its 'Living Stones' – the local Christians – rather than simply visiting sites of religious or historic interest. Attend Sunday worship in one of the local churches, and share a special moment of affirmation together with the local Palestinian congregation.
- In order to appreciate truly the heritage, richness and diversity of those local Christians, invest in a copy of *Living Stones Pilgrimage with the Christians of the Holy Land,* co-authored by Alison Hilliard, Head of Religion at the BBC World Service in London. It was published by Cassell (UK) and endorsed both by the Church in Jerusalem and the Middle East Council of Churches.

THE SPIRIT IN THE WORLD
2. Sending us to each other

Notes based on the New Revised Standard Version by
John Pritchard

John Pritchard has been a minister in West Africa (Côte d'Ivoire), England and China (Hong Kong). A former Africa Secretary of the British Methodist Church and General Secretary of its Overseas Division, he is now superintendent minister of the Croydon Circuit in South London.

This week we read from Luke's account of God's Spirit working among the early Christians, and how they discerned and responded to the Spirit's call and direction. The 'Acts of the Apostles' are sometimes, with reason, re-titled the Acts of the Spirit'. But the Spirit's activity was not a peculiar phenomenon of the apostolic age. Sunday's reading describes Isaiah's encounter, centuries before Jesus' day; and two millennia later the Spirit still (to use Isaiah's key words) 'calls', 'touches', 'sends'.

Trinity Sunday, June 18   *Isaiah 6.1-8**
Who will go?
It was, then as now, a troubled and uncertain time in the Middle East, and Uzziah's death made matters worse. In Uzziah's lifetime already Isaiah had had visions (1.1) but now, in his despair, his whole being was assailed by God: his eyes saw, his lips felt, his ears heard. He was

- seized by a sense of God's glory,
- assured of God's forgiveness,
- summoned to God's service.

So today

- in a world disfigured by conflict and wanton destruction, the splendour of the eternal God is undiminished;
- in a world contaminated by greed and brutality, forgiveness is Jesus' way to deal with sin;
- in a world fragmented by selfish competitiveness, the Spirit still sends us to each other: to welcome, care, love, serve, challenge, encourage, support.

* *You may not want to send me far, Lord;*
  you may want me to make a phone call or send an e-mail.
  You may not want me to go anywhere;
  perhaps you want me to stay put
  and welcome whoever you send.
  How shall I know, unless I focus my whole attention on you,
  and let your Spirit touch me?

Monday June 19   Acts 6.1-7

Share the load

'The task is too heavy for you; you cannot do it alone,' said
Jethro, Moses' father-in-law (Exodus 18.18). 'Look for able,
trustworthy, God-fearing people who will bear the burden with
you.' The apostles knew their scriptures, so when history
repeated itself they knew what to do.

According to Luke the idea was that the twelve should concentrate on prayer and preaching while the seven would have a
practical, diaconal role. Yet when next we meet them, Stephen and
Philip (the only two of the seven we do meet again) are expounding
the scriptures. From the very first, it seems, it has been impossible
to keep separate the servant ministry and the ministry of the word.
Practise what you preach. Say why you serve.

If *you* are one of those in your community with too many
responsibilities, it's time to share the burden. No-one else will do
the job the way you do it; but it can be done differently.

If you are someone with fewer responsibilities, ask how *you*
can help to share the load. You don't have to do it exactly as your
predecessor did; God's Spirit will use your particular gifts and
aptitude.

* *What have you in mind for me, Lord?*
  A new sphere of service?
  The same job done more conscientiously?
  Or something I should let go of?
  Help me to discern wisely.

Tuesday June 20   Acts 8.26-40

No idle chat

Who knows what had attracted the Ethiopian to Jerusalem? With
its splendid Temple and spectacular Jewish festivals, the city
drew people from afar just as the Oberammergau Passion Play
brings crowds to Bavaria today. It was a place of pilgrimage,

tourism, worship, and curiosity. This man's means were enough for him to acquire a copy of the Scriptures (or at least the book of Isaiah) to take home to Africa. He was reading it as he began the journey home.

It is fascinating to observe what people read on the train or bus – newspapers, novels, Bibles and prayer books, textbooks and specialist magazines. 'Do you understand what you are reading?' is a brusque and unlikely way of starting a conversation (and Luke has doubtless abbreviated Philip's story) but travelling together – as commuters or holidaymakers – still provides openings for faith-sharing.

It sounds as though the chariot had made a halt when Philip came across to speak. Soon he was given a lift, and on they went together. Their conversation may have begun with Isaiah, but before long Philip was talking about Jesus, with such passion that the African resolved to become a disciple himself. Then they went their separate ways. It's a plain, human story – in which the Spirit is clearly at work. Travellers to Oberammergau this year may have comparable experiences.

✳ *Grant me, Lord, sensitivity and respect*
for those I meet on my travels,
and the words to share my faith with those who search.

Wednesday June 21   *Acts 11.19-30*
Mission and service
The Spirit operates in many ways. The only direct reference here is to inspiring the prediction of a famine. But see the Spirit at work in Antioch:

- prompting those Jewish believers to talk about Jesus with Greek people;
- moving a large number to become 'Christians';
- in the choice of Barnabas to go and build up the church;
- in Barnabas' approach to Saul (not yet known as Paul) to be his co-worker: even Paul started as a curate!
- inspiring their famine relief effort.

What a lot of 'firsts' there are in this brief account:

- The disciples were first called 'Christians'.
- There is the first recorded 'missionary appointment': Barnabas was officially sent from the Jerusalem church to work in Antioch. Like the vast majority of missionaries, he was sent to follow up work already begun informally and spontaneously by lay Christians living their daily lives.

- There is the first organized 'inter-church aid' project, extending the practice of sharing which was a hallmark of the Christian community from the outset (2.45).

* *A prayer for Midwinter's Day (in the southern hemisphere):*
  Lord, as the sun's rays begin to warm the earth again,
  and life bursts afresh from the ground,
  let the fire of your love warm my heart
  and the hearts of my neighbours,
  and let your life bloom in us as it did in Antioch long ago.

Thursday June 22   Acts 16.1-10
Them and us
Once again we wish we had more details, for much is unexplained.

- An assembly in Jerusalem had just accepted Paul's argument that converts from a non-Jewish background did not have to be circumcised to become Christians, and Paul was doing the rounds to convey the assembly's decisions. But Timothy had to be circumcised to give him a chance of influencing the local Jewish communities. How far should Christians adopt local customs and the practices of other faiths, to gain a hearing for the gospel?
- Events occurred in the Roman province of Asia, and on the borders of Bithynia, which they interpreted (or at least Luke, writing with the benefit of hindsight, interpreted) as signs from God: 'No Entry' signs. Are there times when the guidance of the Spirit is to refrain from witnessing to the gospel?
- At this point, unannounced, Luke joined the mission band. Suddenly he writes 'we' rather than 'they'. Can you say with conviction, not 'God had called them' but 'God has called *us*' to proclaim the gospel?

* *There is a time to speak and a time to be silent.*
  Lord, show those who cross frontiers in your name
  when to speak boldly
  and when unobtrusive lives of love are the best witness.

Friday June 23   Acts 16.11-15
Sent and welcomed
It was a man of Macedonia who appeared to Paul in a vision. It was a woman of Macedonia who welcomed Paul's message, and

welcomed the messengers into her home. To those travellers in an unfamiliar land, Lydia must have seemed 'a godsend'. Not only were they sent to her, she was sent to them.

Not all Christian missionaries have met with such a welcome. Many of the Tongans who took the gospel by canoe to Fiji were slaughtered. Some of the African preachers who trekked north to Zimbabwe (then Rhodesia) were killed. There have been European martyrs too. Yet it is remarkable how many, arriving in foreign lands and inhospitable climates, were given facilities which enabled them to survive, build homes, learn the language, and explain their mission.

Sadly that hospitality to foreigners is not always as evident in Christians as it has often been in those who, like Lydia, received the message. But it is integral to the way of Jesus. 'I was a stranger and you welcomed me' (Matthew 25.35).

✳ *When I want to bar my home and my heart*
against those who would intrude on my peace and comfort,
remind me, Lord, that you too stand at the door and knock.

Saturday June 24   *Acts 20.17-28*

A last meeting

Paul described himself as a 'captive to the Spirit' (verse 22), the Spirit who commanded all his journeys, closing some doors and opening others, driving him forward. He had endured all the sufferings of which he wrote in 2 Corinthians 11.25-27. He could only expect more of the same. But the Spirit would not allow him to retire to Tarsus. As Jesus had once set his face towards Jerusalem, well aware of the hostility of the authorities there, so now did Paul. He would not come to Ephesus or Miletus again. After years as a roving bishop, planting and supervizing churches in Turkey and Greece, others would now take up the reins. The same Spirit who was taking him away to new adventures had provided new leaders to shepherd the church of God.

Think about your local church, the leaders of the past who have now gone, the leaders of the present who need your prayers, the leaders to come in whom the Spirit is already working. Has the time come for you to move into some form of leadership, or to move on to something new?

✳ *Make me a captive, Lord,*
and then I shall be free.   *George Matheson (1842-1906)*

FOR REFLECTION – alone or with others

- Who has been sent among you in the last few years – not by some formal arrangement, but by the Holy Spirit – maybe someone from across the road who has joined your congregation or one of your meetings? What gifts of the Spirit does she bring? Are you cultivating or stifling them?
- To whom does the Spirit want to send you – perhaps for an hour a week, or just once for a specific purpose, or for a longer-term, more demanding assignment?

FOR ACTION

Think about the questions, and if you still don't know what to do, find someone to talk it over with.

THE SPIRIT IN THE WORLD
3. Giving life

Notes based on the New International Version by
Ebere O Nze

Eberechukwu Nze, a Nigerian theologian and former Principal of the Methodist Theological Institute in Umuahia, has travelled widely and represented the Methodist Church Nigeria in many international conferences, workshops and seminars. He is now Bishop of the Abakaliki Diocese in Ebonyi State in Nigeria.

According to biblical tradition, life is to be celebrated, especially in the light of the redeeming and liberating gospel of our Lord Jesus Christ. The Gospels record that in his ministry, Jesus forgives sin, feeds the hungry, raises the dead, releases captives, befriends outcasts and preaches good news to the poor (Luke 4.18). He offers the very life of God to a distressed world (John 5.24-30). He proclaims the coming of the Spirit who makes life more meaningful and generates hope in hopeless situations. Jesus comes to heal the whole of life.

In our meditation this week let us, with the eye of faith and a trusting mind, share the vision that in this much celebrated year 2000 the Holy Spirit will renew our lives as he transformed those of the first church in Jerusalem.

Sunday June 25   *Mark 4.35-41**
Life in the midst of death?
The disciples' panic is typical of our natural human response to such situations. On the other hand, restoring calm in the midst of wind and waves symbolizes what the power of God can do in seemingly impossible situations. Although it may be difficult today to accept miracles, Jesus demonstrates here that he is Lord of all creation, and that there is life and peace to be found in experiences of death and danger.

In many parts of the world today, innocent people pass through terrible suffering and persecution; whole families are killed in senseless wars and ethnic conflicts. They must be asking, 'Lord, don't you care if we perish?' God seems to remain silent. Yet in the silence of darkness, he brings peace in the storm of sorrow; peace when life's problems involve us in the tempests of doubt, tension, uncertainty and anxiety.

In ways we often do not recognize, the Holy Spirit is at work in the world renewing all creation and enabling those who recognize the Spirit's presence to know the peace which Jesus gives and which makes life more meaningful. Have you experienced that peace? If not, listen to his words, 'Quiet! Be still!' And he adds, 'Why are you so afraid? Do you still have no faith?' Remember that the peace which Jesus offers is eternal and remains part of us for ever.

✳ *Come, Holy Spirit, and as you renew the whole creation, renew our faith so that we may trust what the power of God can do in our lives, through Jesus Christ our Lord.*

Monday June 26   Romans 8.12-17*

Living by the Spirit

The word 'obligation' in verse 12 reminds us that the Christian life must be opposed to all forms of evil. If you live by the flesh, you live with despair and fear which bring death. The Christian is to stay on the side of the Spirit. The line of the battle is drawn, but the Christian's victory is assured.

If we live by the Spirit we become true sons and daughters of God. The Spirit confers upon us the right to inherit with confidence all that God has promised. The Christian therefore cannot expect a life of ease and security, but will be prepared to enter into the suffering of Christ, and even suffer with him. The good news is that through the victory of the cross, we shall also inherit the life and glory God has bestowed on him.

The Spirit of God is moving across the world, reviving many lives. Will yours be one of those the Spirit will touch and renew for more effective mission in this year 2000?

✳ *Gracious Lord, may this day be an opportunity to overcome in your strength the power of self and sin that I may see your glory. Amen*

Tuesday June 27   Galatians 5.16-26

The Spirit and human nature

Paul has argued that we are set free from a life that is controlled by desires for self-gratification and from that legalistic bondage to religious tradition which meticulously reckons good deeds as a kind of slavish obedience. We have been redeemed and set free to respond to God's loving Spirit at work in us. No one can be compelled, or forced by the law, to love. Love by its very nature is always freely and spontaneously given.

Notice the phrase 'fruit of the Spirit' in verse 22. The process of bearing fruit starts from within the soil, from the planting, the decay of the sprouting seed, until the plant or tree produces fruits. The Spirit plants the Word of God in our hearts and nurtures it so that 'the fruit of the Spirit' which Paul lists is seen in us. When we surrender our lives to the work of the Spirit within us, we are set free from the power of sin. Jesus said, 'By their fruit you will recognize them' (Matthew 7.20).

Paul warns that those who allow their 'sinful nature' to take control will 'not inherit the kingdom of God' (verse 21). It is significant to realize that each of the vices listed can, independently of the others, completely destroy one's life. 'The fruit of the Spirit', on the other hand, is complementary.

But what do you think St Augustine of Hippo meant when he said, 'Any virtue without love is splendid vice'?

✳ *Come, Holy Spirit, I need you;*
Come, sweet Spirit, I pray;
Come in your strength and power;
Come in your own special way. Amen

Wednesday June 28   *Galatians 6.1-10*
Caring is a fruit of the Spirit
Paul gives some practical ways by which we can be renewed by life in the Spirit. Aware of the situation on the ground in Galatia, Paul recommends some caring actions to bind the Christian community together: gently restoring one who errs (verse 1), carrying one another's burdens (verse 2), and sharing good things with those who teach the word (verse 6). Practical caring of this kind fosters a sense of belonging and reassurance. It renders support, generates hope and stimulates love. If all churches were like this, what a caring world it might be.

Paul ties up his teaching on life in the Spirit by focusing on the reward of eternal life, the hope of every believer. The beauty of living in the Spirit in this life is that it is a foretaste of the glory of God that awaits us, and for which we are preparing now. The Spirit energizes us to continue in well-doing for that purpose.

What harvest will you reap?

✳ *Eternal Father, help us to play our part in creating*
a living fellowship in which caring is the main object
of our mission, in the name of Jesus. Amen

Thursday June 29   Ephesians 6.10-20

Wearing the armour of salvation

Like any good preacher, the writer of this letter draws images
from the world around him to clarify his message. While in prison,
he would have watched soldiers parading their military armour.
But he knew that such armour could not overcome his faith, nor
would it ever save the world, and so he prescribes armour to
protect us against the powers of evil.

Sometimes one wonders whether Christians today understand
the enormity of the battle in which we are engaged – against the
power of Evil through the relentless schemes of unjust rulers and
authorities. However daunting this may seem, God provides
armour strong enough to protect us when we enter the struggle.
Tighten up the belt of truth; wear righteousness; the Word of God
together with prayer are your sword. With the shield of faith and
the helmet of salvation, you will know that you are on the Lord's
side.

✳ *Victorious Lord, may your strength keep our strength*
and may your power be the source of our victory
in our daily battle for your Kingdom. Amen

Friday June 30   Revelation 3.14-22

The sin of lukewarmness

The church in Laodicea was accused of being lukewarm. The city
was a wealthy one, known for its banking establishments,
medical school, textile industry, and it was well-known for its eye-
salve. Although the church there prided itself for its inherited
wealth, it could not see its lack of true spirituality: that it was poor,
naked and blind. Fear of losing status and a self-indulgent
lifestyle kept its members from a living encounter with Christ.

The story is told of a wealthy Nigerian who, when his daughter
greeted him one day, 'Good morning, Daddy', replied, '1.5
million'. She retorted, 'I said – Good morning!' Her sharp
challenge brought him to his senses and he replied, 'Good
morning, my daughter.' Individuals, families and nations often fall
into the trap of materialism. Yet wealth cannot buy happiness nor

health. It cannot bring comfort in sorrow, nor fellowship in loneliness. When Christ enters our lives, we cannot be lukewarm. Our priorities are transformed: 'where your treasure is, there your heart will be also' (Matthew 6.21).

✳ *Lord Jesus, open our eyes to see the poverty of our worship, the emptiness and blindness of our spiritual lives. Take us with you on a journey of faith that we may surrender our will to yours. Amen*

Saturday July 1   *Ezekiel 37.1-14**

God, the Source of life

Just as the Creator breathed into the first person's nostrils the breath of life, 'and the man became a living being' (Genesis 2.7), so did Ezekiel's prophecy in verse 9 'Come from the four winds, O breath...' give life to the dry bones of his vision. The Hebrew word *ruach* is translated as 'breath', 'wind' or 'spirit'.

In this vision Ezekiel saw his people, scattered and disconnected by their Babylonian exile, being renewed by the Spirit of God, brought together as a living body, fit to return to rebuild their homeland. The very presence of God brings hope to the hopeless and life to those who have lost their vitality.

In many parts of the world today where there is ethnic, political or religious conflict, God is at work bringing hope to broken lives, breathing new life into hopeless situations.

✳ *Our dear Lord, you have created us to worship you for ever. Mend our broken lives and may your Holy Spirit be ever near to give the strength we need to cope with life's struggles.*

FOR REFLECTION – alone or with a group

Can you identify in what specific ways God has shown his presence in your church and community during the last year?

FOR ACTION

Form a small group, or use an existing one, and develop an outreach programme through which the Spirit of God may bring new life to those who have lost hope in your neighbourhood.

IBRA INTERNATIONAL APPEAL

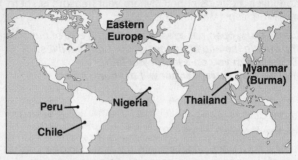

In five continents you will find Christians using IBRA material

Some Christians will be using books and Bible reading cards translated into their local language whilst others use English books. Some of the books are printed in this country but more and more of the books and cards are printed in their own countries. This is done by the IBRA International Fund working through churches and Christian groups and Christian publishing houses overseas.

Each year we receive more requests for help from the IBRA International Fund, with greater emphasis on helping our overseas friends to produce their own version of IBRA material.

**THE ONLY MONEY WE HAVE TO SEND
IS THE MONEY YOU GIVE,
SO PLEASE HELP US AGAIN BY GIVING GENEROUSLY.**

Place your gift in the envelope provided and give it to your IBRA representative, or send it direct to:

The IBRA International Appeal
1020 Bristol Road, Selly Oak
Birmingham Great Britain B29 6LB

Thank you for your help.

WORKING FOR A BETTER WORLD
1. After war and exile (Nehemiah)

Notes based on the Holy Scriptures by the
Jewish Publication Society of America, by

Albert Friedlander

Albert Friedlander is the Dean of the Leo Baeck College in London and the Emeritus Rabbi of the Westminster Synagogue. He is a Fellow of the Wissenshaftskolleg, Berlin's Institute of Higher Learning, and has been a visiting professor at many universities. His books on theology and history have appeared in various languages. He is the Honorary President of the World Conference of Religions for Peace, and co-editor of 'European Judaism'.

Nehemiah and Ezra are the great examples of leaders who return from exile and rebuild their old communities. Nehemiah came as a royal courtier, with the authority of Artaxerxes, king of Persia, who appointed him governor and permitted him to rebuild Jerusalem; Ezra came quietly to rebuild the Jewish faith. The book of Nehemiah is his autobiography, self-indulgent, but a clear picture of the time and its challenges to both of them. By 444BCE the walls of Jerusalem were rebuilt, with a tool in one hand and a sword in the other, against all opposition. As we shall see, the brilliant politician Nehemiah was able to achieve his goal without war, and Ezra restored the *Torah* to the centre of Jewish life. Their co-operation secured the future of Jewish faith in the homeland, just as it continued in the Diaspora.

Sunday July 2   *Nehemiah 1.1-11*

Challenge to comfort

Living in exile from one's homeland can be a pleasant experience. Nehemiah, the 'cupbearer to the king', enjoyed the king's confidence and the lavish life of the palace. After war and exile, it is good to live in safety and to assimilate a new world. But what happens to a person's soul when bad news comes from home? 'The people are suffering...the wall of Jerusalem is broken down... the gates are burned with fires.' Nehemiah's soul is afflicted. He feels guilty, and prays to God. He had lived only for himself, and had forgotten his people and his faith. If one denies the past, one denies one's own identity; and then one denies

157

God. And so Nehemiah prays to God, and admits his sins – sins of omission, actions he had not taken, and these are as serious as the evil one does. An inner resolve grows within him: he must now serve his people. But can he break away from his life of luxury and of service to the king?

✳ *God, let me be aware.*
Let me not assimilate into a world which gives me so much
that I forget my obligations to others.
Let me not fall into a comfortable life
and abandon my beliefs and my duties.
Teach me to come back home,
to restore old dreams and to search for new ones.
God, restore my faith and bring me back to You. Amen

Monday July 3   *Nehemiah 2.1-10*

Initiative

Nehemiah appears before the king with a sad countenance, which rulers do not like to see. 'Why is thy countenance sad? This must be sorrow of the heart,' says the king. Nehemiah replies that he 'mourns for his destroyed city', for his fathers' sepulchres; he knows that rulers do not want to be abandoned, but do want history to remember them as builders rather than destroyers. 'What do you request?' asks the king; and Nehemiah makes his request as a royal plan which will involve the ruler as a builder of cities: 'Send me to the city of my fathers' sepulchres, that I may build it...give me letters to the governors beyond the River (Euphrates) to let me pass through...and to the keeper of the king's park for timber for the gates...and the walls of the city...and a house...' The king grants him a set time – he wants the faithful servant to return to him and adds officers and soldiers to show this is his own wish. Sanballat and Tobiah, the enemies of the Jews, are angered but also afraid. Dare they act against the king?

✳ *O God, help us to distinguish between*
the forces of good and evil which govern our world.
Let us act with wisdom and care,
so that, with awareness of the needs of others,
we can accept responsibility and find a way
in which the good is achieved without violence.
But give us also the courage to remain firm
against the threat of war,
if our cause is truly righteous. Amen

Vision

One of the greatest scenes of biblical history takes place here, and one wonders why artists have not painted it many times. Three days after arriving in Jerusalem, Nehemiah and a few of his loyal followers ride out into the night to inspect the ravaged city, and he describes this in detail: 'I went out by night by the valley gate, even toward the dragon's well...and viewed the walls of Jerusalem...broken down, and the gates...consumed by fire. Then I went down to the fountain gate and to the king's pool; but there was no place for the beast that was under me to pass... Then I went up in the night in the valley and viewed the wall, and returned...and did not tell the rulers...the Jews...the priests nor the nobles, nor the rest who did the work. '

After that night ride, Nehemiah and the faithful few looked at each other and said: 'Let us rise up and build!' Sanballat and Tobiah heard of their plan and mocked them. They could describe the rebuilding of Jerusalem as a rebellion to the Persian rulers. And Nehemiah had an answer for them: 'The God of heaven will prosper us...but ye will have no portion, nor right, nor memorial in Jerusalem!' Those who had returned from exile had remained true to the past, while those who had stayed in the land had forgotten that it was holy soil.

✷ *Sometimes, in the darkest night, a vision comes to us*
   and places us on the way of serving our people
   and returning to our faith.
   Help us, O God, to remain steadfast
   when all seems against us, and the vision fades.
   Our trust in Thee sustains us, and our testimony will rebuild
   the sanctuaries which restore holiness into life. Amen

Strong leadership

The task seemed impossible: there were too many breaches in the wall, and so much rubble that it seemed impossible to remove it. A few had come home from exile; those who had remained were filled with despair. And still the work of rebuilding commenced, and a small citizens' army joined Nehemiah. They rebuilt the gates, even their own houses, and Jerusalem emerged out of the rubble. Their enemies assembled for action, but, as Nehemiah reported: 'We made our prayer to God, and set a watch against them day and night,' although some said, 'The strength of the bearers of burdens is decayed, and there is much rubbish; so that we are not able to build the wall.' The enemies' plans were set: 'They shall not know, neither see, till we come into the midst of them, and slay them, and cause the work to cease.' Nehemiah heard of their plans and called to God to help: the enemies trembled and ceased, and the work continued so that 'all returned to the wall, everyone to his work'. Their enemies were confused, but Nehemiah was confident in his leadership; and the people trusted him. He shared with them a vision which could fashion a new world for them.

✴ *O God, give us strong leaders,*
but not those who are headstrong.
Let them be blessed with perception for the needs
of their people,
and with an awareness of that righteousness
which comes from Thee, the Giver of Truth,
and the Rock of our lives. Amen

Thursday July 6   *Nehemiah 4.10-23*

Diplomacy

Can one strive for peace in a world at war? Nehemiah found a way: 'half my servants wrought in the work, and half of them held the spears, the shields and the bows...everyone with one of his hands wrought in the work, and with the other held the weapon.' Next to Nehemiah stood a man with a trumpet, to rally all to him if the enemy attacked; in the meantime they kept building. Nehemiah himself, his staff and his soldiers stayed inside the city; they did not take off their garments, but stayed on the job to give courage to all who had joined them.

There have always been religious armies fighting for their cause – even bishops carried religious tools which could become weapons. Sometimes war and conquest blotted out the religious vision and religious fanatics committed crimes in the name of God. Nehemiah's small army was different: they wanted their holy city, and wanted to return to the ancient faith of Moses which was renewed by Ezra who stood alongside Nehemiah. Nehemiah won their battles by diplomacy and not by murderous wars. The city of God is not built upon human bodies.

✴ *God, save us from fanaticism.*
We live in a world of wanderers, where homes are lost
and ancient dreams ache for fulfilment.
Let us not ignore the rights of others,

but keep us strong in our quest for identity
as we move from exile towards home.
Thou, O Lord, art our home;
and all humanity is Thy people.
Help us all to move into a world of peace,
bringing us ever closer towards Thee. Amen

Friday July 7   *Nehemiah 5.1-13*
Vision of justice
As the work of rebuilding the city and its walls continued, Nehemiah realized that he had another task: to rebuild the people who had lost the vision of an ethical society. There was no social justice; the rich had turned the poor into economic slaves. An angry Nehemiah consulted his council and told the people: 'Ye lend upon pledge, everyone to his brother... According to our ability we have redeemed our brethren the Jews, that sold themselves unto the heathen; and would ye nevertheless sell your brethren, and should they sell themselves unto us?' And the people were silent in their shame. After Nehemiah had spoken, they said, 'We will restore them, and will require nothing of them; so will we do, as thou sayest.' The priests took their oaths, and the people said, 'Amen'.

A people cannot be changed in one moment, with one action; but they can take a step forward and begin to sense their capabilities. Those who were opposed to Ezra and Nehemiah began to see that there was something special in this return from exile. A new spirit had entered into the people Israel. In Babylon, the prophet Ezekiel had seen the skeletons in the 'valley of dry bones' come to life. In Jerusalem, Nehemiah recognized that the people came to life as they confronted the teachings of justice in the *Torah*.

✴ *O God, give us the opportunity to renew ourselves.*
 We have entered a new millennium,
 and must use it as a way of returning to our religious visions
 and ideals. Help us as a people to discover
 what we may yet become: Your children. Amen

Saturday July 8   *Nehemiah 5.14-19*
Integrity
The next twelve years became a time of rebuilding, with Nehemiah as a governor who did not enrich himself from the crown or from the people. As he described it: 'I and my brethren have not eaten the bread of the governor. But the former

governors...laid burdens upon the people, and took of them for bread and wine above forty shekels of silver; yea, even their servants lorded over the people; but I did not so, because of the fear of God.' Nehemiah had heavy expenses, but his rule was without corruption. He did not speculate in land purchases, and even supplied the food needed for the hundred and fifty people of his household, the administrative staff and workers, out of his own pocket. Nehemiah had come to realize that the government needed to be reformed and not only the people. If he had left a comfortable exile to serve his people, he had to set an example. And he could pray with all honesty: 'Remember unto me, O my God, for good, all that I have done for this people.' And it was remembered by God, even if the people so often forgot this. The reward was the knowledge that he fulfilled the vision which he had seen in exile, far away from the graves of his ancestors.

✳ *God of our ancestors and of our daily life,*
help us to preserve the ancient truths.
Whether I am one of many, or a leader for a moment,
stand alongside me and strengthen me to make sacrifices
when they are needed, and to be true to the task. Amen

FOR REFLECTION – alone or with a group

● We live in a world of vast migrations. Should all borders be open to asylum seekers? Do newcomers have the right to challenge existing patterns in the lands which have received them?

● Are there 'sacred lands' which have special claims upon their children who live in 'exile'? The Irish people in Boston or New York take an active part in Ireland's politics. Are they right to do so? Jews all over the world have very special ties to Israel. Is this part of their religion? Their culture?

● The Israeli/Palestinian conflict has resulted in several wars in our time. On one side, the argument emphasizes a 'war of defence'; on the other, *jihad,* 'a holy war', involves many Muslims who never lived in the area, but who yearn for their holy places in the land. How can the conflicting claims be justified? Resolved?

Sunday July 9   *Nehemiah 6.1-16*
Betrayal
The Bible becomes a contemporary text here: it speaks of dirty tricks as political weapons. Sanballat and his allies want

Nehemiah to meet them in one of their villages, and he rightly suspects them: 'I am doing a great work, so that I cannot come down; why should the work cease whilst I leave it and come down to you?' They urge him to come to them four times, and finally present rumour as facts known to everyone: 'It is reported among the nations...that thou and the Jews seek to rebel; for which cause thou buildest the wall; and thou wouldest be their king...and hast appointed prophets to proclaim in Jerusalem "There is a king in Judah"; and now shall it be reported to the king.' In other words – blackmail. Nehemiah goes to the house of Shemaiah, a friend, who tells him that the enemies will kill him unless he flees with him into the Temple and leaves the work of building the city. He realizes that here, too, betrayal is at work. Shemaiah is the prophet paid by Sanballat to show Nehemiah as a usurper king. Surrounded by enemies, he turns to God for help; and, with that help, the wall is finished and all now see 'that this work was wrought of our God'.

✳ *Out of the depths I cry unto Thee, O Lord.*
Save me from slander and betrayal.
I live in a world of many betrayals, and am perhaps tainted
by the evil which fills the air around me.
Cleanse me from these sins,
that I may not go about as a tale-bearer and destroy others.
Help me not to destroy myself,
but lead me into ways of righteousness. Amen

Monday July 10   *Nehemiah 8.1-3, 9-18*

Rebuilding the people

Jerusalem has been secured. A census has been taken of those who had achieved the vision Nehemiah had beheld in exile, and another vision can now be realized as Ezra steps forward. 'And when the seventh month was come (i.e. the New Year) and the children of Israel were in their cities, all the people gathered themselves together as one into the broad place that was before the water gate; and they spoke unto Ezra the scribe to bring the book of the Law of Moses, which ADONAI had commanded to Israel...so that all could hear...and he read therein...in the presence of the men and women and of those that could under-stand; and the ears of all the people were attentive unto the book of the Law.'

The time had come for the people to be rebuilt; they had to be reunited with the *Torah*. Next to Ezra were the Levites and interpreters to explain and translate, since many now knew the Aramaic language better than the Hebrew text. So they read 'distinctly, and they gave the sense, and caused them to understand the reading'. The people had forgotten much, and wept for joy and for shame; but Ezra, Nehemiah and the priests encouraged them to rejoice, for they had also returned to their homeland, the *Torah* text. They read the text through, and learned that after the New Year came the time of harvest rejoicing. The laws were published for them, and so they went out 'unto the mount, to fetch olive branches, and branches of wild olive, and myrtle branches, and palm branches, and branches of thick trees, to make booths, as it is written.' The walls of the city had been rebuilt and now the walls of the ancient customs surrounded and guarded the people.

✻ *God, make me secure in my religious observances.*
Help me to restore the Bible into its place of honour
within my home, and let me rejoice in my faith
and in my traditions. Amen

Tuesday July 11   *Nehemiah 9.1-14*

Returning to prayer and reflection

Israel, returned from exile, had learned to pray again upon the soil of the Holy Land, and the prayer of this text is still part of the synagogue liturgy: 'Thou art ADONAI, even Thou alone; Thou hast made heaven, the heaven of heavens, with all their host, the earth and all things that are thereon, the seas and all that is in them, and Thou preservest them all; and the hosts of heaven worship Thee.' And then the prayer continues as a recital of the history of the people, of the way that led to Egypt and out of Egypt into the wilderness, and into the promised land. Our text reaches a climax with the description of Mount Sinai, and with the giving of the Ten Commandments through the hand of Moses. Later commentators compare Moses the Lawgiver with Ezra the Scribe who brought the people back to the observance of the ordinances and commandments which had accompanied Israel through its history; but all knew that there had been no one like Moses 'who had seen ADONAI face to face'. What mattered now was that Israel had to relive its history, had to remember how it had strayed from the right path and had gone into exile. Now, they had returned and were given another chance to be 'the people of the Book'.

In history, Christians are also a 'people of the Book' and can examine a history which leads through the millennia.

*✶ God, grant me encounters with the sacred text
and with the message which travels through time and space.
Let me into the sanctuaries of our days, and await Thy voice.
Let me be among those who can listen. Remind me daily
that I, too, belong to the people of the Book. Amen*

Wednesday July 12   *Nehemiah 9.32-37*

Renewing the vision

The people assembled before Ezra and Nehemiah were
reminded of the sins committed by them in their past. No journey
towards the future can ignore the sins of the distant past or the
immediate present. They had to atone for them: 'Neither we, nor
our kings, our princes, our priests, nor our fathers kept Thy law,
nor hearkened unto Thy commandments...for they have not
served Thee in their kingdom...or in the large and fat land Thou
gavest them...' And so the dominion and the land were lost, given
to other rulers, and those assembled to hear the *Torah* knew that
their own distress was great.

Moments arise in the history of a people, and in the history of
the world, when a community recognizes that it has lost the way.
It is easier for an individual to confess the sins of daily life than for
a community to acknowledge that one generation after another
has walked the wrong way. And it is easier for a person to follow
a multitude to do evil, or to be passive and fit into a pattern which
has forgotten the ideals and visions of earlier days. The people
discovered a great leader in Nehemiah, and a blessed teacher in
Ezra. And so they learned to repent and regained their role in
history.

*✶ May we, as a people, regain the identity
which has been granted to every nation, O God:
to be witnesses for truth, to recapture the early visions,
and to bring Jerusalem into our land. Amen*

Thursday July 13   *Nehemiah 9.38; 10.28-39*

Tithing

A great event had taken place in the life of the people: they had
rediscovered the religious vision which had started them on their
journey through history. Now it had to be secured by a system of
laws and ordinances, a constitution to govern the life of a nation.
'And yet, for all this we make a sure covenant, and subscribe to it;

and our princes, our Levites, and our priests, set their seal unto it.' More than lip-service was required: there had to be a system of taxation, and the various festivals with their observances had to be part of the public structure. As in the past, the first-fruits of the soil and the first-born sons had to be brought into the Temple. The priests had to be supported in their work, since the tribe of Levi was not given a share of the land itself. The people, themselves, had to tithe, and the funds were brought to the treasury of the Temple to support the rites and the priesthood, and to ensure the continuance of music and ceremony in the House of God. It was an ancient insight: religion exists within the hearts of the people, but there must be sanctuaries in which the light of religion burns to rekindle the hearts of worshippers.

✳ *O God, teach us to show respect*
for those who dedicate themselves to Thy work.
Let our sanctuaries live in the middle of our community;
and let them not fall into disuse because of us. Amen

Friday July 14   *Nehemiah 13.15-22*

Restoring the Sabbath

Nehemiah had returned to the royal court, a faithful servant to the Persian ruler. He thought the system in Jerusalem had been established properly, and Ezra would inspire the people to follow in the pathways of the *Torah*. Gradually, reports came to him that all was not well in the land of his ancestors. He was granted a new appointment as its governor, and returned to Jerusalem. Much had gone wrong in the intervening years. The House of God was forsaken and the singers had fled. Taxes were stolen, and some of his enemies had made themselves comfortable in the Temple. He cast them out, and then realized that the fault was not only in the sanctuary, but also in the community: the Sabbath was forgotten and ignored! And so he re-established it officially: 'And it came to pass that, when the gates of Jerusalem began to be dark before the Sabbath, I commanded that the doors should be shut, and commanded that they should not be opened till after the Sabbath.' He placed guards upon the wall, and the merchants had to stay outside the city, with the warning that they would be punished if they came in and dared to trade on the Sabbath. He writes: 'From that time forth they came no more on the Sabbath day. And I commanded the Levites that they should purify themselves, and that they should come and keep the gates, to sanctify the Sabbath day.'

Throughout history, Israel has been reminded: 'Even as you have kept the Sabbath, so the Sabbath has kept Israel.'

✴ *O God, we have forgotten the Day of the Lord in our society.*
Commercial considerations have eroded public piety,
and many of our sanctuaries stand empty.
Bring us back to the awareness of faith in our lives;
let us return to worship Thee, just as a people returned
from exile to the Holy Land.
Help us in this inward journey. Amen

Saturday July 15   *Nehemiah 13.23-31*

Dilemma

How can a people of faith maintain itself in a world of idolatry? The Israelites had a vision of the One God, the Creator of humanity. The nations which surrounded them prayed to idols and had many gods. Often, the people of Israel had brought foreign gods into their homes. Nehemiah remembered that corruption could begin at the top: 'Did not Solomon king of Israel sin by these things?...God made him king of all Israel; nevertheless even him did the foreign women cause to sin.' Nehemiah blamed the erosion of Jewish faith and culture upon the inter-marriages where wives from other traditions brought up their children without the Hebrew language and belief in the One God. He took harsh measures against those who had committed 'great evil, to break faith with God in marrying foreign women'. He made them divorce their wives, which divided the people and caused problems. His enemies used it as an issue to incite the people against him.

They obeyed him, but we still feel compassion for the loving couples torn apart. The issue remains alive, as minority groups try to stay separate from the host society. We accept the reality of inter-marriage now, but appreciate the problems of couples and children divided by religion. And we can understand Nehemiah's grim action in his battle to preserve his people and his faith, even when it fills us with sorrow.

✴ *Dear God, we feel much pain*
when we behold the battle between religions.
Help us to understand that there are many ways to Thee.
Give us understanding for others, but let us also learn
that our own prayer towards Thee
is the way to our neighbour. Amen

FOR REFLECTION – alone or with a group

● Last year, the Archbishop of Canterbury asked the British community to embrace refugees and criticized the media for whipping up fear and hostility towards them. What are your feelings in this matter? Do you know any asylum seekers? Has your community taken any positive actions?

● Today, many places of business stay open seven days a week. Do you think this is right? Should the community give more support to places of worship?

● How do you feel about the forced divorces decreed by Nehemiah to 'purify the religious tradition'? Many refugees and expatriates all over the world try to maintain their old traditions by building 'fences' around their children such as setting up their own schools. What value do you see in this tendency? And what value do you see in children of different cultures being educated together in the same schools?

FOR ACTION

The book of Nehemiah is autobiographical. Do you feel that opponents like Sanballat are treated unfairly? Ezra appears only briefly, but has his own book in the Bible. Try to read it, and compare the two leaders. Whom do you prefer? Why?

WORKING FOR A BETTER WORLD
2. People with disabilities

Notes based on the New Revised Standard Version by
Alison Beever

Alison Beever is an Anglican priest working in a parish in Reading (UK). She is chaplain to a local women's centre, and has a particular concern for the way the Church treats people who are perceived as 'different', especially those with disabilities and those who have survived sexual abuse. She has used a wheelchair for some years, and wrote these notes shortly after having a leg amputated.

In today's world, where medicine appears to heal almost anything, people with disabilities and impairments are often seen as different: they do not conform to what others consider to be 'normal' life. When Jesus heals a person with disabilities, we need to ask what else is happening – what are we being taught, shown, encouraged to do? We are not just to applaud the miracle. This week, using different accounts and experiences of disability, we will ask: what have we to learn from this about ourselves and our spiritual journey?

Sunday July 16   *2 Samuel 9.1-13*
In whose interest?

'People like that shouldn't be out.' 'Why isn't someone looking after them?' These are just two of the comments I have heard when shopping with friends in our wheelchairs. They remind us of times when people who were 'different' – physically, mentally, morally – were locked away 'for their own good'. In reality they were kept 'out of sight, out of mind' so that their 'difference' could not disturb, offend or challenge the ordered world of 'normal' people. Today elderly or disabled people are sometimes still treated in these ways, for our convenience. We do not find the time or language to ask, 'What do you want or need to live your life?'

Although David's treatment of the crippled Mephibosheth seems like an act of kindness, Mephibosheth was not consulted. In the culture of his time he was probably grateful for his life, but was he really being cared for? Is not David really serving his own needs – salving his conscience by apparent kindness, whilst in effect keeping Mephibosheth under effective house-arrest by controlling his household and having him eat at his table? Has Mephibosheth any real independence or fullness of life?

How often is what you do for others related to your need, and not theirs? Do you make assumptions about what is best for someone, without consulting her? Do you avoid those whose 'difference' challenges you?

✳ *Lord, help me to be honest in the ways I treat others.*
  Help me to find ways of understanding
    those I fear as 'different'.
  Help me learn to live fully the life you give.

Monday July 17   *Luke 13.10-17*

Liberated by wheels

Most of us are imprisoned by something. It may be a painful experience deep in our minds (which we thought was past history) that still negatively affects us. Perhaps it inhibits something we need to be doing, or makes us continue an unfortunate habit we wish we could stop. Sometimes we are imprisoned by other people's attitudes. One attitude I have fought against since I began using a wheelchair is that which thinks, in headline letters, 'CONFINED TO A WHEELCHAIR'. So, although this is some people's experience of life on wheels, it has not been mine. Once I admitted my need for help with mobility, I discovered the difference wheels made: they liberated me. I still can't climb a flight of stairs...but I can shop all day and only have sore thumbs at the end! I have mobility again, and enjoy life. Now when someone refers to me as 'confined', I think that perhaps he is the one who is 'disabled', and who needs to be liberated from the limited understanding which imprisons him and others. They would discover a new freedom to enjoy the friendship and insights of people who look at life from other perspectives.

That is part of the healing Jesus brings in this miracle. 'You are set free...' He heals, and also challenges the insularity of those who complained about his action. The woman's liberation comes not only in the healing, but in changing the attitudes of others that she might find acceptance, another basic human need.

What cripples, or confines, or imprisons you? What needs to happen for you to hear the words, 'You are set free'? How could you free someone else to hear words of acceptance from Jesus, and from you?

✳ *Lord, free me to live in your way,*
  and to bring freedom to others.

Open up
A friend's deaf five-year-old knows exactly how to wind his mother up: when she signs a telling-off to him, he shuts his eyes so that he cannot 'hear' what she is saying! He turns the tables on her, making her the disabled one! That's sometimes how we treat God as he tries to communicate with us. Deaf to his voice, we shut our eyes to other ways in which we might hear him: through his word, his world. We shut our hearts to hearing through feeling and insight. We disable both ourselves and God by our closed minds. At such times we need to be taken aside, and told 'Be opened', and hear the sigh of Jesus over our deafness and need. Then we will also find healing for our spiritual deafness. With our ears and hearts open to hear God, we may also learn to speak – for just as a deaf child finds speech hard to learn, because he cannot hear his parents' words, so we find it impossible to speak the way of God until we hear it for ourselves.

How are you closing yourself to God? How deaf do you make yourself?

✳ *Lord, help us listen to your way.*
Teach us to speak your words.

What do you see?
A familiar story tells of blind men asked to describe an elephant. Each took the part he could feel and experience to be the whole, and described it: 'An elephant is a tree trunk', 'a piece of rope', 'a flapping piece of leather'. Each was limited, not just by his physical vision, but by his perception.

If you heard something described as having 'two small wheels which seem to go where they will' it could bring to mind a child's pushchair or a supermarket trolley, either of which could seem confirmed by a description of handles at pushing height. But, as in the first story, it describes only part of a wheelchair – and is a limited perception of its use.

Today's reading reminds us that we have to 'look intently' to see. For our spiritual sight to function there has to be obedience and willingness – and an openness to see more than our piece of the picture, to want the fullness of our sight restored so that we see our world with the eyes of God, and can pray and act more appropriately in accord with that vision.

Thursday July 20   Mark 9.14-29

Scatter the darkness

Many people fear those who have a psychiatric illness or learning disabilities. They confuse the two and think they experience the same problems because their behaviour is 'different'. In England some of this fear and ignorance are expressed when new sites are suggested for care homes, or holiday homes for people with learning disabilities: 'You can't put people like that here.' 'What about our children?' 'It won't be safe to go out any more.' We still have not learnt to accept one another 'as God in Christ accepts'.

In Jesus' day, fear and lack of understanding meant many illnesses and disabilities were believed to be the work of demons. This led to further fear and isolation for the sufferer and family. Perhaps fear made the disciples powerless. But once Jesus enters the situation he somehow normalizes it. Of course things can be changed: he deals with the child, family and crowd, and tells the disciples that the missing ingredient in their care package is prayer. In your dealings with other people, especially those experienced as different, how often is prayer the missing ingredient? How often (honestly) do you choose to hold on to your fears and presuppositions, rather than risking the change in yourself and others that prayer might bring?

✳ *Lord, teach me how to pray and what to pray!*

Friday July 21   Luke 14.7-14

Finding the right perspective

Some years ago, I was asked to organize a carol service for a local disability support group. I proudly thought I'd organized everything – wheelchair access to church, seating so that wheelchair users and their families could be together; toilet facilities; large print service sheets; readings chosen to celebrate Advent and our shared disability rights agenda. Success was on hand...except for a few oversights! In all my planning I'd only been aware of the needs of one group of people – those whose needs I shared. Where, in my planning, was a signing choir for those who used sign language? Where were the Braille carol sheets? What about an invitation to the learning support unit? Because they were not a part of my immediate world, they had not been included. This was a painful lesson in how limited was my understanding of disability, and how much my experience had actually distorted my vision.

Today we are called to know ourselves without distortion, thinking neither too highly nor too lowly of ourselves. If we try to see ourselves as a loving God sees us, we should find it possible to own our limitations and hidden impairments. We then discover our invitation to the banquet of life where our 'difference' becomes a place of celebration not of fear.

✳ *Lord, help me see myself as you see me, and believe it.*

Saturday July 22   *Romans 12.3-8*

Me, myself; you, yourself

One of the greatest needs I felt, especially as I experienced increasing pain and disability, was to be accepted. And one of the loudest shouts I hear, in all aspects of my ministry, is 'Accept me!'.

Accept me, with my pain which you cannot change.

Accept me, and your inability to change what is happening.

Accept me, though I cannot express myself in language you can understand.

Accept me, though to you I smell, and cannot control my body.

Accept me, though I cannot think as you do, nor express my thoughts.

Accept me, though I challenge all that is 'nice' and 'decent' in your world.

Accept me, though in your eyes what happens to me is my fault.

Accept me, though you judge that I do nothing to help myself.

Accept me, though I fail, and fall short, and fall down.

Accept me, though your friends would not understand, and you risk ridicule.

Accept me, though I choose to be different and not obey the rules you set.

Accept me, and take the risk of finding that I accept you.

Accept me, and risk finding that I too am a part of the body of Christ,

and that the body of Christ stumbles, and cannot find words, and dribbles, and is different,

and that this is so because you are part of the one body,

and I am part of the one body,

and all whom we find difficult and different are part of the body too, and without any one of us, this body would be diminished, and this work of God would be incomplete.

Accept me, for I am gifted too, though the gifts God has given me to offer you may be harder to understand, more threatening to accept, more fulfilling to explore.

'We, who are many, are one body in Christ...members of one another.'

✳ *Thank you, Lord, for accepting me as I am now.*

FOR REFLECTION – alone or with a group

- As you consider 'disability' in all its forms, where do you find God?
- Think how much God, in incarnation and crucifixion, shares our impairment. How might this change your understanding and faith?
- Does 'healing' have to mean becoming someone else's idea of 'normal'? What is 'healing' for people with disabilities?
- If possible, ask someone whose disability is different from yours to share with you their answers and reflections.

FOR ACTION

Discover what, in your area, most disables different groups of people. What can you do to help change it? Contact local disability campaign groups and see if they are involved in any action in which you could engage.

WORKING FOR A BETTER WORLD
3. Health for all

Notes based on the Good News Bible by
Magali do Nascimento Cunha

Magali do Nascimento Cunha, a Christian journalist and educator, has worked for over ten years in ecumenical projects in Brazil, and now works with the Methodist Church, among poor communities on the outskirts of Rio de Janeiro City.

Jesus said, 'I have came in order that you might have life – life in all its fullness' (John 10.10). What does Jesus mean by 'life in all its fullness'? When we read about Jesus' actions we see that he worked to restore people's physical and emotional health. If we feel ourselves to be committed to work for a better world, following in the steps of Jesus, the physical and emotional health of others has to be one of our targets.

Sunday July 23   *Mark 6.30-34, 53-56**
Sheep without a shepherd
Jesus' love and mercy for the people, his care and attention, brought large crowds searching for him wherever he went. It was almost impossible to find a place to be alone and rest! (Verses 31-33). Most were forgotten men and women, discriminated against on the basis of religious traditions often associated with ritual purity. That is why Jesus felt pity as he saw poor people as 'sheep without a shepherd' (verse 34).

In his ministry alongside poor people, Jesus saw health as a major issue. Everywhere he was followed by 'sick people lying on their mats', trying at least 'to touch the edge of his cloak'. Jesus' humanity (he felt pity!) was made concrete through acts of solidarity. He showed that God cares and that salvation is more than the salvation of souls: God means people to live life to the full, and health is essential for that!

✳ *Thank you, Lord, for being our shepherd and for caring for us.*
Help us to express our humanity in practical acts of solidarity with those who are sick. Amen

'Is the Lord with us or not?'

Although Brazil is irrigated by many rivers, the land of the north-east interior around the Amazon – one of the largest rivers in the world – is very dry. Every year the *sertanejos* (land workers from the backwoods who inhabit that area), suffer severe drought and spend months asking the government for projects and investments to irrigate the land, to save their plantations and cattle, to feed their children and give life to all of them. The answer is silence. There seems to be no way to bring change. No political will. Every year the *sertanejos* kneel down on their land and pray for God's mercy to help them to water the soil. Sometimes the answer is rain; sometimes there are concrete acts of solidarity from people in other parts of the country or the world. Until when?

Water is life. The Israelites suffered a lack of water in the desert as they searched for their liberation in the promised land. It is still the experience of peoples in many parts of the world today in their search for liberation, peace and health. Every day, as we turn on our taps – an ordinary action – let's think of them, as a simple act of solidarity.

✳ *Almighty God, we know that you are with us.*
   Have mercy on us, and on our brothers and sisters
   who lack the water of life that you provide for their bodies
   and souls. In Jesus' name. Amen

The right to live

It is almost impossible to read the biblical narratives of disease-carriers and not to think about the religious prejudice and discrimination which marginalized these people. According to tradition, they or their parents must have sinned. Skin-diseases, especially, were thought to make people ritually unclean, and so they were discriminated against by a society that linked spiritual purity with physical cleanliness (Leviticus 13.1-45).

The situation faced today by those who suffer leprosy and who are HIV carriers is little different. We need to look at the example of Jesus, someone who, in God's name, acts more than speaks. In the Gospel of Mark Jesus is always travelling, healing, caring, and saying little: 'filled with pity', stretching out his hand, touching the sick man and saying to him, 'I do want to. Be clean!' This has to be for us Christians a model of how to work for a better world. Jesus, for the sake of this act of solidarity, according to the Jewish law, made himself unclean by touching the 'untouchable'.

Our world, in a new millennium, will only become a better place when we demolish the barriers that we ourselves maintain: when we stretch out our hands and touch those who, because of mental or physical disease, are isolated and discriminated against. These brothers and sisters have the same right to live as all of us who are healthy. The Lord wants it so.

✳ *Forgive us, Lord, when we ignore barriers which isolate those who need our hands and our touch.*
Show us the way to follow in your steps and to do your will.

Wednesday July 26   *Mark 5.1-20*
God is kind
It is common in poor communities to find people with emotional or mental problems. Life is so hard. Difficulties which frustrate survival grow every day: the search for a job or a way to earn some money, lack of food, bad housing conditions, sick people at home (especially the elderly and children), violent husbands, wives who have lost self-esteem, demons that occupy people's minds and hearts and make them suffer...

There is something seriously wrong when such people in their search for acceptance and love are dismissed by a church or religious group with the attitude that their symptoms of depression and confusion are nothing less than demon-possession which needs to be exorcised. While it is true that the performing of special rituals helps some people to find peace and wholeness, the majority return home and find their real problems – broken or difficult relationships – are still there.

We learn with Jesus that the local church has to be a therapeutic community, where those who suffer depressive illness may find peace among people who are kind to them as God is. Solidarity through befriending, sensitive listening, providing a space where all feel accepted and welcomed, are the most effective therapy and help the healing process.

✳ *Loving God, teach us to be kind as you are,*
to share attention and patience with those brothers and sisters
who lack peace and emotional stability.
Have mercy on them and on us all. Amen

Doing God's will

As we reflect on the theme 'Working for a better world' it is impossible not to think of contemporary poverty. A better world will inevitably include many who are not so well off as others, but their basic needs will be met, and human rights guaranteed. Yet what we see in many areas today is the complete exclusion of the poor and a denial of their rights – a forgotten people – at a time when to be a citizen of the globalized world one has to be a consumer, at least to have a credit card. More and more poor people become ill and die. We may be helping some but the problems continue for others and for those yet unborn. This is not God's will. Jesus came to bring abundant life, not for a privileged group, but for all. God wants health for all; and that means work, food, clean water, houses, time and facilities for leisure... To work for a better world means to work and struggle to make God's will for all people a reality. How are we to do it?

✳ *Lord, forgive us when we confine our caring*
to a select group and forget others in their need.
Show us the way to make your will concrete.
Renew our commitment to build your Kingdom. Amen

An image for us

What a beautiful image from Ezekiel! Life comes from the Temple... A 'Temple' is to offer water for refreshment to the thirsty and to nourish trees that provide food and shade: a challenge to our Christian communities today.

The world is far from being what God intends it to be. The communities we build, and that we call God's communities, need to be places like that described by Ezekiel, spaces to offer refreshment to the thirsty and to irrigate our arid world; spaces to provide food and shade to those who are hungry and tired.

Read the words of Jesus: 'Whoever is thirsty should come to me and drink. As the scripture says, "Whoever believes in me, streams of life-giving water will pour out from his heart"' (John 7.37-38). More than ever these words have to be owned by Christian communities as an invitation to all who are sick, 'tired from carrying heavy loads', to come and find relief.

✳ *We praise you, Lord, that you are our life-giving water.*
Bless our communities that we may be a source of refreshment
and food for all who are in need. Amen

'Be strong and do not be afraid!'

The situation of Judah was far from good at the time when these words were spoken. War and death surrounded the land; kings were unjust; people, especially the poor, were suffering. The prophet shows that a new order is possible and hope can be kept alive. This command is appropriate for us today: 'Be strong and don't be afraid!' (verse 4). Seeing the order of things in our world we are tempted to give up and not believe that it can be changed. Poor people in Latin America have found, in their study of the Bible, words like these of Isaiah that show how the Word of God is alive and can feed us in situations of sorrow and grief as the people of Israel experienced.

Let's read this passage again, again, and again, to renew our hope, and for inspiration to work for a better world.

✷ *We do not have words, Lord, to praise you*
for your mercy and love. Thank you for showing us
the 'Road of Holiness' where we want to walk
and follow in your footsteps. Amen

FOR REFLECTION – alone or with a group

● Have you experienced ill-health, yourself or in your family? How difficult was it? Have you had any kind of support? How important was the support?

● Is your Christian community a therapeutic community, following in Jesus' steps and God's will for the 'Temple'? If you say 'yes', share how it acts. If you say 'no', share how you think it should act and with whom specifically.

FOR ACTION

Invite someone in your area who spends time in solidarity with sick people to come to your group to share the experience and encourage members of the group to interview him/her. Aim to discover ways to engage in a similar caring ministry.

WORKING FOR A BETTER WORLD
4. Bread is for sharing

Notes based on the New Revised Standard Version by
Simon Barrow

Simon Barrow is Associate Secretary of the Churches' Commission on Mission at the Council of Churches for Britain and Ireland.

For some in our world bread is a luxury, while others take it for granted. These readings ask us to reconsider what gives substance to our lives, to ask what Jesus as 'the bread of life' requires of our churches and societies, and to rediscover our Hebrew heritage as we prepare for the Feast of Life for a hungry planet. These notes were prepared in the aftermath of the eighth assembly of the World Council of Churches in Harare, Zimbabwe. When Christians from every continent come together we have a chance to glimpse the community of God which requires us to hunger and thirst for righteousness.

Sunday July 30   *John 6.1-21**
Breaking and freeing

This famous passage (which parallels Mark 6.34-52) contains two of the best-known incidents in the New Testament: Jesus' walking on water, and the feeding of the five thousand. But the key to the true significance of these stories in John's *schema* lies in the two verses (14-15) which do not appear in Mark's account. Here we read that Jesus rejects attempts to make him a worldly king, and instead he is recognized as 'the prophet who is to come into the world'. But what does this mean?

The renowned Old Testament scholar, Walter Brueggemann, has talked about two very different dynamics running through the Hebrew Scriptures. One – associated with Moses and the prophets – was a radical movement, critical of the Temple cult and of attempts by priests and rulers to manipulate faith and ritual for their own ends. Another was the monarchical tradition which upheld the established religion in matters of statehood as well as piety.

In this passage, John is placing Jesus firmly in the first camp. The preceding references to Moses (5.45-47) make this even clearer. In showing Jesus calming and crossing the sea of Capernaum, the writer is associating his Lord directly with the Exodus event and the parting of the Red Sea. Similarly, the feeding of the multitude recalls the manna in the desert and demonstrates that Jesus has come to offer (as John also reminds us) life in its fullness. Here is not just a one-off satisfying of his followers' hunger, but a dramatic promise of bread and freedom for the world. Jesus' followers are amazed, but they are also puzzled. Like us, they want to know how and when these promises will be fulfilled.

✷ *God of the multitudes,*
May your presence feed our hope in a world freed for sharing.

Monday July 31   *Genesis 18.1-15*

Feeding and laughing

To laugh or not to laugh? Sarah, quite naturally, has difficulty in seeing how the promise that has been made to Abraham – fertility where there is dryness, a future where none seems available – can possibly come true. For a Christian reader the appearance of bread and water and the promise of a son point us towards those images and realities (they are both) which the Gospel writers subsequently wove into their portrait of Jesus as the one in whom God's purposes become clear.

But for Abraham, the father of a universal hope of deliverance born among the most unlikely of peoples, things are far from certain. The sagas of the patriarchs in Genesis 12 to 36 are all about trust, perseverance and the hope of restoration for an ailing generation. Abraham sees in his unexpected guests a possible sign of God's favour, and his sharing of food and hospitality becomes the vehicle for this most unlikely of blessings. As so often in the Scriptures, the breaking of bread becomes a moment of revelation. The Covenant relationship, in which all can find a place (cf. Genesis 17.4-5) will even visit an old and barren woman – one of the least respected members of the community.

Where we take our leave of this episode is at a point of uncertainty, however. Knowing what will happen, we may rightly see Sarah's womanly laugh as one of ultimate triumph. But for her at this moment it is a cry in the dark, and she is sorely tempted to deny it.

✷ *God of surprises,*
Show us how to rejoice in your fertile future.

Hungering and thirsting

The liberated people of Israel have dared to cross the sea (their 'Rubicon') to leave behind the oppression of imperial Egypt, but find that freedom does not come cheaply or easily.

Earlier in the same chapter (verses 2 and 3) the people challenged Moses with their persistent stomach pangs – and with a certain nostalgia about the 'fleshpots' of consolation which they enjoyed in the old days of captivity. Perhaps Jesus remembered their pain when he chose to bless those who 'hunger and thirst to see right prevail' (Matthew 5.6, REB).

In any event, the God of Exodus does hear those rumblings of hunger, and provides a very strange food (manna, literally 'what is it?') – something to nourish the people for the next part of their sojourn, but not such as to allow them to institutionalize it into a system of organized luxury (verses 20, 21). When so much of our world is based on 'future markets' and on planned extravagance for the privileged few, perhaps Moses' 'theology of enough' (to adapt a phrase from the missionary theologian, John V Taylor) sounds strange to our ears. We, like the freed but frustrated Israelites, need to realize that the bread that truly satisfies is for what we need, not for what we try to grasp.

✳ *God of deliverance,*
Nourish us to hunger for what is right for your world.

Eating and talking

At the heart of this reading lies an injunction not to forget God's purposes in times of prosperity. This warning is apt. The Deuteronomic texts comprise reminiscences, exhortations, songs, appeals, forebodings and legal frameworks suited for a people who have arrived on the plains of Moab, just forty days away from entering the promised land.

This is the context for that famous saying, echoed by Jesus, 'one does not live by bread alone, but by every word that comes out of the mouth of the Lord' (verse 3). The point is not to drive a wedge between the physical and the spiritual. The stuff of life and the fullness of life belong together. But that is just the point. To concentrate on worldly ease and the desires of the stomach is to miss the richness of life that is possible in God, our ultimate destiny, who binds the bread of today and the bread of tomorrow together.

The intention is to train and discipline a wayward people on the edge of maturity (verse 5) to make the best use of the rich resources that are about to be theirs (verses 7-10). The lesson of the manna is that, by clinging to our own needs, we risk losing the rich gifts God provides. The spirit of trust, generosity and 'enough' is God's way – a way which offers life for all, together, as a community. But as we are reminded elsewhere in this book, unless an ethic of giving is at the heart of the household, the poor (those who are excluded and marginalized) will remain, and the God-driven spirit will not find peace in the land.

The land of milk and honey, of fertility and plenty, is certainly promised, but not on the basis of self-seeking or exploitation. As the span of history shows, we human beings are slow to learn God's lesson and quick to hog the bread of life to ourselves – with disastrous consequences.

✳ *God of unveiling,*
Blind us to all that blurs our vision of the promised land.

Thursday August 3   *1 Kings 17.8-24**

Emptying and filling

In turning today and tomorrow to the two books of Kings we are moving from the threshold of the promised land to the time of monarchy and settlement, roughly spanned by the death of King David to the fall of Jerusalem in 586 BC.

The editorial setting for the history of the Kings is similar in tenor to the warnings of the Deuteronomist. The rulers are judged not according to their imperial achievements, wealth or success, but in terms of their fidelity to Yahweh, the God of Exodus. This means that the concerns of the poorest people – whom the Indian theologian M M Thomas called 'the last, the lost and the least' – remain of paramount importance. For God is continually being revealed as a universal deity, not a tribal one.

So it is that in the moving story of the widow of Zarephath, her unexhausted jar of meal and her wonderfully revived sick son, the central character is this poor woman from Sidon, an ancient Canaanite stronghold. Jesus recalls this story after his sermon in Nazareth, along with the cleansing of Naaman the Syrian in the time of Elisha (Luke 4.26-27). The point is that God's love is poured out not just on the religiously acceptable and upright, but on those who are despised by the upholders of 'true religion'. This sentiment, that the bread of life is not ours alone, led to Jesus' violent ejection from the synagogue, and it played a crucial role in the conflicts and trials Elijah had to endure.

✳ **God of gifts,**
Pour out your love on those who least expect it.

Offering and transforming

Here is an often overlooked incident concerning a man from Baal-shalishah who brings the first fruits of his produce to the prophet Elisha. This is a remarkable act of faith for, as the name of his village suggests, this man is probably not a worshipper of Yahweh but of Baal, the fertility god who was used by the priests and rulers of Canaan to give religious sanction to their monopoly of the land. Maybe this food was originally intended as a Baal sacrifice. It would certainly have been destined for a priest rather than a prophet. That the man came to Elisha at all is therefore extraordinary, and testimony to his evident goodness.

That goodness is instantly seen when Elisha orders his servant to share bread with the hundred people gathered in that place. In a similar way to the feedings of the multitudes by Jesus recorded in the Gospels, and in accordance with the Mosaic tradition, the food is duly distributed and turns out to be more than sufficient. We are reminded of Gandhi's famous saying that there is enough for the world's need, but not enough for the world's greed.

But there is more. Again we see that the physical giving of food to a neighbour becomes an occasion of grace, an instance of God's bounty transforming human meagreness and fear into plenty. And in saying this, we should recognize that we are not 'spiritualizing' the story, but describing an enlarged reality – a new way for a whole community to be in companionship with God. Appropriately enough, therefore, we should remind ourselves that the Latin term *cum pane* from which we derive the word 'companion', means 'with bread'.

✳ **God of grace,**
Take our poor offerings and turn them into food for life.

Feasting and befriending

The religion of Proverbs is practical and pragmatic – if sometimes a little paradoxical. Rather like the person who is apt to say one thing to one group of people and something quite different to another, according to the circumstances, the Wisdom Movement in Israel tailored the message to the moment.

In this startling passage, Wisdom (who, in contrast to the patriarchy of the culture, is characterized as a wealthy woman) talks about building up a huge feast in a fine building – and then throwing the doors open to all who may come, even the simple and the senseless. Stupidity is, of course, a cipher for those most rejected in the society of the Wise, but the writer still can't resist calling a spade a spade. There is a combination of earthy generosity and unsentimental honesty in these verses.

The moral is straightforward: to 'lay aside immaturity (or simpleness)...and walk in the way of insight' (verse 6) is to share widely both the substance (bread) and the excess (wine) that are offered in the midst of life. The mixture of these two (verse 5) reminds us of the Last Supper, and that the nourishment and joy symbolized by bread and wine can also require the flesh and blood of One who will not submit to an order that denies the gifts of God for whosoever needs them.

✳ *God of simplicity,*
Confound our wisdom with your overflowing love.

FOR REFLECTION – alone or with a group

● What do you hunger and thirst for most at the moment, and why?
● In what ways is it possible, even for people of faith, to deny the bread of life to a hungry world?

Hiroshima Day, Sunday August 6   *Isaiah 25.6-9**

Choosing and cherishing

Throughout the Scriptures we find an argument being waged between particularity and universality in the purposes of God. At some times and in some places it seems as if the love of God is directed particularly to 'the chosen', and is actively withheld from others. Such is the case with the particularly bloody diatribe against the Moabites which follows this passage from the great prophet Isaiah (cf. verses 10b-12). How do we square this with the glorious, inclusive vision of verses 6-9, which say unequivocally that God will create a feast for all peoples on the holy mountain?

First it is important to recognize that the judgement which thunders forth from Isaiah is not a counterpoint to God's universal love, but a feature of it. A thirst for justice requires intolerance of injustice; a quest for peace involves a condemnation of war. The context of these writings is also, it must be recognized, a struggle for survival by a remnant in treacherous circumstances. It is understandable that God's stern love might be mixed (not judiciously, we might feel with hindsight) into a melting pot of vindictiveness towards the national enemy.

Jesus was aware of this problem, and so he made enemy-love a key component of his renewing Way. He also lived to the full this extraordinary, poetic and deeply compelling vision of food for all (verse 6), the swallowing up of death and the wiping away of tears (verses 7 and 8). For Isaiah this is the ultimate purpose of God to bring all creation to fulfilment in Godself.

Along with Micah's 'swords into ploughshares', the tree of life in Revelation, and Julian of Norwich's assurance that 'all manner of things shall be well', this is a definitive 'last word' within the tribulations, triumphs and sorrows which make up the biblical tradition. In place of a shroud of death (verse 7), a tablecloth for feasting is offered.

Whenever we, like (sometimes) the people of Israel, are tempted to think of ourselves as chosen *alone*, when we confuse God's judgement with our sectional interests, we need reminding that the banquet of the Kingdom is for all.

✳ *God of life,*
Deny us our instincts to punish others for wrongs we choose.

Monday August 7   *Hosea 14.4-8*

Harvesting and having

Like Isaiah, Hosea was concerned to show that God's assurance of forgiveness will finally bring restoration in the face of apostasy. Both prophets vigorously condemned the neglect of the poor, foolish involvement in superpower alliances, injustice and the faithless accumulation of wealth for its own sake.

The emphasis in this chapter is on God as the source of life and its renewal. Divine love will 'heal their disloyalty' (verse 4), and divine protection will enable the people to 'live beneath my shadow' (verse 7) – the darkness of night is transformed into the darkness of God. Divine faithfulness 'like an evergreen cypress' (verse 8) will restore their trust. The suffusion of the material world with the Spirit of God foreshadows the age of fulfilment in the vision of the prophet.

The components of that time of renewal (dew, blossom, lilies, forests, olive groves, gardens and trees) are as much to do with beauty as with physical nourishment. The renewal of the aesthetic world accompanies an ethical reformation. The reference to the vine (verse 7b) echoes Isaiah's dream that 'everyone under their own vine and fig tree will live in peace and unafraid'. That is, as the Latin American writer José Portifa Miranda points out, all people will enjoy the benefits of their labour in a way which is free of exploitation and suffering. In an ever more complex, technocratic and commodified world we do well to remember that work and its produce (like the Sabbath) were made for humanity, not the other way round.

✳ *God of beauty,*
Keep us from gorging ourselves on the glorious feast of life.

Tuesday August 8   *John 6.22-35**

Now and then

On the basis of these verses it seems that the Word became, not just Flesh (1.14) but also, in a certain sense, Bread. In other cultural contexts we might easily say, as one Japanese theologian put it, that 'God is Rice'.

What we are talking about here is a symbol of the core and substance of life – the energy of God that makes itself known in manna (verse 31) and in loaves (verse 26), but which in no way is confined to or exhausted by them (verse 27). There is far more than sustenance to be found in Christ; there is overflowing abundance (verse 33). Yet the physical nature of the imagery prevents us from disengaging the things of the spirit from the stuff of the universe. One transcends the other, to be sure, but in the direction of fulfilment rather than negation.

Since John is a relatively late Gospel, many commentators suggest that passages such as this one embody the growing sacramental and liturgical understanding of the Johannine community which produced it. We are not wrong, therefore, to see the bread of eucharist (thanksgiving) and communion (unity with each other and with God) in Christ's words here (see also verse 51). As we break the bread, in church and in the world, in remembrance of Jesus' brokenness, we enable new life to be shared – and we experience his power, presence and purpose with us, in the community and at the table, inviting all to the Feast of Life.

✳ *God of communion,*
Spare us unity at the expense of others.

Wednesday August 9   *John 6.36-51**

Food and faith

The clues to understanding Jesus' continuing discourse in John 6 are his words in verses 45-48. Throughout his Gospel, the writer dramatizes the good news as a continual struggle between true faith and false religion, between the life that has been revealed in Christ and the death-dealing of the current world order.

Certainly we know that Jesus, while remaining thoroughly faithful to the religion of his forebears, directly challenged the right of religious leaders to determine who was and who was not acceptable in the sight of God. Faith (trust) is enough, says Jesus, to be embraced in the eternity of God (verse 47). By denying the efficacy of worthiness and works (cf. verse 29, and the mocking words of his opponents in verse 42), Jesus challenged the power of the cultic elite, rather unhelpfully generalized by the writer as 'the Jews' (verse 41). This is also confirmed by his avowal that, as the prophets emphasized in contrast to some of the priests, 'they shall all be taught by God'. No religious system, doctrine or representative will obstruct the relationship between the humble person and the Lord of all. This life-giving truth is enfleshed for us in Christ. This is why he is 'the bread of life' (verse 48) in whom God is transparent (verse 46). As we might say, employing a different metaphor, 'the proof of the pudding is in the eating'.

✳ **God of eternity,**
   Confound our limitations with your freedom.

Thursday August 10   *John 6.52-59**

Flesh and blood

The sacramental terminology of John 6 is even stronger in these verses, which form the apex of a long discourse on life-giving bread from the life-giving God. John's Gospel is addressed to the philosophical Gentile world as much as to its own Jewish religious environment. So it is hard not to see in these words ascribed to Jesus the Johannine community's own justification for its practices of the Agape (Lovefeast) and Eucharist.

Jesus' images form a deep and uncompromising language of participation. To be 'in Christ' (to use Paul's phrase) is not merely to subscribe to a belief or to place one's trust in a particular person; it is to share tangibly in the very power, presence and purpose of God-in-Christ. Only words of the utmost physicality and down-to-earthness can begin to do this justice. They are not signs (disconnected from what they point towards), but symbols (participating in the reality which they still cannot fathom).

Perhaps, with our contemporary scientific language, we can begin to understand the larger implications of this fleshy, incarnational faith. For we already know that there is a sense in which 'we are what we eat', and we have come to discover that the stuff of dead stars is also the stuff of the carbon-based life through which we humans take our form. Similarly, Jesus says here that the communion which unites him to God, and us to him and to one another, is a kind of mutual in-dwelling, a sharing of the very substance of life.

We are left in the realms of mystery and metaphor, but they help us to understand the sheer extent of the interdependence of creature and creation, and the liberating dependence of all on the life of God. If we can begin to live this out in our own lives and communities, then we shall begin to see the 'kin-dom' (sic) of God taking flesh among us.

✳ *God of indwelling,*
Grant us unity with all that draws us to you and your will.

Friday August 11   Acts 2.42-47
Serving and saving
We may dismiss this famous post-Pentecost picture of the early Church as a little *too* ideal. If so, the rest of the Acts of the Apostles serves to remind us that imperfection, disagreement and vulnerability were as much part of the weft of the Christian community in its early days as they are now!

Even so, we are right to be intrigued and attracted by the purity, simplicity and integrity of the Gospel vision which lies at the heart of this account of the first believers in their common life. The unity, which is both practised and subscribed to, is of the fleshy kind which fully accords with Jesus' vivid symbolism of the bread in John 6. At its heart is the 'breaking of bread': in the context of worship (verse 42), in the distribution of goods to the community (verse 45) and in the household (verse 46).

Here is no divorcing of prayer and work, piety and service, but a new society, based on for-giveness, the predisposition to share without limits (verse 44). It generates goodwill in the world (verse 47a), and its attractiveness is in its inherent divine value rather than in evangelistic technique (verse 47b).

Is it too naive to believe that the churches in our modern, complex urban world need to recapture the vision and practice of the Acts community if they are to begin to convince the world at large that they seek to share the bread of life?

✳ *God of purity,*
Make us clear about what builds up our common life together.

Saturday August 12   Romans 12.9-13
Creating and stirring
The final word in our exploration of new life in Christ, the bread of life, belongs to Paul in his letter to the Christians in Rome. At the heart of a burgeoning imperial system the Apostle commends an entirely new way of living, a common life in both senses of the word – one rooted in the extra-ordinariness of ordinary things, and one based on sharing that which has been received from God. In this entirely new order strangers become friends and outsiders become insiders (verse 13); people do not try to outdo each other, except in multiplying virtue (verse 10); pursuit of goodness is the core motivation (verse 9); service, rejoicing, hope, perseverance and prayer are the principal aspirations; and ultimately (verses 20-21) enemies become friends and good overcomes evil.

As Stanley Hauerwas has said, 'Understood rightly, the Church does not have an ethic, it is an ethic.' If we take Paul's words seriously, we have not just a new loaf in Christ (if you will pardon the pun) but a recipe for the whole new creation which takes shape in him. Having entered the third Millennium, the need to rediscover a vocation to be the Church in and for (rather than over and against) the community becomes ever more pressing. Our tendencies to division and sectarianism are an immense scandal in a traumatized world. We need people who can share bread (life), and share it now.

✳ *God of blessing,*
Show us the ordinary way to live eternity today.

FOR REFLECTION – alone or with a group
● Orthodox Christians talk about service to the world as 'the altar beyond the altar'. How can our churches better integrate worship and work into their common witness?
● What is it that feeds and strengthens our participation in Christ, and what difference should our neighbours reasonably expect this to make?

- What would people in your neighbourhood recognize as 'the bread of life' for them?

FOR ACTION

- Plan a church or community event around a common meal, or invite people to make food or to use their gifts in different ways to share with others at the end of a church service.
- Talk to a development agency, or Christian service organization, about food security for vulnerable people in another part of our still hungry world. What programmes, projects or actions might your church support as part of its common life?

BUILDING COMMUNITY
1. In the Church (1 Corinthians)

based on the Revised English Bible by
Bernard Thorogood

Starting his ministry in the islands of Polynesia, Bernard Thorogood served with the London Missionary Society for 18 years, and then in 1970 became General Secretary of the Society when it developed a new form, the Council for World Mission. From 1980 for twelve years he served the United Reformed Church (UK) as its General Secretary. After retirement in 1992 he settled in Sydney as a minister of the Uniting Church in Australia.

Corinth was a noisy, bustling, sometimes violent city. It had a bad reputation. The port attracted people of many races who followed many religious devotions. And there, in Corinth, was a small Christian fellowship which had been founded by the preaching of Paul. They had written to him, asking their questions, and Paul, probably in Ephesus, replied. We have that reply before us in these three weeks; it is a wonderful letter which still speaks, but needs some translation from that world to ours.

Sunday August 13   *1 Corinthians 1.1-17*
Called into fellowship

Paul begins with his calling (verse 1) and moves on to the calling of the church (verse 9). So the starting point is the action of God in Jesus Christ, who calls disciples. Paul was able to remember his calling, for it was the most dramatic thing in his life. The Corinthian church could remember, too, for they had heard this strange preacher and responded with amazement and trust. Sometimes we forget that all Christian fellowships exist through this calling, for they often seem human creations, sustained by habit, divided into parties. Then we all have to be recalled to that first call, which is the voice of Jesus.

The parties in Corinth followed their teachers. It was like saying, 'I am a Lutheran', or 'I am a Wesleyan', or 'I am a true-blue Calvinist', and so putting another name before that of Jesus Christ. Paul reminds the Corinthian church that he tried to avoid this party fervour by refusing to baptize; for he knew the risk that some would then claim to be 'Paul's people'. To offer Christian leadership without creating a party of followers is a grace we all need today.

So the letter begins with the call of God to become a united community where Christ is central. Much of what follows develops that theme.

✳ *Lord God, you called us and we came.*
We saw a light, we heard a voice, we felt a touch,
we knew a liberation, we entered a home,
we were fed at a table. Thank you, Lord.

Monday August 14   *1 Corinthians 1.18 to 2.5*

God's call and Paul's voice

To many people in that ancient world, with its many philosophies, shrines, prophets and temples, Paul must have sounded like just another foolish preacher. He spoke of the coming of the great God to earth (not such a new idea to the Greeks), but not as a powerful hero ready to do battle. Here in a despised province of the empire was the divine presence in a poor, wandering teacher who was executed for treason or blasphemy, and then who was alive again. It is no surprise at all that so many people found this to be foolishness.

'But to those who were called' this was the profound wisdom and love of God. So we have a picture of this community gathered by the power of the message, not the charisma of the preacher. The believers came from the poorer part of town. How often this has been the way of the Word, touching first those who are the despised, ignored and powerless in the community. Why is this? Surely because Jesus comes to heal those who know their wounds, their despair or their fear. 'It is not the healthy that need a doctor, but the sick.'

And it is the cross that Paul preached as the central message: the wounds, the suffering and the fear are all there in the wounds and pain of Jesus, which are the wounds and the tears of God. That was radical preaching for Corinth, and for us all.

✳ *In the cross of Christ we glory,*
but teach us, Lord Jesus, to live
the resurrection too;
to know victories of life over death
in all our daily struggles.

The mind of Christ
There are many different ways of looking at the world around us. We can look the scientific way, seeing the materials and organisms and their development, and our place in the natural world. Or we can look the economic way and see capital and labour, poverty and wealth, and people as caught in the jungle of industry. But here Paul points to the specific Christian way of looking at the whole creation, that is the 'hidden wisdom' in verse 7. We possess the mind of Christ: a tremendous claim.

The Spirit reveals this hidden truth. Paul reflects his own experience, that all the learning of the Pharisees in which he had trained did not reveal the ultimate nature of God, but it was the Spirit, opening his eyes to the Christ, that enabled him to see into the heart of the Creator of all things. This revelation is open to all who travel the Christian way of faith, so that wisdom, in Paul's meaning, is given as a grace of God. Here is a clear NO to the ancient thought that by education, research, and investigation we can uncover the purpose of life. Is this still true?

✳ *Spirit of God, give us light to see life truly,*
   and to know ourselves as we really are.

God's garden
In this and the next passage we read two images of a Christian community, as Paul tried to lead the Corinthians on from their first steps in faith towards maturity. We know from Acts 18.11 that Paul had stayed in Corinth for eighteen months, laying a strong foundation of teaching. Yet it was only a foundation. As the believers met all the hard questions of their neighbours – the temptations of the city, the party spirit that had grown among them and the doubts of their own hearts – they could have been overwhelmed.

Apollos was a powerful preacher, a Jew from Alexandria, who had helped to sustain the public witness to Christ (Acts 18.24-28). But all preachers can do is to plant and encourage the growth of the seeds of faith; the power of growth is not theirs. All priests, pastors and evangelists need to hold this word in their hearts; they are not the workers of miracles. If people believe, if they are renewed and given new life, then it is the Spirit at work, and the preacher is just the gardener.

* *Great Teacher, help us to grow;*
  to move on from childish things
  and meet the complexity of life
  with compassion and confidence.

Thursday August 17   *1 Corinthians 3.10-23*

Builders of the temple

In the Old Testament we read about the building of the temple of Solomon, with great detail of the materials used (1 Kings 6). This is the background of the image in Paul's mind. He looked on the congregation as the temple of the Spirit of God. Each person is part of it and each pastor a builder of it. So the quality of workmanship is bound to vary, and only the very best will stand the strain of severe tests which are to come.

Persecution has been one such test. Christians in the Roman empire through to Christians in this century have had to face the assault of those in power. The cultural revolution in China was one such time, when it was very dangerous to be a Christian or to own a Bible, and no public worship was possible. I read of one old lady whose only contact with the Church was a little cross made of two sticks which she kept in the pocket of her gown. But she was in touch with the cross, and Paul would say that she was the pure gold of the building of God, and was the wise one amid chaos.

* *Our hearts are thankful for the wise builders*
  of the temple of the Spirit.
  May we be there with our devotion
  all our lives.

Friday August 18   *1 Corinthians 4.1-13*

Testing the apostle

'The glorious company of the apostles praise you,' we sing in the old hymn called *Te Deum*. We may have a picture of these fine bearded figures, wearing long white robes, with haloes around their flowing hair, all chanting in heaven. But today we read what the reality was like for Paul. It was a hard, unprivileged, often criticized life, with people ready to accuse.

And that may be what lies behind this passage. In the letter which the Corinthians wrote to Paul, there may have been some hard words about his apostleship. 'Some people here claim that we need not obey you because you are not a true apostle; they say that you live on the charity of the church; they prefer other teachers. Of course, Paul, we don't believe them, but you know how people talk.' It may have been like that. Here Paul is strong in his defence. Hungry, thirsty, in disgrace, beaten up, worn out, persecuted – that's the life of this true apostle.

✳ *Lord of all faithful people,*
   we thank you for those witnesses
   who have carried a cross and died a death
   out of love for Jesus Christ and his Kingdom.

Saturday August 19   *1 Corinthians 8.1-13*

One fellowship – two opinions

It is not long in any group of people before divisions emerge; human beings are built that way. Even when we try to follow conscience we find that it speaks with different voices. So this passage is an illustration of how to deal with division.

Part of the church was sure that any food which had been presented in a heathen temple was banned. Others could not see this; they saw that the food was just as good, not tainted, available, so why not use it? Paul's word is plain. Those who feel at liberty must respect those who feel bound by conscience, for to act in a way that wounds the conscience of a sister or brother is to wound Christ again.

The church is slow to learn. There are many debates in churches about sexuality and sexual ethics, where there is little regard for those who do not feel free from old conventions. They may be abused or derided as relics of the past. But those who do feel free should read this chapter and ask whether they might be wounding the fellowship of God's people. Paul is not saying that freedom is wrong, but that it must not be used to hurt others.

✳ *When we are deeply divided and led in different ways,*
   may your Spirit of unity and caring keep us together;
   one flock and one Shepherd.

FOR REFLECTION – alone or with a group

● Paul sees the Corinthian church as an extraordinary creation of the Spirit, made up of ordinary people. Is this how the Church seems to us? We look ordinary enough, and we could list our weaknesses, but can we see the wonderful gift that is true community?

- Think of the major divisions that have hurt the Church in your experience; and consider the way that Paul commends in chapter 8. Would that change the way we debate and argue a case?

Sunday August 20   *1 Corinthians 10.1-13*

Trials in the wilderness

At the end of chapter 9 Paul wrote of the example of athletes who have to prepare for the games. Next month the Olympic Games will be held in Sydney and we will watch people who have trained hard for many years to reach the top level. In the same way the apostle calls us to prepare for the journey of discipleship.

Then he turns to the journey of the Israelites through the wilderness, their Exodus. Paul regards them as struggling with God, hearing God's voice but often disobedient, looking for miracles, pining for the past, distrusting their leaders. So many were lost; but some did remain faithful and entered the land across the Jordan.

There are testing times for all of us. Nobody escapes the hardness of life, the loss of loved ones, times of sickness, failures at work or at home, and so on; and through all the human journey we are never alone, for God is with us. The providence of God is that, through all the hard times, faith can grow; there are always possibilities that lead to peace.

✳ *Lead us, Lord, lead us on life's journey,*
and when the hard times come
keep us trusting in your good purpose for us.

Monday August 21   *1 Corinthians 10.14-22*

Holy food

Paul here responds to another issue that was evidently troubling the church at Corinth – the conduct of the Lord's Supper. There are further, more detailed, references to this in chapter 11. In this passage the issue is the distinction between the holy meal in obedience to Christ and the food that is offered in many of the pagan temples.

For us the concern is rather different. We may think of the hands which did some bad work during the week, or were soiled by violence; or of the tongue which spoke bad rumours about a neighbour; and are we then to take the holy food as though this is

197

all quite acceptable to the Lord? Verses 16 and 17 are the key for us to think about. We can think of a loaf of bread on the table and a cup of wine, very ordinary things, but made exceptional through the action of Jesus and the power of the Spirit. Paul is clear that for those who eat and drink in faith there is a real sharing in the life of Christ; we are – in Paul's phrase – 'in Christ' and Christ is in us. And since we share the one loaf we are bound together, just as a family is at the meal table.

By stressing the meaning of the Supper as an act of unity, Paul shames us. We have made it, all too often, a cause of division. Christ must weep as we put barriers around his table.

✷ *Lord Jesus Christ, forgive us, challenge us,*
 renew us and make us all one.

Tuesday August 22   *1 Corinthians 10.23 to 11.1*
Follow my example
We return to the same subject of food! How important this was – and still is – for Jewish people who need to follow dietary laws. But in Paul's time the Gentile people (Greeks, Romans, Egyptians, Syrians and so on), who were joining the churches, were not at all fussed about their food. So the origin of food could easily become a cause for separation and dissent.

Paul's advice is to be considerate towards others but not to be too fussy. You do not have to raise awkward questions about this piece of mutton and that piece of stewed goat. But if you can see that the questions are troubling some people in the community, then have a care for them and refrain from that dish. How challenging the final verse is! Few of us would ever dare to say it. But we have to ask ourselves, if others followed me then would they be any nearer to Christ?

✷ *When you desire to be with Christ*
 what do you see in me?
 I'm afraid, Lord, of that question;
 help me to show you more clearly.

Wednesday August 23   *1 Corinthians 11.17-29*
At the Lord's Table
At a date when there was no written liturgy, before the four Gospels were circulated, when apostles and other teachers were carrying their own versions and when little congregations were widely

separated – then we can imagine the diversity of worship. Evidently in Corinth there was a mix of a social meal and the holy supper. The common meal was a sign of the fellowship of the church, sharing their food; and we know how important this still is, for eating together is a necessary part of hospitality, of neighbourliness.

The Corinthians had spoilt the occasion by selfishly grabbing at the food and drink. It sounds as though they had some riotous meals and so, when they came to the bread and wine of the Lord's table, they were in no mood to receive the sacrament. We are grateful to Paul for this earliest account of the Last Supper and it is his only extended quotation from Jesus; it was something that was supremely important for him. We note how simple the words are. They are for everyone. The very life of Christ is shared so that we become his body in the world.

✳ *Thank you, God of the Feast,*
   that when we hunger and thirst for righteousness
   we are filled by the passion of Christ.

Thursday August 24   *1 Corinthians 12.1-11*
Unity and diversity
By the Spirit, some have been given passionate songs and dances, while others, by the same Spirit, have been given the blessings of silence and contemplation. Some, by the Spirit, find the presence of God in the richness of the liturgy, while others, by that same Spirit, know God best in the sound of wind in great trees. Some find blessing in the great congregation, others in the intimate house church. So we know the reality of Paul's words and can give praise to God for the many gifts of the Spirit.

We do not all have to be alike. It is part of our human nature that we have different ways of receiving the deepest influences in life, and of expressing the deepest thoughts. God speaks to us, and acts through us, respecting our diversity; and the Church must respect that also.

✳ *Spirit of God, use all our gifts*
   and bless all our offerings
   that we place at your disposal.

Friday August 25   *1 Corinthians 12.12-31*
Body parts
There are many images of church fellowship in the New Testament but this is the most detailed. Paul elaborates this

image of the body so that there can be no mistake about his meaning. The members of Christ's Church belong together as completely as the limbs of the body do. There is health for the body as a whole or pain for the body as a whole; it is one entity. How hard we find it to live like this! If Christians in the Sudan are suffering greatly, then we are hurting too. If another denomination of the Church has found growth and zeal and healing, then we are blessed too. I do not always think like that or pray like that, for I too readily concentrate on our group or my little patch.

This passage leads us to review our understanding of the body of Christ, so that we may cherish all our links and put energy into all our ecumenical relationships. Verses 27 to 31 remind us to value all sorts of ministry that are commissioned by God; there are many fingers to do God's work.

✳ *Lord Jesus, head of the body,*
I am not on my own and not my own master,
I am a member of the body.
Help me to pray and act with others
as your Spirit gives us life.

Saturday August 26   *1 Corinthians 13.1 to 14.1a*

The eternal gift

This passage is so familiar and so wonderful that we do not need more words about it. What a present it was to those first Christians in Corinth, a great poem of faith which speaks of God to every generation. God is love. This is what God's love is like, transcending all other qualities, outlasting all empires, overturning all ambitions. This is love; it is also life for the human family.

Let us read the passage again, slowly, and let us be fed and nurtured by it.

✳ *O love of God, how deep and great,*
Far deeper than man's deepest hate;
Self-fed, self-kindled like the light,
Changeless, eternal, infinite!

O love of God, our shield and stay
Through all the perils of our way;
Eternal love, in thee we rest
For ever safe, for ever blest!   *Horatius Bonar (1808-89)*

FOR REFLECTION – alone or with a group

● Your church has a way of celebrating Holy Communion that is familiar; other churches may show differences and seem strange. What are the strengths in these different ways of sharing?

● One body, many limbs and organs. Can we see all members of the Church as having special gifts and graces which the Spirit brings?

Sunday August 27   *1 Corinthians 14.1b-12*

The gift of language

Evidently the Corinthian Christians were disturbed by their experience of what is called 'speaking in tongues' and asked Paul's advice about it. This spiritual gift was singing or speaking in a language unknown to the speaker or the hearers, quite mysterious noises unlike normal speech. A parallel gift was the ability to interpret what had been spoken. This strange experience has recurred occasionally throughout Christian history when people have been caught up in the Spirit.

Paul sees another gift, that of prophecy. That is speaking in ordinary language but with great spiritual insight and power. And for Paul, that is the more important gift, since it builds up the fellowship. So his concern is not to stop the ecstatic utterance but to encourage what will strengthen discipleship. The image in verse 8 stays in our minds and we are grateful that Jesus spoke in words so clear that all the world may hear. Who, in the modern world, has the clearest trumpet-call?

✳ *Bless us, Lord, with the Spirit's gifts:*
the right word to speak,
a heart to bring peace,
and a touch to speed healing.

Monday August 28   *1 Corinthians 14.13-25*

With mind and with the Spirit

Although Paul continues here to deal with the gift of 'tongues', and stresses the need for interpretation and clarity, the strong impression of this whole chapter is that worship in Corinth was something exciting. It was not orderly. They did not follow any written liturgy and probably had little skilled leadership. But something was happening; the Spirit was active; lives were changed; there was a sense of wonder and joy. It needed care so that it did not descend into chaos, and Paul could see that.

But the contrast with much modern Christian worship is great. For many of us there is plenty of order but not so much enthusiasm. When I have shared in African or Caribbean worship, I have found something closer to Corinth, with movement, spontaneous harmony and praise from the heart. Intelligence and emotion, order and freedom, all together, praise the Lord!

✳ *Move us, worshipping Spirit,*
to sing and pray and read
with heart and mind,
with our whole being,
and with the living Word on our lips.

Tuesday August 29   *1 Corinthians 15.1-11*

The risen Christ

As we begin this tremendous, but difficult, chapter we are brought directly to the experience of the apostles. They were witnesses of the resurrection. That was the heart of their preaching, and it was because of the risen Christ that they travelled the world to proclaim him as Lord. The details in verses 5-7 are not easy to match with the Gospels. There were evidently several versions of how and when Jesus appeared and spoke to the apostles. But Paul was sure of this, that Jesus came and spoke to him on the road to Damascus.

Verses 9 and 10 spell out the heart of Paul's apostleship. He could never claim to be like the twelve who followed and listened and learned and sat at the table with Jesus, for then he was in the other camp, hostile, hard, prepared to be brutal. But the miracle of grace for him was a true revelation of God; he knew without any doubt that Jesus was all he claimed to be: Messiah, Healer, Saviour, Son.

✳ *I have not heard that heavenly voice*
and my eyes have not been blinded on the road,
and I was not there in the upper room;
but I believe you are the living Lord.
Hold me, Jesus, in faith today.

Wednesday August 30   *1 Corinthians 15.12-20*

Faith and fact

Just as today, so in ancient times there were many sceptics who denied any possibility of resurrection. Probably there were some in Corinth who poured scorn on the Christians for their conviction that death is not the end. Paul's way of dealing with this is to point to Christ. In his empty tomb, his word of peace in the upper room and his scarred hands, Paul saw a reality: that death is not the final act of the human drama. If, then, we deny all resurrection, we deny Christ, and the whole of our faith collapses like a building shaken in an earthquake.

Is Paul's argument sound? Could we not say that Christ was so exceptional that his resurrection is one-off, not a sign of God's goodness to all, and not a model of the Christian community? After all, we do not argue from the detail of the birth stories to claim the same for ourselves. This is a serious question; Paul begins to answer it in tomorrow's passage.

✴ *'Blessed are those who do not see me, and yet believe.'*
Help us to know, dear God, that there is life from the tomb,
that you deal in commas, and not in full stops.

Thursday August 31   *1 Corinthians 15.21-34*

New creation

We are all one humanity: one breathing, loving, laughing, struggling, exploring, fearful, wounded human family. Just as we have that unity from a natural process (or, as Paul says, from Adam), so there is a new humanity which comes from the Son of God. The new creation is the realm or Kingdom where God's justice and love reign, and where death is no longer the feared enemy. So for Paul the question is, are you within that realm of new creation? If, by faith, you are, then you share the glory of resurrection with Jesus.

Verse 29 is difficult. It seems as though some Christians were eager to include within God's blessing their loved ones who had died without knowing Christ. So they had a form of baptism for the dead. It was a custom that very quickly disappeared from the Church. Paul does not say he approves of it; he just points to the belief that there is indeed a life beyond death.

✴ *Christ, the first-fruits, then...*
go before us, Christ, into tomorrow,
into a new century, into a new arena;
lead us into your Kingdom life
which is for ever.

Spirit and body

To approach this difficult passage it is helpful to recall that for people in the Greek tradition the physical body was a prison cage for the spirit. The life we know in our body is brief, often painful, and subject to passions of all sorts; but when this body dies then the spirit will be free. Many thought (and some still believe) that the spirit after death falls back into the universal spirit, as a drop of water falls into the ocean, and all individuality disappears.

Paul preaches another vision. When he writes of a 'spiritual body' he does not mean that every bone and muscle lives on for ever. He is writing about our individuality, our being as persons. Just as we now know each other within a physical body, so, beyond death, we shall still be known. I will be I and you will be you. So Paul can say: Away with all the shadows and ghosts and auras; the risen Christ is the Jesus of Nazareth; we know his name and he knows us. That is the new confidence which is the gospel news.

✳ *God of grace, so much is hidden from us,*
and we wonder, as we get older, what lies ahead.
So thank you for the assurance
that we are with Jesus today, tomorrow and for ever.

Victory song

Paul brings this great chapter to a close on the note of joy, wonder and victory. This is hardly prose at all but a song that should be set to triumphant music. To get the full flavour of it, think of what Paul wrote in Romans 7.24: 'Wretched creature that I am, who is there to rescue me from this state of death?' That is the low point of human experience. In depression, despair, self-hatred, or in the agony of guilt, or in the weakness of chronic illness, many people could echo Paul. So beside that rock-bottom point we read now of victory, and Paul lived it as well as preaching it. There was victory over his past, victory over hardships, over fears, over illness, and all has come to him from the Lord. Jesus meets us, not at the top of our powers and self-confidence, but when we are brought low, for 'he humbled himself, and was obedient, even to the point of death, death on a cross!' So he brings us with him into resurrection joy.

✳ *Lo, Jesus meets us, risen from the tomb;*
lovingly he greets us, scatters fears and gloom;
let the church with gladness, hymns of triumph sing,
for her Lord is living, death has lost its sting.
Thine be the glory, risen, conquering Son,
endless is the victory thou o'er death hast won.

  Edmond Budry (1854-1932) tr. Richard Hoyle 1875-1939)

FOR REFLECTION – alone or with a group

● In chapter 14 we have read a lot about worship. What do we
   see as the main purpose of worship? Is it for education and
   improvement, or for public witness, or is it an expression of
   joy? Or is it something else?

● What are the common attitudes to death in your community?
   How do they look when compared with the confidence that we
   find in Paul?

FOR ACTION

We have been reading about the life of a Christian community,
with all its problems and its joys. It was a community of the Spirit
which crossed old social divisions. What divisions still break the
human family apart? Is there one such division which we can
begin to overcome here and now? By an act of friendship, by a
common task, by a plea for justice, by a generous letter, by a gift
of love?

BUILDING COMMUNITY
2. No generation gap

Notes based on the New Revised Standard Version by
Rosemary Wass

Rosemary Wass is a laywoman and former Vice President of the Methodist Church. She and her husband have a farm in North Yorkshire. Rosemary has travelled widely, meeting and learning from women worldwide.

Community today is made up of more generations of people than ever before. Higher standards of living and advances in health care mean that in many countries people expect longer life. Children are privileged to know and remember great-grandparents as well as grandparents! But what do the generations say about each other? 'It wasn't like that in our day.' Acceptable social behaviour and patterns of life have changed while technology offers new freedoms and dangers. Our readings this week help us to think again about life and why such importance is laid upon 'telling the coming generation' (Psalm 78.1-4).

Sunday September 3   *Deuteronomy 4.1-2, 6-10**
Helping history to come alive
The writer of Deuteronomy says it is important to remember and not forget what God does for his people. Memory is the foundation for the present and the future. God is extremely generous. He gives the people of Israel their land, a gift for all time, stability and permanence to those who keep faith. Obedience is essential: it will offer an example to others and draw them to God. To tell the story is to remember, so that the young might hear and in turn repeat and tell the story again. Oral tradition is an important vehicle of communication, linking one generation to another. Remembering all that God has done in the past and is doing in the present gives foundation and trust for the future. What he has done, he will continue to do as long as people are obedient to him.

✳ *For the way in which you have sustained us*
from one generation to another,
we praise you, loving God.
Help me to remain obedient to your way,
and may the stranger who meets me
see your life in mine.

No substitutes

Obedience to the law of the community is a significant part of the cultural heritage of all peoples but Jesus challenges customs, rituals and rules which do not reflect the values of the Covenant God made with his Jewish ancestors. *Corban* (verse 11) is an Aramaic term for a practice which allowed children to make a monetary offering to the Temple. This absolved them of any obligation to care for their parents. The Temple gained to the detriment of parents in need. Jesus does not spare anyone his feelings on this matter! He defends the vulnerable members of community. The building of community is about caring for all ages and generations of family with dignity. This is also about fulfilling the commandment: 'Honour your father and your mother, as the LORD your God commanded you, so that your days may be long and that it may go well with you in the land that the LORD your God is giving you' (Deuteronomy 5.16).

✳ *Loving God, thank you for all that you have given to each of us,*
and for those who have cared for us throughout our childhood, giving us time and love to learn important truths for life.
Help us to be as loving and caring for them,
especially when frailty and increasing age become a burden.
Grant us generosity of time, patience, and a quiet spirit,
so that they may see their love for us reflected in our caring.

Christianity and contrasts

Here are three thoughts on which to ponder today:

– God is the giver of every good and perfect gift (verses 17-18);
– we are to live by the word of God and allow this to permeate our attitudes and behaviour (verses 19-25);
– our faith challenges us to work for the rights of others (verses 26-27).

Christianity demands a way of life contrasting worldly values and patterns of living. The test of faith here is whether we have the confidence to 'challenge the norm' and to live by new options and alternatives. 'Jubilee 2000' has been one of the ways of learning about and campaigning for justice for the poorer nations of the world. When people protest, even governments take notice. The easiest place to be a Christian is in the Church.

✳ *For all that we have inherited from you, O Lord, thanks!*
For all that you are able to achieve in our lives, thanks!
For your patience with our failings,
  and for your forgiveness, so readily available, thanks!
So, continue to nurture and help us
to see your exciting alternatives for life in this third millennium.

Wednesday September 6   *1 Timothy 4.6 to 5.2*
Bridging the generations with respect
Timothy is God's gift to the early Christians. He has several possible barriers to overcome – not least his youthfulness. Paul does his best to reassure him that God's purposes are blind to age. Human expectations and judgements are a detail once Timothy has won their trust and respect. Timothy is tutored by Paul on how to behave towards his elders.

How do we feel when younger people try to tell us something we thought we knew already, or challenge us about something we do in the life of our church? Do we feel intimidated or patronized? Can we begin to think what a difficult time Timothy faced? Are we able to think of the positive gifts that Timothy brought to the early Christians? Is there a 'Timothy' in your congregation? How can you help and encourage this gift of God today?

✳ *Make a list of people in your church with whom you get on easily, those whose comments you find abrasive or irritating, those you feel you help, those who help you. What will it take to be 'Timothy' to everyone?*
Pray about it and thank God for the example of Timothy.

Thursday September 7   *Mark 9.33-37**
Vision and values
If you can find time, read Mark 10.35-45 to reinforce expectations and a measure of greatness in human terms. How often do we allow ourselves to feel flattered when something 'important' comes our way, when perhaps we should be asking other questions?

The measure of importance is when Jesus takes a child, a member of another generation, and gives her pride of place. A child, powerless and vulnerable, is taken from the margins and brought into the centre. Jesus cares for the undervalued in society. He encourages and respects women and children and gives them dignity and real value. A child does not have to wait for adulthood to be of worth. A child is precious. Community is incomplete without every generation being fully appreciated and valued. The images are powerful, humbling and challenging. What do they say to us today? How do we treat people who are younger or older than ourselves?

✳ *Why are we so stubborn, Lord,*
so sure of ourselves and our own self-importance?
Forgive us, Lord. Make us more aware of our poverty
and help us to live in the way we were so clearly shown
by your Son, Jesus Christ.

Friday September 8   *Luke 2.41-52*
Fulfilling the prophecy
Mary and Joseph are brought up with a start. Jesus was growing up fast. They had brought him up to be truly Jewish. The Jerusalem visit was a requirement of the law. At the celebration of Passover, it was important to remember their history of God's saving of the Jewish nation. The gathering in Jerusalem witnesses the coming together of the Jewish community. We can imagine family chatter – comparisons of children of similar ages by parents, young people congregating together to talk at their level. The time comes to return. Jesus is not in either of the caravans of pilgrims. We can sense the increasing anxiety.

Jesus has grown beyond recognition. Mary is looking for her child, but he has become a man. He will probably help to provide for her and the family in the intervening years until his public ministry.

✳ *Thank you, God, that one generation after another*
celebrated your rescuing of the nation;
for the ways in which Jesus was brought up as a Jew,
learning the Scriptures and history of your people;
for the way in which Mary, like every parent,
had to love and let go;
for all that he meant to a community reluctant to believe him,
and for the way in which the story has continued to be told
throughout every generation.
Help us to be sure of our inheritance and prepare us
to be ready to recognize the signs of your presence among us.

All are equal
Jesus' family come to find him. Jesus is used to people looking for him – sometimes because they want their friends to be healed, or they want to hear Jesus firsthand, or to ask a question. Some come to harass him – the Pharisees and elders of the law. The family still see Jesus as an important member, but Jesus has been busy enlarging his family. This does not make his immediate family less important, but places them in a wider setting. His disciples may also think that they are 'extra special' in Jesus' eyes. They are 'family', and this has taken his natural family by surprise. How easily do we admit people into our family circle? Are we genuinely inclusive towards others? What are the hurdles to be overcome?

✳ *In Jesus you taught us new values and ways of being 'family'.*
Forgive our apathy, and fear of failure before we begin.
Fire us to be brave, and to be bold in your strength.
May we not be satisfied
until we have played our part in building a community
where all ages are welcomed and valued,
and justice, peace and love reign supreme. Amen

FOR REFLECTION – alone or with a group
- Does the church to which you belong take every age-group seriously? Where do you meet all generations of Christians other than at worship?
- Which age-group of people need the most support at this time? Are there ways in which you are able to encourage one generation to help another?

FOR ACTION
Invite a group of mixed ages for a meal or a get-together. Steer the conversation round to their perceptions of 'church' and see what each can teach the other!

BUILDING COMMUNITY
3. No one excluded

Notes based on the Revised English Bible by
Mary Cotes

Mary Cotes is minister of the United Church, Pontypridd, and part-time chaplain to the mental health unit of her local hospital. She lectures in feminist theology at the University of Glamorgan and broadcasts regularly on radio.

'Good news for all throughout the earth'. We sing it in our hymns, affirm it in our prayers, declare it in our preaching – but do we really believe it? Many looking in on the Church from outside might be forgiven for thinking that we have created instead a cosy introverted clique for ourselves and developed strange customs and practices especially to put outsiders off! The readings for this week invite us to look again at the gospel of God's all-inclusive love and examine ourselves in its devastating light.

Sunday September 10   *Proverbs 22.1-2, 8-9, 22-23**
You did it for me

I confess that I'm rather uncomfortable with this passage, just as I am with any 'carrot and stick' method of spiritual teaching. 'Do good and what a good reputation you'll develop! But do evil and think of the punishment in store.' Certainly such warnings can offer very effective methods of controlling people. I dare say it's the way many of us train our children to stay out of mischief and eat their dinner! But the 'carrot and stick' mentality can be destructive in terms of motivation. If we're not careful, we end up doing good works for the glow of pride we feel afterwards. Such pride is enough to poison a church's mission, no matter how successful it is.

The true reason for 'sharing our food with the poor' is not to earn ourselves a good name, but because God's love extends to all people. Indeed such is God's identification in Christ with the powerless that Christ comes to us in the young addict, the schizophrenic and the jailed criminal. 'Truly, anything you did for one of these, you did for me.'

✳ *Teach me, Lord,*
  to find you in ever new and unexpected places.

Lord, when did we see you?

For most of us, a new-born child draws our love. We utter sweet
nothings to her even though she may not be able to speak back;
we cuddle her even though her nappy may be full; and we put her
over our shoulder even though she might dribble and puke down
our back. So for once, Jesus' words don't seem to be that difficult!
But if in this passage Jesus was inviting us to receive someone
equally powerless, such as a person in the late stages of
Alzheimer's disease – as speechless, dribbly and incontinent as a
baby – perhaps we might begin to understand how his words rub.
Of course we accept that the powerless need our practical support,
even though offering it is often far from easy. But Jesus' point is not
that the powerless need us. It's we who need them. Their gift to us
is to challenge our selfishness, expose our fears and pound at our
heart's fortress door. Until we are ready to embrace the very
poorest, Jesus says, we'll not find the Kingdom of God.

✳ *Batter my heart, three-person'd God, for you*
   As yet but knock.   *John Donne*

Room at the inn?

Well, here's Jesus telling the Samaritan woman loud and clear
that true worship is never place-oriented. And here are we,
followers of Jesus, embellishing our buildings, arguing over what
colour the walls are painted and spending lots of money on
renovations! Have we got our priorities wrong?

Perhaps Jesus' teaching is not so much about the places
themselves as about the danger of their becoming exclusive. The
presence of God doesn't belong to one particular area or building
any more than to a particular people. Of course we know this, but
our church buildings often tell a different story. Situated in a
remote corner of town, miles off the nearest bus-route, they can
proclaim that only people with cars or strong legs can come. They
may have no toilets for the disabled or assistance for the hard of
hearing. If we believed the gospel was for all, how would we
change our premises?

✳ *Lord Jesus, our gate is barred,*
   our steps are high,
   our seats are cold.
   Help us to hear you calling still:
   'Behold, I stand at the door and knock.'

'Behold I stand at the door and knock.'
Papercut by a student at Nanjing Theological Seminary in China.

Broken but loved

Most clubs or organizations demand that the people who belong conform to certain criteria: they must be good at art or running, or rich enough to pay the membership fee. But the only thing that church members have in common is that they are drawn together by the love of God in Christ. And whereas in many cultures couples who marry choose one another, those who belong to the church have no such choice! Consequently we are thrown together with others who may be very different from ourselves, have very different opinions, and with whom we may find it hard to get on.

But the fact is that we need one another – not just to visit when we're lonely, or to pray with us when we're sick, but to reveal to us who we are. This is the work of God. Without others in the fellowship we might never discover what gifts of listening we have, or indeed how selfish we are. Yet by their faithfulness to us, our brothers and sisters in Christ remind us that no matter how broken we might be, we are still loved. And therein lies the joy and the pain of being the Church.

✳ ***Praise to the Risen Christ who, knowing how poor and vulnerable we are, comes and prays in us the hymn of his unchanging confidence.***   *Brother Roger*
From Meditations on the Way to the Cross (Mowbray)

My neighbour and myself

Impartiality – what a challenge! The truth is that we find it well nigh impossible. No matter how much we may lecture ourselves about the universal love of God, there are always people with whom we feel a natural affinity, and others we go out of our way to avoid. We demonstrate the same tendencies in relation to our own natures. There are elements of our personalities with which we're glad to be friends, and other parts of ourselves that we'd rather push into the shadows and forget.

We need to realize that the two are linked. God's love encompasses all – and each one of us in our entirety. The sooner we grasp this, the sooner we're ready to face those sides of our natures we prefer to hide from. And the more we face and welcome both the light and the dark in our own selves, the more we learn to encompass in our love the light and the darkness of others. Loving our neighbour means loving ourselves too. Public and private faces are images one of the other.

* *Lord Jesus, when I push others away,*
  help me to see what I push away in myself.
  And in seeing myself more truly,
  may I also see you,
  hidden in the shadows,
  your arms open in pain and embrace.

Friday September 15   Luke 13.22-30

Love the sinner, hate the sin?

Who are these people huddled together on the doorstep, howling
to be let in? Are they a motley group of individuals being punished
for their wicked ways? Or do they represent a local church who,
for all its feasting with the master, has still not understood the real
meaning of his all-inclusive love?

The terrible irony is that often churches are so anxious to be
loving and inclusive that they tolerate extreme behaviour which
actually damages the body from within. On the grounds that 'after
all, none of us is without sin', we bend over backwards to
appease the insatiable critic or do what the bully dictates. The
result is the slow but sure poisoning of the fellowship. Is it really in
the name of inclusive Christian love that we make space for
wicked ways? Or is it because deep down we're frightened of
standing up to the person in question? Or worse: is it that we're
so used to their strategies and to our own conditioned responses
we don't notice them any more?

* *Lord Jesus, I'm cast in a mould others have made for me;*
  unable to shift, unable to change;
  so accustomed to it, I hardly know it's there.
  Come with all the violence of your love
  and smash it to splinters;
  then melt me down and remake me in your image.

Saturday September 16   Luke 14.15-24

Believing without belonging

What sort of excuses would be made today for not wishing to
come to the feast? In Britain it might be something like this: 'If you
want to hold a feast, you carry on. But I'd rather do my own thing.
I don't want to be tied down.' Loyal participation in communal
activity is out of fashion, and clubs and organizations of all kinds,
social and political, are feeling the pinch. The Church is no
exception. No matter how hard we preach and practise an all-

inclusive gospel, the simple fact is that many people don't wish to be included. They may believe – even have a strong personal faith – but they don't want to belong.

This raises serious questions for the future of the Church as an institution, and I'm not sure what the answers are. For committed church members, the situation can easily induce a panic which manifests itself in possessiveness, pressurizing newcomers and suffocating others. But this is never God's way. God leaves us free to come or go. So perhaps the challenge of the current climate – though not the solution – is for us to learn from the loving Christ who remains constant even to those who always choose to walk away.

✱ *Reflect: **A father complained to the Baalshem that his son had forsaken God. 'What, Rabbi, should I do?'**
'**Love him more than ever**,' was the reply.*

FOR REFLECTION – alone or with a group

● In Christ, 'there is no such thing as Jew and Greek, slave and freeman, male and female.' If we were to write a similar formula for baptisms today, what great divisions would we want to say Christ challenges?

● How would you describe the 'culture' of your church service? What sort of people would find it attractive? Who would be put off by it?

● Name some of the most marginalized people in your area. How could your church develop ways of relating to them?

FOR ACTION

Take a decision to visit or befriend someone you find difficult.

INTERNATIONAL BIBLE READING ASSOCIATION
1020 Bristol Road, Selly Oak, Birmingham, Great Britain B29 6LB

ORDER FORM – For 2001 Books

Please send me the following books: *Office Ref: 21001*

Name: _____

Address: _____

_____

_____ Postcode: _____

*To qualify for 2001 books at the prices shown, this order form must be used (photocopies not accepted). Your order will be dispatched when **all** books are available.*

Code	Title of Book	Quantity	Unit Price	Total
ZYW0971	Words for Today 2001		£5.00	
ZYL0972	Light for Our Path 2001		£5.00	
ZYL0973	Large Print Light for Our Path 2001		£9.00	
ZYF0897	Finding Our Way Together Book 1		£6.50	
ZYF0910	Finding Our Way Together Book 2		£6.50	
ZYF0938	Finding Our Way Together Book 3		£6.50	
ZYF0974	Finding Our Way Together Book 4		£6.50	
ZYF0897-SET	Finding Our Way Together series (4 BOOKS)		£20.00	
ZYP0975	Preachers' Handbook 2001		£5.50	
ZYE0213	Everyday Prayers		£5.50	
ZYM0325	More Everyday Prayers		£5.50	
ZYF0495	Further Everyday Prayers		£5.50	
ZYI0889	Invitation To Read		£2.00	
ZYL0575	Looking at the Cross		£4.50	
ZYL0781	Living Prayers For Today		£12.50	
ZYM0902	More Living Prayers For Today		£12.50	

I enclose cheque (Payable to IBRA)
Please charge my MASTERCARD/VISA/SWITCH
Card No:

Expiry Date: _____

Signature: _____

Total cost of books	
Post – UK free Overseas – add £2.50 airmail per book	
Donation to International Fund	
TOTAL DUE	

Payments in Pounds Sterling, please

The INTERNATIONAL BIBLE READING ASSOCIATION is a Registered Charity

INTERNATIONAL BIBLE READING ASSOCIATION

Help us to continue our work of providing Bible study notes for use by Christians in this country and throughout the world.

The need is as great as it was when IBRA was founded in 1882 by Charles Walters as part of the work of the Sunday School Union.

Please leave a legacy to International Bible Reading Association.

An easy-to-use leaflet has been prepared to help you provide a legacy. Please write to us at the address below and we will send you this leaflet – and answer any questions you might have about a legacy or other donations. Please help us to strengthen this and the next generation of Christians.

Thank you very much.

**IBRA, Dept 298, 1020 Bristol Road,
Selly Oak, Birmingham B29 6LB Great Britain**
Tel: 0121 472 4242   Fax 0121 472 7575

Our solicitors are Pothecary and Barratt,
Talbot House, Talbot Court, Gracechurch Street,
London EC3V 0BS

Charity No. 211542

BUILDING COMMUNITY
4. Forgetting self

Notes based on the New Jerusalem Bible
Joseph G Donders

Joseph Donders, a Dutch priest of the Society of Missionaries of Africa, is Professor of Mission and Cross-cultural Studies at Washington Theological Union. He was formerly Head of the Department of Philosophy and Religious Studies and Chaplain to the Catholic Students at the State University of Nairobi, Kenya.

The word 'forget' is a combination of two words 'for' and 'get'. The first one is not our modern preposition *for*, but an older element in the English language, indicating a negation. So *to for-get* means literally 'not to get' or 'to lose one's hold on', and metaphorically 'to lose one's memory of'. 'Forgetting self' then means 'to lose one's hold on self'. In Matthew 10.39, Mark 8.35 and Luke 9.24, Jesus asks us to lose our lives for his and the gospel's sake. He also asks us what good it would be losing ourselves to gain the world!

Sunday September 17   *Proverbs 1.20-33**
The warning!

Last year, in a discussion on the existence of God in a British journal, an author dismissed any belief in Jesus. How can you believe, he wrote, in someone who threatens you with the hell-fire of Sodom and Gomorrah if you do not obey him? At first reading, he seemed to be right. Yet he is wrong. Take the case of parents who want to warn their child against bad company, and the drugs she has started to take. The child doesn't seem to listen. Aren't they then going to warn her about the consequences of her behaviour?

This is what this first chapter in the book of Proverbs, a Wisdom Book, does. Wisdom walks through the streets; it passes through market places and shopping centres. It warns: do not forget who you are, do not forget yourselves. If your lifestyle is only influenced by those streets and market-places, and if you continue your over-simplifying, materialistic approach to life, you are not going to make it. It is the type of warning we should be grateful for! It intends to keep us together.

✸ *Almighty God, let us not forget where we come from,*
and where we should be heading.
If we forget we will come to nothing.

Monday September 18   Psalm 116*

Undoing fetters

She wrote him a letter of thanks. Her husband had been overseas. Without her and his family, he had felt very lonely. He began to drink. The stories about his drinking bouts had scared her terribly.

But when he came home, he had overcome his drinking and he had told her how. One of his friends had taken the courage to take him apart in one of his lucid moments, telling him the risk he was running. The friend opened his eyes; he undid his fetters. She wrote that letter to thank the friend for the service he had rendered, for the love and friendship he had shown.

I remember an old man who once told me, 'Your real friend is the one who is willing to tell you that you are going wrong when you threaten to slide down the slippery slope into nothingness.'

The psalmist does not write a letter to God; he writes a poem to thank God for having undone his fetters like a good friend would do!

✸ *Gracious God, Abba,*
let us understand better the liberating role
which Jesus, our brother and friend, plays in our lives
indicating the way to live. Amen

Tuesday September 19   Isaiah 50.4-9*

Lending God your mouth and ear

Isaiah asks God to give him a disciple's tongue and ear. It is a splendid prayer. It is a petition we all should join. It is also a risky prayer. God might hear us and give us that mouth and that ear.

So many stories in the Bible are about people who, listening to God, became God's mouthpiece. Hearing them pray like that, God answered, 'If that is what you are asking for, lend me your ear!' They had to listen with God's ear, listening to the cries of the poor. That is what Jesus did.

Once you listen with God's ear, you will have to use your mouth accordingly, as Isaiah tells us. Having a disciple's ear, your mouth will comfort the weary. Your words will not only touch the air, making it vibrate with your voice. They will be followed by your deeds privately and publicly, personally and politically. Isaiah calls this 'saving justice'. It was the work Jesus wrought in our midst, asking us to join him to finish the task he began 2000 years ago.

✳ *Almighty and gracious God,*
help me to be more aware
of what is going on in the world around me,
and help me to share in your universal love.

Wednesday September 20   Luke 12.13-21

Forgetting self

A farmer had a windfall. His harvest was so abundant that it was too much for the barn in which he usually stored his yield for the year. Thinking about how to use this bonanza, he only thought of himself. The words 'I', 'myself' and 'my' are used ten times in this short parable.

At first hearing, the farmer did not forget himself. Yet that is exactly Jesus' point: the man forgot his own condition! He overlooked what Jesus mentioned before he told his story: 'Life does not consist in possessions, even when people have more than they need!' That was not the only reality the farmer overlooked. He also forgot about others.

Jesus does not leave it at that. He tells what the hoarder should have done; he should have become 'rich in the sight of God'. Or, as Jesus points out later in Luke's Gospel: use your money, tainted as it is, to win you friends, and so make sure that, when it fails you, they will welcome you in heaven (Luke 16.9).

✳ *God, Creator of the goods of this world,*
who left their distribution to us,
inspire us to find a way to do that
and to make sure that all your children
have what they need to live and prosper.

Thursday September 21   2 Thessalonians 3.6-15

Self-sufficiency and mutual dependence

Paul insists that the Thessalonians should earn their own living, as he had done when he was living with them. He paid for his room and his board, working day and night making tents. He did not want to give anyone a pretext for not working. He preached self-sufficiency: people should go on quietly working, earning their food, avoiding being busybodies and poking their noses into everyone else's business.

There is, however, an exception! In case some are not willing to follow the way Paul urged them to walk – in the name of the Lord – the community should give them notice, and if need be even avoid them. This does not mean that the community should withdraw their love from them, but gently try to bring them to change their lives.

The challenge of these exhortations is the need to strike a delicate balance between independence and dependency. This is the warp and woof of each society, and definitely of a Christian community that lives up to Jesus' standard.

✳ *Gracious God, make me strike the balance*
   between care for myself
   and for those around me.
   Do not let me forget myself
       because of my care for others.
   Do not let me forget others
       because of my care for myself.

Friday September 22   *2 Timothy 2.1-13*

Remembering

Paul's last letter to Timothy asks him to remember – not Paul – but the good news Paul had brought him. Paul's letter is addressed to an individual, but through Timothy he is writing to all of us.

Jesus' last words also had been about not forgetting. He asked his disciples to do something to remember him, his body and his blood. Remembering him, they would forget neither Jesus Christ, nor their Christian identity.

Paul uses examples to insist on this faithfulness to Jesus and to oneself as a Christian. A soldier who is mixed up in civic affairs will not be a good warrior. An athlete who does not compete according to the rules will be disqualified. The hardworking farmer will gather the harvest, and – by implication – the lazy one will not.

Soldier, athlete and farmer have to labour to succeed, just as a Christian has to do to win through for the Lord. Paul reminds Timothy of the chains he is wearing because of his faithfulness to Jesus, the unforgettable presence in his life.

✳ *Lord Jesus, let your Spirit lead me*
   by my memory of you
   in my work and my play,
   by day and by night,
   my whole life long.

Losing in order to gain

Repeatedly we find in the Gospels the paradoxical statement that we have to lose our life in order to save it.

It takes the form of a beatitude, 'Happy are the poor in spirit, the kingdom of Heaven is theirs.' Then again, we hear that we have to leave father and mother, brothers, sisters, and children in order to follow Jesus and carry our cross. How do we understand these sayings?

It has to do with our spiritual priority list. God has to come first, and not any other attachment. Once you have detached yourself in that way – some spiritual authors call this state 'holy indifference' – you are free to listen to God. Of course, one of the first things God will ask you is to love the ones God entrusted to you, your family and community! You will do that naturally out of love for God. And your loving will be enhanced by God's love. So neither loving God nor loving the other as yourself is the only mission in your personal and professional life. Together they will constitute your chore or cross on the way to the Kingdom.

✳ *Gracious God, bless all of us,*
my family, my friends, my colleagues,
and all those for whom Jesus taught me to pray!

FOR REFLECTION – alone or with a group

- Do you ever see your love for others in the light of Jesus' love for them?
- Do parents see the educating of their children as spreading the light of Jesus' teaching?
- How many politicians and voters regard their responsibility as an extension of Jesus' mission in gathering the community of God?

FOR ACTION

Write a letter of appreciation to someone in your community whom you know as a community builder.

BUILDING COMMUNITY
5. Honouring marriage

Notes based on the Revised Standard Version by
Brian Haymes

Brian Haymes, Principal of Bristol Baptist College, is the author of the 'Looking At' series published by IBRA. He has served as President of the Baptist Union of Great Britain.

Forms of marriage are found in every human society. People instinctively feel that this is one of the major building blocks for building community. But all round the world the understandings and practices of marriage are undergoing change.

Because marriage is such an important part of human community life, we would expect the Bible to have significant insights for us, as the people of God have thought on what it is to be married, to be unmarried, and to be members together of one community. The scripture passages for this week invite us to reflect on what Paul in particular says about marriage and human sexuality as he writes to the situation in Corinth. What he says will encourage us to think about marriage in our time and place.

Sunday September 24   *Proverbs 31.10-31**
Righteous partners

This is a hymn to God in praise and gratitude for a 'capable wife'. A pious Jewish husband would sing this psalm before every Sabbath in thankfulness. A 'capable' man is described in Psalm 112.

What makes these people so special? Both of them care for each other, recognizing they have responsibilities to each other and to their children. Yet some marriages can become less than God intends when the couple become 'wrapped up' in each other. But partners can also be concerned about others, especially the poor and vulnerable in society. As a married couple they do not live for themselves and 'their own', but they are concerned for righteousness and they take pleasure in doing good. In this way, among others, they show that they are godly people.

There is no split in their minds between their religious duties of prayer and worship and those of doing God's will in the everyday concerns of life. Finance, public duty, housekeeping chores, work and leisure – all are lived out before God. No wonder such a woman's works bring her praise.

✳ *Thank you, loving God,*
  for all those marriages secure enough to care for others.

Take care of marriage

There is no mistaking the apostle's mood here. It has come to his notice that there is a case of immorality in the Corinthian Church. The Corinthians know and tolerate it. But Paul is quite clear. Marriage is being defiled. Their church is being corrupted, and the people concerned are in a serious situation before God. Action, not tolerant indifference, is what is required.

Marriage is so important to Paul that he knows the Church cannot be casual about it. It is no answer, as perhaps the individuals at Corinth had claimed, that their new freedom in Christ set them free to follow whatever desires they liked. The corruption of marriage has far-reaching consequences for the rest of the Church and society. Paul's seemingly hard judgement has a profound moral base in his understanding of marriage as God-given and God ordered. Community discipline is called for, not simply in order to punish, but to keep whole and healthy what is necessary for human well-being. Paul's discipline here is marked by pastoral care both of the church and the individuals involved.

✳ *Thank you, living God, for your laws.*
  Save us from the folly of self-deception.
  Help us to live out your truth in family life.

Body and spirit

Then and now there is a great deal of extra-marital sex. Paul is again arguing with those who say they are free to do what they like with their bodies. A modern form of this approach comes from those who say it does not matter what two people do together so long as they both want to act in the way they do and no one else gets hurt.

This is not a possible position for a Christian to take. Paul gives three reasons. First, there is no dualism between body and spirit as if we are talking about two separable entities. Our bodies matter, and to abuse them is to dishonour our Creator and the Saviour who took flesh for us. Second, our bodies are the sanctuaries, or temples, of the Holy Spirit, the indwelling presence of God. Third, we are not our own to do with just as we please. Let our bodies glorify God.

In summary, what Paul is arguing is that what goes on in the body has an effect on the spirit and vice versa. This is obvious with toothache. But it is also the case in all our relationships. What we do in our flesh is not separated from God. What we do in our bodies affects the people we are and are becoming.

✳ *Creator God, may I honour you in my body.*

Wednesday September 27   *1 Corinthians 7.1-9*

Realism about sex

The Corinthians have raised some questions about discipleship with Paul and the first among them are to do with sex in marriage. As we saw yesterday, Paul cannot contemplate sex outside of marriage as being honouring to God. But what about our sexuality in marriage?

We can guess that some people at Corinth, due to an over-sensitive 'spirituality', thought that sex is somehow tainted and belonging to their earlier life. Some may even have been abstaining from sex in marriage. Paul replies with a healthy sexual realism. He commends those who mutually agree upon a time of celibacy for prayer. But, to deny one another the joy of making love is unnecessary and unrealistic. Paul knows the power that our sexuality is. If there is denial in marriage there will be severe temptations. Behind this is the view that sex is not inherently wrong but is one of those great gifts of God which can be so easily corrupted. So the love in marriage is to be enjoyed.

And that realism is there in the case of unmarried people. Paul's pastoral guidance is realistic but also shaped by the thought that Christ is coming soon. Sex is a great gift but not the greatest. And no one adds to their salvation by being either married or single.

✳ *O God, thank you for all the joys*
that come to us through human relationships.
And thank you for your gift of Christ Jesus.

In every condition

It is possible that some Christians in Corinth had thought about leaving their married partners, probably for what they thought were good religious reasons. Paul is against this and cites a command of the Lord.

It is not for the Christian to take the first step towards separation from a non-Christian partner. After all, the Christian was in this state when God called him or her into the new life in Christ. In fact, some Christians were married at conversion, some were single, some had been circumcised and others not, some were slaves and others were owners of slaves. The great reality is the saving call of God in Christ. To that they have responded in the condition in which they were. Again, Christians are not going to add anything to their salvation by changing their condition, least of all in marriage.

It is in marriage that the love of Christ may show through to the unbeliever. Too many Christians upon conversion try to change everything. Some aspects of the old life will need to be changed, but stay with the marriage, says Paul. It is an 'honourable estate', God-given and ordained. Stay there with God, and live out the life in Christ.

✳ *O God, may my life, married or unmarried,*
  reflect your love and celebrate your salvation.

Live always before the coming of Christ

Paul's thinking is shaped here by his thought of the impending return of Jesus Christ. That explains his change from otherwise fundamental behaviour. So Paul suggests that it might be better for all the unmarried to remain single. Earlier he had suggested that people should marry if that is their overwhelming desire. But in view of the Lord's return it would be better if people were utterly free from the inevitable responsibilities which marriage brings.

In all things the crucial matter is to live a life pleasing to God. Single-mindedness is essential here. But notice how Paul still does not counsel separation. His high view of marriage will not allow this. The key is marriage and singleness in the Lord.

Paul's chronology was mistaken, for the Lord had not returned as he seems to have imagined. That means we must inevitably read his words carefully. When we do, the pastoral care for married people and single people, honouring both before God, remains. Unless one has received the gift of celibacy then sexuality expressed in marriage is the norm, until Christ comes. Both marriage and celibacy are seen by Paul as gifts of God.

✳ *Living God, wherever we are, and whoever we are with,*
may our lives show a winsome holiness in your service.

Saturday September 30   *Song of Solomon 2.8-13**
The joy of being in love
Have you ever had to wait at a rail or bus station or an airport for the one you love? You stand on tiptoes, straining to catch a glimpse. Your heart beats faster. Your whole body is alive. Then you catch sight of your love and the world is transformed.

Being in love means recognition. It means being totally absorbed in the other person. It means secret whispers and sharing. It involves a growing trust, for with all intimacy there is risk. But you gladly run it because of the beloved.

A tragedy happens when such love is taken for granted. So lovers seek to spend time with each other, for love does not grow without such contact. There is a secrecy in love, not to be abused by easy exposure, for in the end what is most essential of all cannot be said, only experienced.

And this is what is given in marriage. It is given in friendships too. And it is a reflection of the relationship with God that he seeks for us all. No wonder being in love and worship are so closely related. No wonder lovers develop their own kind of language. No wonder we recognize in marriage and before God that we are on holy ground.

✳ *God, our lover beyond all deserving,*
thank you for human love.
Thank you for amazing divine love in Jesus.

FOR REFLECTION – alone or with a group
● What makes for difficulties in marriage today and how can the Church help its members to face them?
● What other Bible passages can you think of that help us to understand marriage?
● How would you suggest the Church helps people prepare for marriage today?

✶ *God our beloved,*
born of a woman's body,
you came that we might look upon you,
and handle you with our own hands.
May we so cherish one another in our bodies
that we may also be touched by you;
through the Word made flesh, Jesus Christ, Amen
Janet Morley, All Desires Known (SPCK)

FOR ACTION

Encourage your church

- to take more seriously the preparation and support of people in marriage, and
- to ensure that those who are single are fully integrated into the life of your church community.

BUILDING COMMUNITY
6. Sharing suffering
(The book of Job)

Notes based on the Hebrew Bible by
Jonathan Magonet

Jonathan Magonet is Professor of Bible and Principal of the Leo Baeck College, a Rabbinical seminary in London. His books on biblical subjects include 'A Rabbi Reads The Psalms' and 'The Subversive Bible'.

Because Job is a classic examination of human suffering, it may be hard to approach. The language is difficult. The different arguments are often lost in the torrent of words. It is an attack on a wisdom tradition that conceals as much as it reveals about the workings of God, so Job has to break through the words with their false certainties to the God who exists beyond them.

For the author this life is all that we have and here is the place in which we have to work through our destiny. So Job's arguments and honesty are particularly important today in a secular world deeply uncertain about the traditional 'consolations' of religion.

Sunday October 1   *Job 1.1-22**
The Eternal gave, the Eternal took away

The story is uncomfortable. What kind of God gets into this sort of wager with one of his servants? Worse, the 'adversary' has the right arguments in this case as Job himself reveals. The fact that he makes a daily sacrifice 'in case they sin and curse God' exactly reveals the nature of his view of God and their relationship. His welfare depends on appeasing God in advance of any possible problem – Job has himself defined the issue and the inevitability of the test.

Job's anxiety becomes reality, and paradoxically reveals his real strength of character. So far he is merely a cypher in a legendary story, somehow not yet real with his perfect wealth and perfect family. Now, with the terrible losses and his stoic response, he shows an extraordinary degree of resignation: 'The Eternal has given, the Eternal has taken, may the name of the Eternal be blessed.' My Bible teacher, Dr Ellen Littmann, disapproved of using this text at a funeral. It was not for a preacher to say, she pointed out. Only the one who mourned might one day be able to say it. Job's journey has begun.

✳ *Source of existence and of all human strength, we do not rely on our own good deeds but on Your great mercy as we lay our needs before You.* *Jewish Daily Prayer*
Forms of Prayer Vol 2 (Reform Synagogues of Great Britain – RSGB)

Monday October 2 *Job 2.1 to 3.4**

Shall we accept good from God and not evil?

The fairy tale character of the narrative continues with the identical verses describing again the visit of the 'sons of God'. Even God's words to the 'adversary' are identical – childishly boastful in the context and provocative. What is God trying to prove, and to whom?

The 'adversary' takes up the challenge with another test for Job, but God sets tough conditions: Job must survive the ordeal. The Rabbinic tradition likens the 'adversary's' nigh impossible task as 'to break the cask without spilling the wine'!

If God's aim is to bring out the qualities of Job, this ploy too succeeds. Job's wife on earth plays the role of the 'adversary' in the heavenly assembly, but not even her words can touch his faith: 'Shall we accept good from God and not evil'? Despite this fervour, something within Job may have moved: he no longer speaks of 'the Eternal' but of '**the** God', or simply 'God'. Rabbinic tradition distinguishes the names – the former represents God's compassion and love, the latter God's strict justice. Whatever the change may mean, Job's words hint at the bitter anger that will now spill out in the presence of his visitors.

✳ *Our living God and God of our ancestors, help us hold fast to the good within us and to good deeds, and bend our will and our desires to serve You.* *Jewish Daily Prayer*
Forms of Prayer Vol 2 (RSGB)

Tuesday October 3 *Job 3.11-26*

That which I feared is come upon me

Job reveals the problem at the heart of his own theology. It was already evident in the 'prologue' – his obsessive sacrifices on behalf of his sons in case they might have sinned (1.5). 'My worst fear has come true,' he cries (3.25). In fact by his own account his life till now had been dominated by such fears – 'I was never at ease, never quiet, never rested – but trouble came.'

Job lives in a cause and effect universe dominated by a God who rewards good behaviour but visits each sin with appropriate punishment, measure for measure. As head of the family Job is responsible for the behaviour of his children, but seems to have overextended his concerns. Indeed, how far has he been trying to play God in their life with his excessive precautions? Where does natural parental concern drift over into a kind of control that leaves no room for them to make mistakes and ultimately take responsibility for their lives? Since they seem to be forever feasting, this might well reflect a degree of over-indulgence on Job's part! In ironic contrast, the 'real' God of the prologue seems to give too much freedom to his 'children', the 'sons of God'.

✱ **Blessed are You, our Living God, Sovereign of the Universe, who has not made me a slave.**

Wednesday October 4   *Job 4.1-17*
Eliphaz – 'A word to the wise...'
Eliphaz's well-intentioned remarks would fail him on a hospital visitor counselling course.

He congratulates Job on all he has done for others. We can, however, already feel the 'but' that is coming. And the 'but' is Job's own theology thrown back in his face: a world of mathematical precision where the good are rewarded and the bad punished. It does not help Eliphaz's argument that he is rather pretentious. 'The lion roars and the fierce lion howls...' It is a nice metaphor, but barely appropriate in the circumstances. It just makes him seem pompous.

To add weight and drama he introduces a visionary experience: whispered messages and hairs standing on end. Since the message is standard theology, it hardly needs a nightly visitation to justify it. Perhaps he is trying to persuade Job by the other-worldly source of his words, but Eliphaz's self-importance comes across instead. Here is someone used to being heard and admired for his wisdom – and slipping into his usual rhetorical style.

The fact that the author of Job portrays Eliphaz as a bit of a buffoon does not mean that his message is unimportant – but we await it already with a degree of scepticism.

✳ *Our Living God, let no evil within us control us, and keep us far from bad people and bad company.* Jewish Daily Prayer
Forms of Prayer Vol 2 (RSGB)

Thursday October 5 Job 5.5-27

Man is born into trouble

Eliphaz finally gets to the point and spells out his basic religious assumptions with authority and certainty. Not only is his doctrine true but he himself has witnessed it. God is in ultimate control of the universe and of human actions. The 'wise' may make their plots and plans, but God protects the poor and unwary from their schemes. In passing he manages, presumably unwittingly, to infer that Job is a fool (5.3) whose children were inevitably destroyed (5.4). Ouch!

His advice is to turn to God, because his troubles are God's way of offering correction. Accept this and God will protect you. Famine, sword, destruction, beasts of the earth – none of these can harm you. Moreover, all shall be restored – numerous offspring and life to a ripe old age. He seals his advice with the assurance that his own research has validated the theory. QED.

For all his crass insensitivity, Eliphaz is sincere. The global theory must inevitably ignore the individual circumstances. But it is not advisable to assert at the bedside the truths one thunders from the pulpit, as Job is about to point out in no uncertain terms.

✳ *Our Living God, may my ears always hear and my heart always weigh what my lips are about to say.*

Friday October 6 Job 6.14-30

My brothers have dealt deceitfully

Job is furious, and the anger he could not direct against God he can now hurl at his friends. His wife had given him a way out of his suffering – curse God and die (2.9). But Job refused. The anger turned in on itself and his bitter mourning began.

The words of Eliphaz opened the floodgates – but against a safer target. He had cursed the day of his birth; now the friends are the object of attack.

For all their wisdom they had not understood that there is a time to comfort and another time to preach, a time to speak and a time simply to hold someone's hand and listen.

Perhaps what was most galling for Job was to hear his own religious beliefs offered to him, beliefs that he must have been struggling to comprehend in his awful situation. But Job also knew from his losses, and through the pains that wracked his own sick body, the difference between theory and reality. He had moved into personal experience, to a place beyond wisdom and the certainties of traditional belief. Now he needed something totally different.

✳ *Turn us back to You, our Living God, and we shall return. Renew our days as of old.*   Based on Lamentations 5.21

Saturday October 7   *Job 7.7-21*

What is man that you test him?

With nothing to lose, Job is free. And since he wants to die, why not provoke God in the hope that death will come? Death, which comes to all, and which he describes in all its grim finality, would give him the release he wants.

Why does God treat him as an enemy (verse 12)? He describes his painful days and restless nights before attacking God again with a sarcastic re-working of Psalm 8. The psalmist expresses his awe that God has set humanity at the pinnacle of creation: 'What is man that You remember him, the son of man that You visit him!' In Job's spiritual agony God's attention is the last thing that he wants: 'What is man that You raise him, that You set Your heart upon him, visiting him every morning, testing him every moment!' (verses 17-18).

At the end even his poetry fails him. For the first time the elegant parallelism of his verses disappears and his words become bitter prose: 'If I sin what does it matter to You?' God the Creator of the first people should have left well alone in his case. Forgive his sins! Let him finally escape from this life – and the God who so burdens him.

✳ *Will You hear my voice, You who are far from me? Will you hear my voice, wherever You are; a voice calling aloud, a voice silently weeping, endlessly demanding a blessing.*   Rachel
       Quoted in Forms of Prayer Vol 3 (RSGB)

FOR REFLECTION – alone or with a group

● How should Job's friends have acted?
● What was the basis of Job's faith in his God?
● How do we understand the existence of suffering in this life?

Bildad – Does God pervert judgement?

Bildad may simply be naive and pious. He cannot bear Job's attacks on God and his first reaction is to want to shut him up.

For him, it is all black and white and he is not sensitive enough to be careful with his words. Job's sons sinned and that is why they died. The matter is closed. Job needs to accept this basic truth and turn back to God. After all we have this on the authority of tradition, even if in the present moment it may be hard to explain. Clearly Bildad has never read Jeremiah with his challenges to this simplistic truth.

Yet again he breaks into metaphor to sell his message to Job – plants die without nourishment; people die who are not nourished by their trust in God. So trust, and all will be well.

By the end he waxes poetic. Like Job, he too can paraphrase a Psalm! (Compare Job 8.21 with Psalm 126.2). But his enthusiasm goes too far since Job's problem has nothing to do with 'enemies' or 'the tent of the wicked'. Bildad is temporarily overcome by piety which makes his response even more irrelevant.

✵ *God, hear my prayer, listen to my cry! Do not be deaf to my tears! For I am a stranger with You, just a guest, like those before me.*   *Psalm 39.12*

How can man be just with God?

Job struggles with two theological commonplaces that are usually taken as proof of God's benign governance of the world. God is creator and master of the world, so everything is in God's direct control, all natural powers in the universe, but also the just regulation of the world. Job draws forcibly the logical conclusion: if evil and injustice flourish, the fault must ultimately be God's.

Secondly, all human beings are inevitably impure and sinners in the face of the justice and righteousness of God. But for Job, God uses this factor of human existence in a cruel and arbitrary way to bring punishment and suffering on people. Worse still, how can someone take God to court to demand satisfaction, when God is both judge and jury?

What drives Job to such conclusions is that his own experience of life till now has been of success, clearly, according to his religious beliefs, because of God's favour. Suffering on this scale is something for which he was completely unprepared and the bitterest part is that it is unwarranted by anything he has done. His entire universe has been turned upside down.

✳ *We are frightened to meet You, fearing Your judgement...*
Hear our songs and the private prayers within them.
Mediaeval Jewish poet – quoted in Forms of Prayer Vol 3 (RSGB)

Tuesday October 10   *Job 11.1-16*
Zophar – Can you find out the deep things of God?
Enter Zophar the Na'amatite. If Bildad has appealed to piety and tradition, Zophar turns to wisdom and common sense. How can a mere mortal fathom the doings of God? Unlike Job, he draws from their shared view of God's power the fact that human beings cannot understand God's purposes, so who is Job to attack and condemn God!

Had he left it at that, he might have reached Job on the basis of a shared humility and bewilderment in the face of God's overpowering otherness. But he spoils the argument by reverting once again to the old theme of reward and punishment.

If God's ultimate ways cannot be known, who is to say that our concepts of good and evil are appropriate ways of understanding how God governs the universe, or at least judges human behaviour? But such an idea is too threatening for Zophar and he cannot follow Job into this disturbing conclusion. So he stays true to the safer convention: that Job has clearly done something wrong to have been punished in this way. He must simply set aside his wrongdoing to be restored to health, to light and hope.

✳ *Oh, God, help me!*
For I have fallen into the hands of the righteous
And the sons of the pious have encompassed me.   *Izak Goller*
The Passionate Jew and Cobbles of the God-Road
(The Merton Press, London 1923)

Wednesday October 11   *Job 13.6-23*
Though he slay me yet will I trust Him
Job is understandably furious with his companions – the 'last wise men on earth!' (12.2). Why do they try to reduce God to conform with their simplistic morality of cause and effect? Are they simply trying to flatter God?! (13.8).

Job is not prepared to undervalue his human right to be heard, to confront God, come what may. For Job has the faith to know that God is also his ultimate refuge and protector – so this gives him, paradoxically, the power to challenge God about his fate. In a true relationship one can risk honesty and criticism. Anything less than demanding truth would actually be an insult to God.

Job has moved from a situation where he wanted to confront God, be killed and escape from his torment and God's constant watching and testing, to demanding that God address him directly and confront him with the sins for which he has been punished. Job has been driven by the unacceptability of the words of his friends to recognize that it is not appeasing God for real or imagined sins that is needed, but a relationship that includes accountability from God as well.

✳ *You have shown me many bitter troubles,*
  but You will revive me again
  and raise me up again from the depths of the earth.

Psalm 71.20

Thursday October 12   *Job 14.7-22*

Man is of few days and full of trouble

Job brings his long speech (chapters 12-14) to an end with an even harsher expression of his bitterness about life. Every hope that a human being has is worn down by God. This life is all we have and death is the end of it. And life itself is a process of decay. In the end we do not even recognize those closest to us or miss them when they disappear. At this low point all that seems to offer comfort is that Job can still compose his complaint with poetic skill and savage precision.

For Job there is no concept of an after-life where somehow things can be made good. The underworld, the grave, is the end where at least one escapes being hounded by God. As far as we can ever know, this life is all that there is, and that is the ultimate truth that we must face. Ecclesiastes also confronts this and invites us to enjoy life while we can. Job focuses on the end when that brief time of pleasure is past. No wonder his friends feel the need to argue against him. Their own hope is also being undermined by his assault.

✳ *God, do not reject me in old age; when my strength is feeble,*
  do not abandon me.   *Psalm 71.9*

I know that my Redeemer lives

Eliphaz, in his second speech (chapter 15), paints a gaudy picture of the torments and destruction waiting for the wicked. Job responds (chapters 16-17) by insisting on his innocence and attacks his 'friends' – those who should at least have comforted him have instead betrayed him because they want to flatter God (17.5).

Bildad (chapter 18) tries to reinforce Eliphaz with even more images of the destruction of the wicked and now clearly locates Job in that position as one who does not really know God.

Job (chapter 19) counters again with the failure of his friends at least to show pity instead of persecuting him as badly as God has done! His suffering has isolated him from others, and forced him to confront what seems to be an unacceptable paradox – that the only one there for him is God, the one who has unjustly punished him but will nevertheless redeem him (19.25), even if it is at the last minute when he is on the verge of death.

In a deeply moving cry, 'pity me, pity me!', he begs his friends to help him precisely because it is God's hand that is against him.

✳ *You are my God; my Redeemer lives!*
the Rock I grasp in deep despair.
You are my banner and my refuge.
You share my cup the day I call.
                Based on 'Adon Olam', a mediaeval Jewish hymn

Can a man be profitable to God?

In chapter 20 Zophar at least acknowledges Job's reproof, but then adds yet another catalogue of the crimes and punishment of the wicked.

Job responds (chapter 21) by displaying the obvious prosperity and success of the wicked. By depicting both views – of the success and destruction that come upon the wicked – the debate has moved into a discussion of whether God does regulate the world according to an obvious justice or not. The bitter conclusion is that the only common denominator between the good and wicked is that both end up in the grave.

In today's reading, Eliphaz changes tactics and outlines the specific wrongdoing of Job: how he exploited the poor and hungry. Is this a fact we have not yet been made aware of, or is

Eliphaz simply following the logic of his position, even if Job really is innocent? Perhaps he even hints that the indifference of the rich, like Job, is actually a cause of the suffering of the poor.

There is nowhere to hide from God, nor can one simply tell God to stay away. So let Job only put away his wickedness and God will hear and restore him.

✳ *Where can I go from Your spirit, and where can I flee from Your presence?* Psalm 139.7

FOR REFLECTION – alone or with a group
● How far is our faith in God tied to our personal comfort and success?
● How do we understand the existence of evil in the world?
● How does a faith in the afterlife affect our actions in this life?

Sunday October 15 *Job 23.1-9, 16-17**
If only I knew where I might find Him
Having complained about God's relentless pursuit of human beings, examining and testing them at all times, Job seems to reverse his approach. Now it is God's unavailability he resents. How can Job present his case, or defend his innocence, before a God who is never there?

He is trapped in mutually contradictory views and, indeed, experiences of God. If God is just and fair, then a well-reasoned defence would be listened to and Job would certainly be acquitted. So God must be deliberately hiding from him to avoid just such a consequence. God's plans for Job are already determined, so no intervention on Job's part will help.

It is as if Job has been party to God's wager with the 'adversary' and knows the secret that his friends cannot fathom: that Job's suffering is purely arbitrary and nothing he does will affect or influence things!

That would be the ultimate terror – in contrast to all the shared wisdom teachings of Job and his friends – to inhabit a universe truly without meaning or purpose. Or worse, it might be one ruled by a God who is all-powerful, unpredictable and either indifferent to or vindictive against the creation itself.

✳ *May the will come from You*
 to annul wars and the shedding of blood from the universe,
  and to extend a peace, great and wondrous, in the universe.
Nachman of Bratslav – quoted in Forms of Prayer Vol 1 (RSGB)

I was a father to the needy

Job describes the paradoxes of God's powers: controlling the whole of nature, suspending the earth in space, setting boundaries to the seas. Yet for all this God is ungraspable, though at times dramatically present (chapter 26).

In a first climax Job turns inside out the premises on which he and his friends have been working. Human wisdom, despite its incredible achievements in manipulating the material universe, cannot comprehend God. Rather the 'fear of God' may lead to wisdom, and righteous behaviour to true understanding (chapter 28).

In chapter 29 Job reverts to pleading his innocence. Once he moved in the highest circles. His wisdom and advice were respected, his behaviour just and honourable. In a dig at his friends he concludes that he at least knew how to comfort mourners! (verse 25). His description gives a hint of the arrogance and patronizing that may come with privilege. Job generously dispenses wealth, advice and justice, but never questions the system to which he belongs. The 'adversary' has rightly seen the flaw in Job's position. Job has played by the rules of cause and effect that his good fortune and power till now have affirmed. But God was playing a different game.

✳ *May we not be blind to the needs of others, nor deaf to their cry for food. Open our eyes and our hearts so that we may share Your gifts, and help to remove hunger and want from our world.*   *From the Reform Jewish Grace after Meals*
Forms of Prayer (RSGB)

Tuesday October 17   *Job 32.1-10; 33.19-28*

Elihu – Beware lest you say: We have found wisdom

In Job's final speech (chapters 29-31) he insists that he has avoided any wrongdoing against others because of his dread that some calamity would descend upon him from God (30.23).

Elihu (chapters 32-37) presents himself as a young man, frustrated at the ineffectiveness of the friends and furious at Job's attack on God. The main thrust of his argument seems little different from that of the others. He insists that all people suffer and inevitably die, though God will always take back the repentant sinner, which seems something of a contradiction.

Chapter 34 shows that Elihu has shifted the argument. It is not Job's past wrong actions for which he is being punished but rather his assertion that there is nothing to be gained from being in accord with God (34.9). Job's crime is now seen as heresy. But Elihu may be closer to the truth than the other friends. For if Job's 'good behaviour' is based on fear of losing God's favour, rather than doing right simply because it is right, then Job is demeaning his own God-given human freedom. The God of the Covenant wants love not dependency.

✳ *God, let me not be like servants that serve their master for the sake of receiving a reward, but let the awe of heaven be upon me.*   Based on 'Pirqe Avot' – Sayings of the Fathers 1:3

Wednesday October 18   *Job 38.1-7, 34-41**

Where were you when I laid the foundations of the earth?

To whom is God speaking in this chapter? It seems to be Job, and that is the view of scholars who assume that the speech by Elihu – who is not mentioned when God finally condemns the friends (42.7) – is a later insertion into the book. God is therefore answering Job's closing speech (31.40). However if we follow the sequence in the book, then it is Elihu the last speaker who is accused of 'darkening counsel with words without knowledge'. Since Elihu is suitably chastised here there would be no need to mention him later with the others.

What is Elihu's mistake that leads to this condemnation? Firstly, that he claims to know Job and his sins better than Job himself. But worse that he defends God, as if he could speak with real knowledge from God's point of view. Elihu knows his theology, but not God. At the end he 'explains' how God works within nature (chapter 37) so it is appropriate that God challenges him, and the others, as to what they could possibly know about God's actions in creating and sustaining the world.

✳ *God, let all the inhabitants of earth recognize and know*
    the innermost truth:
that we are not come into this world for quarrel and division,
nor for hate and jealousy, contrariness and bloodshed;
but we are come into this world
You to recognize and know.   Nachman of Bratslav
                    Quoted in Forms of Prayer Vol 1 (RSGB)

Thursday October 19   *Job 39.1-12*

Have you given the horse his strength?

God's questions undermine the entire wisdom enterprise of Job and his friends by indicating the limits on their ability to understand the mysteries of the universe and the workings of God. God does not attempt a self-justification in reply to Job's challenge. Rather this is effectively a 'Zen' response, forcing the discourse into a totally different dimension. Any attempt to 'describe', justify or contain God is absurd as it simply reduces God to human dimensions.

God's questions refer back to the creation of the world and forward into times yet to come. God's activity covers areas of the earth where no human habitation is to be found, let alone the vast reaches of space. In a further ironic comment on Psalm 8, which hymns human rule over the earth, the questions challenge our vaunted human authority over even the animal kingdom. Could we have created, can we even domesticate, those animals that live in the wilds? Animals act out of their own innate wisdom that God has fashioned and only God can truly grasp. As far as our limited human wisdom is above that of the animals, so much further is God's wisdom above ours.

✳ *Source of our life, what are we? What is our life? What is our love? What is our justice? What is our success? What is our endurance? What is our power? What can we say before You?* Jewish Daily Prayer – Forms of Prayer Vol 1 (RSGB)

Friday October 20 Job 40.1-19

Have you an arm like God?

It is now that God addresses Job directly, and with precisely the invitation he has wanted – to go 'one on one' with God in court. But Job backs down and it is his turn to face a barrage of questions. Whereas Elihu has been confronted with God's powers over the natural world, Job is invited at first simply to acknowledge that God's justice is beyond human ability to grasp let alone duplicate.

Then the text explodes into an extravagant description of two mythological beasts, a reminder that human beings are but a small part of the richness and complexity of God's world. It is as if all the previous images of God's control of nature are still not enough to bring home the truth of God's otherness. For in describing the uncontrollable forces of these beasts God hints also at the controlled passions within the divine, passions that, if once unleashed, none could withstand. Only God can tame such powers, make them speak 'soft words', and bind them in a covenant for ever (41.3-4). In awe we grasp a fragment of the overwhelming nature of God and are forced to imagine something even greater beyond.

✳ *I have sought Your nearness,*
With all my heart I called You
and going out to meet You
I found You coming to meet me.   Judah Halevi
                    Quoted in Forms of Prayer Vol 1 (RSGB)

Saturday October 21   *Job 42.1-17*

The end of the matter

In conclusion Job undermines all the theologizing that has been the basis of his own belief in God and that of his companions. 'I have heard of You by the hearing of the ear but now my eye has seen You.' God is not an object to be talked about, but a subject to be met.

To confirm that Job is correct, God condemns Eliphaz and his two companions for not speaking rightly about God as Job has done, and Job is even invited to intercede on their behalf. Job receives the comfort denied to him till now and in a bizarre 'happy end' finds fortune and family more than fully restored. The twice seven sons reflect the ideal state he enjoyed before, while, in a reversal of biblical conventions, it is his beautiful daughters who are actually named and celebrated.

This end is either the bitterest irony of the entire book or a note of hope in a religious tradition that is notoriously optimistic. But it is a reward granted to Job precisely because he did not aim for it or try to guarantee it through appeasing God. Therein lies his transformation.

✳ **Blessed are You, our Living God, Sovereign of the universe, who forms light yet creates darkness, who makes peace yet creates all.**
                Jewish Daily Prayer – Forms of Prayer Vol 2 (RSGB)

FOR REFLECTION – alone or with a group
● Do 'proofs' from nature still convince us about the existence of God?
● In what ways do our religious traditions or convictions 'limit' God?
● How true to life is Job's 'happy ending'? How might we write the end of the story today?

FOR ACTION
What resources are available in our community for comforting or supporting the bereaved? Is there a project that would create or extend such resources?

VOICES OF CREATION
1. Celebration

Notes based on the Revised English Bible by
Kathy Galloway

Kathy Galloway is a theologian working in the community, and a poet and liturgist. She lives in Glasgow and edits 'Coracle', the magazine of the Iona Community.

It used to be in Scotland that every child was expected to know the *Shorter Catechism* by heart, and to be able to answer the question, 'What is man's chief end?' with the words, 'Man's chief end is to glorify God.' As people of faith, we are called above all to celebrate God. But 'God' is an abstract concept. So we celebrate what we see, God revealed in the creation; we celebrate what we trust, God-with-us in Jesus; we celebrate what we experience, God's Spirit moving among people, reconciling and liberating; we celebrate what we hope for, God's commonwealth of justice and love. And beyond all these, we celebrate the mystery of grace and generosity at the heart of life.

The Bible is full of stories of celebration, of people who honoured, published abroad, made known the God they met, not just when their living was easy but at times of great suffering and grief, stories of people who stopped and looked and wondered, who saw the colour purple in a field and were glad. They were not so different from us, these people.

Sunday October 22   *Psalm 104.1-23**
Making worshippers of us

The instinct to worship in response to the beauty and mystery of the universe is as old as the human story itself. The passionate outpouring of the Psalmist is a song of praise to God the Creator which echoes down the centuries and still resonates today in the hearts of everyone who has ever looked out over mountain ranges folded into blue mist, or at innumerable stars over the desert, or out across a sparkling sea, and wondered. That song of praise for the intricate delicacy of a leaf unfurling, for the massive solidity of granite and basalt, for the corn high in the field and the horse racing across a meadow has moved humankind to express its love for the earth our home in a thousand ways.

In the late Middle Ages, the poets and singers of Scotland were known as *Makars*, 'makers'. It is not too fanciful to imagine the universe as the song of God the *Makar,* a joyous outpouring of energy and creativity and wild ordering and continuous exchange. And it is truly a religious instinct to respond to God's song-making with our antiphon of praise.

Creation makes worshippers of us.

✳ *Almighty God, Creator:*
The morning is yours, rising into fullness.
The summer is yours, dipping into autumn.
Eternity is yours, dipping into time.
The vibrant grasses, the scent of flowers,
the lichen on the rocks, the tang of seaweed –
All are yours.
Gladly we live in this garden of your creating.

Monday October 23   *Genesis 2.4b-14*

Taking care

There is something rather touching about the God we meet in Genesis 2, so profoundly human in his activity – modelling a man out of the earth's clay, animating (literally, 'breathing life into') him, then planting a beautiful garden full of magical trees and treasure for him to live in. But the man himself is as much a part of the earth as all the other forms and species. His very name, Adam, links him with the ground – *Adamah* – of his being. He is created, not creator.

The failure to acknowledge createdness has been a big problem for human beings ever since – and an ever bigger one for the other life forms with which we share the earth. Our tendency to assume that the universe is at our disposal, that it has no intrinsic worth other than its utility to the human species, has made us careless to the point of extreme culpability. In the last twenty-five years alone, we have destroyed 30% of our natural environment. It is a kind of blasphemy. How can we pray to God the Creator with integrity when we are so cavalier with God's creation? We take care of what we value. Celebration involves carefulness.

✳ *Always in the beauty, the foreshadowing of decay.*
Nature red and scarred as well as lush and green.
In the garden also, always the thorn.
Lord, teach us to care.

The ache of longing
Jewish and Christian traditions and a long history of Western theology have viewed woman's creation in Genesis 2 as secondary and derivative, evidence of her inferior status: 'woman created after man; from man; for man.' It is not hard to read in this story not only the patriarchal culture which it represents, but also a curious existential envy which has woman born of man rather than man of woman. This passage has been used to justify appalling abuse and oppression.

And yet, there is an ache of longing here ... 'it is not good for the man to be alone'. The desire for a partner, a companion who will accept our vulnerability, the deep-rooted instinct for intimacy, is both human tragedy and human glory. Tragedy because trust is so lightly betrayed, because belonging 'with' so easily turns to belonging 'to'. Glory because it calls out all that is best in us – tenderness and delight, kindness and care, genuine mutuality and self-giving. As with persons, so with peoples.

✽ *Almighty God, Redeemer:*
the sap of life in our bones and being is yours,
lifting us to ecstasy.
But in the garden that is each of us, always the thorn.
Lord, preserve the unity and dignity of all human beings.

The things we do not know
This God is scary! Who would not, like Job, crumple in humiliation, silenced by such withering sarcasm:

'Have you comprehended the vast expanse of the world?

...Doubtless you know, for you were already born.

So long is the span of your life!' (verses 18 and 21).

The tone reminds me a little of my fifteen-year old daughter: 'Oh Mum, you don't know anything!' I remember as I grew to adulthood, being amazed at how much my mother had learned! It is one of the most painful lessons of adulthood, realizing how little we really know, and how much less we can command. The struggle to impose our will on everything around us, including the earth, causes grave damage to the environment, to other people and to ourselves.

Job is being called to let God be God. Even with all our scientific insight, what we know about the universe is so much less than what is still mysterious to us. The created order in all its complexity and beauty moved a quantum physicist to say that the appropriate response to it is one of sheer wonder and love. But such a celebration requires the dethronement of human ego, and the birth of co-operation with nature rather than domination over it.

✳ *Lord, by the glories of your creation,*
    which we did not devise,
Fan our faith to flame.

Thursday October 26   *Job 39.13-30*
The dialogue of life

In the close and patient observation of creatures in the wild, human beings discover the nature of them, their particularities, their strengths, the ways in which our createdness is similar and yet different. It is in the nature of human beings to be in dialogue, to ask a question, to start a conversation, to yearn for communication. The book of Job is a dialogue between Job and his Creator, and it has huge power still to move us.

Because it challenges a particular kind of pious orthodoxy, the easy linkage of virtue and prosperity and the equally shallow linkage of sin and suffering, both of which still disfigure the Church today, this dialogue speaks to us of real life. It goes beyond cheap grace into painful questions of injustice, beyond the scapegoating of people with AIDS into the mystery of compassion, beyond theological posturing into a faith lived at the limits of experience. That the dialogue continues still, despairing and yet hopeful, is a gift of creation and a cause for celebration. It is the dialogue of life.

✳ *Lord, by the assurance of your freeing us,*
    which we could not accomplish,
Fan our faith to flame.

Friday October 27   *Mark 4.26-34*
The greatness of the small

The mustard seed was proverbial in Palestine for the smallest possible thing. Nowadays, we might refer to the atom. Both are so tiny that it is hard to conceive of the potential they contain, the energy that is needed to take them on their journey of transformation. They shift and change in appearance, in shape, they become different – and yet the harvest is there in the seed, given nurture and openness to the processes of life.

Jesus took his followers on a journey of transformation also. They were not powerful or wealthy, they did not have high status. But he knew the greatness of the small. They went through many changes; they ended up very different from how they had begun, citizens of the Kingdom of the ear of corn. They realized their potential to live fully human lives, to grow in love and courage. In the seed of their faith is the harvest of faithful lives through the centuries.

Jesus embodied the potential of life lived in solidarity with the purposes of God's realm. All that degrades or denies that potential is a kind of blasphemy; all that cherishes and affirms it is praise.

✳ *Holy Spirit, Enlivener,*
In this new creation, already upon us,
Fill us with life anew.

Saturday October 28   *Colossians 1.15-20*

In You, all things

'Invisible we see You, Christ beneath us.

With earthly eyes we see beneath us stones and dust and dross,

Fit subjects for the analyst's table.

But with the eye of faith, we know You uphold.

In you, all things consist and hang together;

The very atom is light energy,

The grass is vibrant,

The rocks pulsate.

All is in flux; turn but a stone and an angel moves.'

                               George MacLeod

I love this great prayer of George MacLeod's. It prays the mystery of the cosmic Christ, a mystery I cannot grasp hold of by analysis but which encompasses me in poetry. This created universe is alive with a life I participate in, and in my participation I am in Christ. In Christ, all things consist and hang together.

The life of our participation in Christ is the Resurrection life. In Christ, the whole created order is raised. God, being earthed, raises earth to heaven.

We are encompassed by the stuff of eternity. Such stuff demands respect.

✳ *I bind unto myself today*
The virtues of the star-lit heaven,
The glorious sun's life-giving ray,
The whiteness of the moon at even,
The flashing of the lightning free,
The whirling wind's tempestuous shocks,
The stable earth, the deep salt sea
Around the old eternal rocks.

Attributed to St Patrick (c.386-460)

FOR REFLECTION – alone or with a group

● What are some of the things you take delight in celebrating?
● What is it a struggle to celebrate, and why?
● What do you think it means to celebrate nature?

FOR ACTION

Walk for fifteen minutes from your home. On the way back, make a note of anything you see that you think needs to be celebrated. Then find a way to do it with other people.

VOICES OF CREATION
2. Protest

Notes based on the New Revised Standard Version
of the Bible by
Edward P Echlin

Edward Echlin is Honorary Research Fellow in Theology at the University College of Trinity & All Saints, Leeds. He has taught at John Carroll University (Ohio), Ushaw College, and Lincoln Theological College. He has written and lectured widely on the Church, ecumenism and ecology.

Broken relationships

People and other earth beings depend on each other. When we stumble other creatures suffer along with us. God, people, and other creatures are in a triangular relationship. Sin disrupts our relationship not only with God but with the whole created community. There are 'natural' disasters beyond our control or fault. But many illnesses, cancers, climate changes, floods, extinctions, famines and general deterioration of our earth are the result of human sin. St Paul and – centuries later – Ignatius of Loyola vividly teach that, despite human malice, God, people and other creatures continue to provide food and shelter: but all creation suffers for human sin.

Sunday October 29   *Genesis 3.1-13*

The snake or sustainable sufficiency?

The snake story is one we learn as children and never forget. It teaches, as only a packed symbol can do, layers of wisdom about human weakness, temptation, foolishness, and the skewed relationships resulting from human sin. We people are so inter-related to God and to the natural world that some philosophers describe people as 'beings in relationships'. As God's image on God's earth we are client sovereigns responsible to our Creator. As man and woman we are related to each other. We function well only when women and men are in community together. We also depend on and relate to other earth creatures, especially animals, and they to us. When we sin we defy God and eat of the forbidden tree. The result, without exception, is broken relationships with God, ourselves, and nature.

Consumerist cultures, large or small, are broken places. God gave us this beautiful earth-garden to care for and use reverently. When we take more than we need, we remain unsatisfied, and our relationships with God and other creatures are in disarray.

Let us learn from the snake story. We can live, under God in God's world, not chasing more than we need, but sharing among people and with other creatures in sustainable sufficiency.

✳ *Lord, help me to take only what I need of your gifts,*
and to return my part of the earth as healthy as I found it.

Monday October 30   *Genesis 3.14-24*

Tension at the centres

The Genesis pictures of the immediate effects of original sin are disturbing. God's distance, the enmity with the snake, the struggle in work, the thorns and thistles among the wheat, the tension between the sexes, pain in childbirth, love with hate – all these are familiar. Here again we are reminded of our inherent triangular relationships: our Creator, people, our fellow creatures. The Bible portrays our fallen condition as total alienation from our Creator, from our work, from the soil, from the other sex, from the responsibilities surrounding the power of procreation.

Deep within the familiar story of the aftermath – or, better, results – of human sin there is the indomitable presence of God's Spirit inviting acceptance.

First, the Spirit moves us to accept the innate propensity to conflict at the centres of deepest relationships.

Second, God's Spirit moves us to accept God's faithfulness even at the centre of our tensions. We repeatedly disrupt the triangular relationship, yet God and our fellow creatures continue to support us.

✳ *Pray often:*
Loving God, help me to accept my weakness
and to be grateful for your faithfulness
and the faithfulness of your other creatures.

Tuesday October 31   *Genesis 4.1-16*

The Church of Abel

The Cain and Abel story is one of the most chilling in the Bible. There is envy, fratricide, lying even to the all-knowing God, and the universal human proneness to violence. There is much for reflection in this memorable story which has become a part of western culture.

We behold even in Cain, despite his horrible crimes and the chaotic nemesis resultant on his malice, the fundamental faithfulness of God and creatures. God will punish the one who harms Cain. Other creatures continue to nourish him, providing a home on earth for this fugitive from God and people.

When the early Christians reflected upon the cosmic scope of salvation in Jesus, they remembered this story. Since at least the fifth century there have been references to the 'church of Abel'. The Second Vatican Council (1962-65) recalled Abel when considering Jesus and other religions. Abel, representing believers at the dawn of our race, responded in faith to Holy Mystery's self-disclosure. The cosmic embrace of God's saving act in Jesus includes people before the Jews and people beyond Christian churches today.

✳ *O God, may our faithfulness assist people everywhere to respond to the seeds of your Word in their lives and cultures.*

Wednesday November 1   *Deuteronomy 28.15-24*

Retribution

The Hebrews attributed most illnesses and disasters, 'pests, famine and war', to human sin. When humans disobey, the result is often disorder. The Bible is not science but there is truth here that can be verified. People are so intimately related to other beings that when we fail they suffer with us. A surprising proportion of illnesses and afflictions are related to arrogant human interference with God's world. Climate change, much asthma and leukaemia, ozone depletion, desertification, loss of biodiversity, animal suffering from genetic engineering – are a few examples.

There are, however, other disasters which we call 'natural' that arise independently of human agency. We now accept that all created beings, including humans, die independently of any pre-historic sin. Some earthquakes, flood and climate change happen independently of human error. Yet even in 'natural' evils the intimate connection of people with all creation is apparent. If we rebel, even lose faith in God because of evil, the evil increases. Two principles assist us when faced with evils.

First, when the evil proceeds from human malice, each of us can repent by not contributing to the structural sin in societies which cause evil and, when possible, by healing.

Second, in natural evils not caused by a human agency we can only accept, in faith and humility, the presence of Holy Mystery who holds us even in tragedies.

✳ *O God, help me to trust in your caring presence*
even in tragedies.

Thursday November 2   *Isaiah 24.1-13*

The cosmic covenant

Throughout the Old Testament and, more familiarly, in the New, are echoes of an ancient covenant. A covenant was a treaty between a ruler and his subject peoples. The Hebrews adopted the idea. There are covenants between God and Abraham, Moses, and David, but also with the whole creation. The first explicit reference to the cosmic covenant is after the flood when God enters on a covenant with 'every living creature...of the earth' (Genesis 9.10).

Initially, it seems, kings ritually secured a covenant with their people and, when they broke it, restored justice and right order to all creation. When there were no kings the priesthood propitiated God for breaches in the covenant. Eventually that responsibility was 'democratized' so that people, as God's image or client sovereigns, became responsible for justice, rightness, and *shalom* (complete peace), in all creation. Isaiah 24 pictures the results of human violation of the cosmic covenant: all creation suffers.

The letter to the Hebrews portrays Christ as our high priest propitiating God. Uniquely in the New Testament it recalls the 'eternal covenant' (Hebrews 13.20-21), echoing the words of Isaiah and of God to Noah. From the mists of ancient Jewish tradition through the letter to the Hebrews the 'eternal covenant' has entered many western liturgies.

✳ *May we realize, as your grateful people in Christ,*
our King and high priest,
our responsibilities for all creation.

Friday November 3   *Joel 1.1-20*

Disasters and worship

The Book of Joel is important to Christians. Peter quotes it, according to Acts, at Pentecost, the birth of the Church (Acts 2.17-21). Joel paints pictures of horrendous catastrophes, a locust plague combined with a withering drought. We notice again the bond, the cosmic covenant, between people, animals, plants and all creation including the weather. We notice the sequence of human crime and the nemesis of plague and drought. Here in northern Europe we experience different plagues in wet springs, of slugs which devour our seedlings while torrential rains cause floods. In frightening times we can learn from Joel.

First, let us ask ourselves if we have caused evil.

Second, we should with repentance worship God.

Third, we offer God bread and wine in which is included the earth community which nourishes us.

Finally, let us realize with Joel that animals (and plants) suffer with us. They too burn and thirst and starve. We remember them in our rituals and our mercy.

✳ *Let us ask ourselves in what way we are implicated in our current ecological crisis, perhaps by wasteful consumption of fossil fuel in car and jet travel. Let us repent and make restitution by healing the earth in our own locality.*

Saturday November 4   *Romans 8.18-22*
The future community
After the flood God entered an everlasting covenant with people and animals (Genesis 9.11). The very creatures who share our frustrations also share our hope. As covenant partners we have relationships with animals and with the rest of creation which remain faithful to us through sin, flood, wars, drought and plagues.

In today's reading, Paul says all material creation groans expectantly awaiting our transformation in Christ. This text provides solace for people concerned about the future, about good works done here, deeds of love, the arts, the beauties of nature, and the animals with whom we share life. Christ is the key to the future of the universe. That future, still to be revealed, includes all creation as does the rainbow covenant.

I care about my own pekinese dogs who have accompanied me here. I hope to be with them, in a way 'eye hath not seen nor ear heard', for ever. They are included in the 'creation' which now longs with and for us.

✳ *May we value all earth's creatures as precious to God and in themselves.*
May we realize they too love life and share our future.

FOR REFLECTION – alone or with a group

- How do we distinguish between 'natural' evils which occur independently of us, and evils to which we contribute?
- How can we widen our healing ministry to include the whole creation?

FOR ACTION

Let us include other creatures in our worship, especially in intercessions, confessions of sin, and our outreach ministry.

VOICES OF CREATION
3. Call for action

Notes based on the New Revised Standard Version by
John Polkinghorne

John Polkinghorne has had a long career as a theoretical physicist and was a Professor at Cambridge University. In 1979 he resigned to train for the ordained ministry. He is both an Anglican priest and a Fellow of the Royal Society. In 1996 he retired from being President of Queen's College, Cambridge. He has written a number of books about science and religion.

Science gives us knowledge and this enables us to do new things and to change our environment. If that technical power is to be used rightly, we must add wisdom to knowledge so that we are able to make beneficial decisions. Not everything that can be done should be done. Religious traditions, including those of ancient Israel, are reservoirs of wise understanding and so they can still help us to make right decisions about how to act.

Sunday November 5   *Leviticus 25.1-7*
The sabbath principle

'Keeping the Sabbath' might today seem to have a somewhat dreary ring to it, suggestive of an enforced and repressive boredom. To think like that would be an unfortunate mistake, for the sabbath principle is concerned with affirming the need for rest and for moderation. Modern society exerts an unrelenting pressure upon us to be ever active, ceaselessly exploiting the next opportunity as soon as it comes along. Ultimately this is destructive of our humanity, for we need times of quiet stillness in which to recuperate, to consider what it is we are actually doing and why we are doing it. The springs of right action lie in reflective assessment.

In this surprising passage from Leviticus, a similar principle is applied to the land itself. It too must have its time of rest, its sabbath. We may wonder whether Israel ever literally left all the fields uncultivated for a whole year, but we can see the principle behind the instruction. Limits must be set to the exploitation of natural resources, which need to be given their chance for renewal. Fishing and forestry cannot be pursued ceaselessly without thought for the future. A principle of sabbath restraint should govern our relationship with nature. Here is biblical endorsement of the call for a sustainable use of the fruits of the earth.

✳ *Lord of creation, grant to us and to all your creatures*
the peace of your sabbath rest.

Monday November 6   *Leviticus 25.8-22*

Stewardship

As the second millennium comes to a close, we are conscious of the inequalities that mark our world society, the disparities between rich and poor, the unequal relationships between the nations of North and South. Part of that scene is the heavy burden of debt carried by many developing countries, with the result that the interest payments they have to make may greatly exceed the financial assistance they are given by way of aid. The recognition of this state of affairs has resulted in a call for some form of release from this crippling burden – a Jubilee act of deliverance from debt.

Today's passage explains the significance of the word 'Jubilee', the restoration of land holdings due to take place in Israel every fifty years. Behind it lies the Hebrew understanding (see verse 23) that the ultimate owner of all things is God and that creation is only on loan to us from the Creator. We do not have absolute rights of possession, but we hold the earth's resources in trust. In our actions we need to bear this truth in mind. Even so strong an advocate of individual enterprise and market principles as Margaret Thatcher was once wise enough to say that we are tenants, holding the Earth on leasehold, and not freeholders with unfettered possession. All, including the generations yet to come, must have a just share in what ultimately belongs to God, the Father of all.

✳ *Lord, give to us, and to all peoples and nations,*
grateful and generous hearts
that readily share the good gifts that you have given us.

Tuesday November 7   *Leviticus 25.23-34*

Discernment

Yesterday we thought about principles. Today we have to think of practice. We can assert that there is a problem of world debt that justice and compassion require must be dealt with. It is another, and extremely complex, problem to say specifically how this should be done. The world economic system is complicated and subtle, with many linkages that are difficult to evaluate and understand. Consequences of actions interlock in unexpected ways and it would be altogether too simplistic just to draw a line through all that is owing.

Exactly what Israel did about the Jubilee is not known, but the complexities that accompany a realistic attempt to apply its principles are illustrated in today's passage. Property in a walled city could not simply be returned after fifty years if a building programme was to be encouraged. Hence special provisions are set out in verses 29-31. In our actions, we have to steer a path between an unworkable idealism, which disregards real problems, and a selfish pragmatism, which disregards moral principles. This will not be easy and it requires attention to the advice of experts as well as a critical evaluation of what they recommend. Verses 18-22 have already promised God`s blessing on those who truly seek to behave in accordance with the divine will.

✷ ***Many problems perplex us, Lord.***
Give us your wisdom
and the guidance of your Spirit
as we seek to discern your will and to do the right.

Wednesday November 8 *1 Kings 21.1-16*

Challenge

When credit cards were first introduced to Britain, one bank marketed them with the slogan, 'Take the waiting out of wanting'. It was a blatant appeal to a consumerist desire for instant gratification. People, who already had many possessions, wanted more and they wanted it now.

The story of Ahab and Naboth`s vineyard shows that this was no mere modern phenomenon. The King of Israel, with all the wealth and opportunities that went with his office, became sullen and sulky because he could not persuade his humble neighbour to let him turn the family possession into a convenient vegetable garden. Ahab`s ruthless wife Jezebel believed that all that was needed was some assertive action. A 'practical' woman of the world, she would soon deal with the little matter of Naboth. Thwarted desire quickly led to deceit and murder. The springs of action lie in what we value and what we are prepared to do to gain it. Wrong inclinations soon lead to wrong deeds; covetous-ness is the seed from which death and destruction can grow. Few individuals would exhibit in their private lives the cruel deter-mination of a Jezebel, yet we often tend to keep silence while nations pursue their own interests and pleasures in ways that pay no heed to the needs of others. Poverty and premature death for many innocent people are the result.

✳ *Lord, we seek your face and long to do your will.*
May your Kingdom be the centre of our desire.

Thursday November 9   1 Kings 21.17-27

Never too late

Ahab and Jezebel seem to have got away with it, but Elijah is sent to tell the King that this is not so. God is not mocked and God has seen what has happened. Deeds have consequences and evil deeds have evil consequences. Those who take the sword are likely to perish by the sword. Today`s passage is concerned, first of all, with judgement. Our actions can bring results beyond those we immediately intended. If we are able to live in a just and sustainable relationship with creation, then nature will nurture us and things will be well. If we are greedy and exploitative, things will go wrong. Failure to control carbon dioxide emissions will intensify the problems of global warming, with climate change and sea levels rising. Failure to control the emission of fluorocarbons will further denude the ozone layer and lead to increases in cases of cancer.

Yet our passage also speaks of the possibility of repentance and restoration. Ahab is smitten by the words of judgement that Elijah utters and he humbles himself before God. The immediate threat is withdrawn, though there are still problems lurking in the longer term. It is never too late to pay heed to what God is saying to us. Repentance can lead to actions that heal and restore.

✳ *Lord, have mercy upon us,*
quicken within us repentance for our sins and errors
and lead us to amendment of life.

Friday November 10   Isaiah 1.2-9,15-20

Choice

The prophet paints a picture of a land and people that are sick unto death. Pollution, corruption, exploitation have devastated the nation that was called to be God`s chosen people. The first thing that Judah and Jerusalem have to do is to recognize the gravity of their situation. Painful as this is, no progress or restoration can happen without it. Action can only be based on reality, on the acknowledgement of how things actually are. The question of truth is a central religious question, just as it is a central scientific question. We have to be clear-eyed, looking at the world as it is and at ourselves as we are.

When this honest stance has been taken, then there is hope. Sins may be as scarlet but if they are seen to be so and this leads to repentance and a change of heart, then those involved can become white as snow. Failure to face up to what is the case can only lead to fantasy and the grave mistakes which result from actions based on unreality. Recognition of what is the case can produce an openness to the transforming power of divine grace at work. In the closing verses of today`s passage, Isaiah sets a choice before Judah, a choice between obedience and rebellion, a choice between flourishing and destruction. We face the same choice today.

✳ *Forgive the sins and weaknesses of the past, O Lord, and renew your good spirit within us.*

Saturday November 11　　　　　　　　　　　　　　　*Micah 6.6-8*
What God requires
One of the most famous passages of Old Testament prophecy sets before us a succinct and powerful description of right action, what it is to serve and please God. We are not called to extravagant ritual offerings, nor to terrible deeds of sacrifice. Instead what the Lord requires of us is justice, kindness and humility.

Justice (verse 8) is the fulfilling of the second great commandment, to love our neighbours as ourselves. Someone once defined Christian love – *agape* – as the due recognition of another`s need and the appropriate meeting of that need. A just society would be one in which that happened. Lest that should seem a little cold and distant, to judgement is added 'kindness'. Here, in fact, the NRSV translation is too weak, for the word used is better translated 'mercy' or 'steadfast love'.

We are not only to act rightly but with warmth and unfailing good will. How this might be possible is given in the final words. None of us is sufficient for this vocation; no human nature by its own unaided powers is able to pursue an unfailing policy of right action. Only those individuals and peoples humble enough to acknowledge this will be able to work with God who longs, through the collaboration and obedient response of human creatures, to bring about the divine good purpose for creation.

✳ *Grant to us, Lord, the grace to do justice,*
to love mercy
and to walk humbly in your presence.

FOR REFLECTION – alone or with a group

● How can we honour the sabbath and Jubilee principles (a) in our lives; (b) in the life of our nation?
● What does it mean to see the earth as under God's ownership?

FOR ACTION

Consider the world of your life and work and seek to fulfil God's desire for justice and mercy within it.

VOICES OF CREATION
4. Hope

Notes based on the New Revised Standard Version by
Martin Lambourne

Martin Lambourne, a Baptist minister and committed ecumenist, has served both in Baptist pastorates and as a Youth and Children's Officer for the Methodist Church. He is now working on projects related to the under-fives, youth work training and family issues as part of his role as Director of Resource Development for NCEC/IBRA.

This week's readings offer glimpses of heaven on earth, expressions of hope written in times of despair. They look to the restoration of harmony through the establishment of justice and reconciliation between humankind, the earth and the Creator – an at-one-ment. 'As it was in the beginning', is not now, but one day shall be! Origen, an early Church Father, had a concept of ends being like beginnings. The world, and humanity especially, had disintegrated and must hope in Christ for reintegration, for wholeness through atonement.

Sunday November 12   *Psalm 146**
The focus of hope

The Psalmist reminds us that all flesh is as grass. Often our dreams and visions die with our dreamers and visionaries. But true vision is eternal, for God, who keeps faith with what he created demands justice, food and liberty for all. In this covenant-relationship we are expected to respond to God's faithfulness in the way we behave to one another.

Is this not a vision of 'at-one-ment'? Indeed, if we are in a right relationship with one another, we would not want anything different. Why, then, are we prepared to put up with the continuing exploitation of the poor, the foreigner, the old, the young and the earth on which we live? We are called, not only to faith, but to faithfulness, and not to desperation but to determination – to see God's Kingdom on earth, as in heaven, and to see all people at-one with each other.

✳ *Lord, let me worship you by fighting greed;*
Let me praise you in serving need;
Let me love you in accepting others;
Let me adore you in seeing all as brothers.

The extent of hope

There is an image here which conjures up desolation. All that is left is a stump! And yet, in a seemingly devastated land, where forests had been ravaged and left for dead, there is a shoot. And while there is life there is hope of restoration, and the possibility of harmony between all God's living things.

Again we have a vision – this time born out of a sense of the impending demolition of a nation by a large enemy. It is a vision of justice and equity for a people who will identify with one who is righteous and faithful. And the vision of harmony extends even to wild animals. The thought of lions eating straw and snakes being tolerant of inquisitive and interfering children may seem a hope too far. But the ideal is of a world content to live and let live, not seeking to hurt or destroy.

Here is a challenge to seek to live alongside people and animals – to create safe havens where lions can be lions, tigers can be tigers, and people of every race can be themselves, each ethnic group free to enjoy their cultural heritage without fear. It means that we may not eliminate what we see as a threat – either among humankind or in the natural world. We are to make space for everything and respect the right of each being or creature to be different. It requires a determination to be governed by hope born of God-given aspirations rather than fear born of basic instincts.

✳ *Lord, help me to create safe havens,*
   Hospitable spaces within the aggression of the city
   And the rawness of the countryside.

Creation's hope

There are still many people much closer to the land than most of us who live in the industrialized areas of the globe. It is tempting for the developed world to see them as 'primitive' or 'under-developed'. Perhaps the reality is that those who still 'feel' for the land have something the 'overdeveloped' have lost – a respect for the whole of creation and a sense of the balance of nature and of the universe.

It is fascinating for those of us who are part of an advanced nation to find that scientists are discovering healing properties in so many common and exotic plants. Discovering? Many peoples closer to the land might be amused to find that what they have known since the beginning of human existence is now being declared as a breakthrough in modern research!

The time is long overdue when those 'high fliers' who have advanced and left the soil behind admit to those who have stayed with their feet on the ground that there is much to learn from communities and peoples who have kept in touch. They have not forgotten the secrets of creation, learned through taking time to explore, experiment and pass on learning and skills in herbal medicine and healing.

Many of us see the raw materials of this world as ripe for harvesting – to the point of exploitation. A precious minority remains which sees the plant world and the soil as involved in a kind of partnership of give and take. They are at-one with the earth. 'Do not fear, O soil!' There may yet be hope for creation if we will learn from those who have not forgotten.

✵ *Help me, Lord, to understand how all creation cries and struggles for renewal, and help me to be part of its fulfilling.*

Wednesday November 15   *Zechariah 8.1-13*
Hope of ages
Verses 4 and 5 appeal to many of us who work at NCEC. We are working for opportunities for children to be given back their childhood – to be freed from the isolation of the computer screen, the pressures of school curricula, the expectations of ambitious parents, the terror of ethnic cleansing and the lack of safe spaces to play, so that they can be themselves.

Other organizations fight a similar battle for older people and for a quality of life which means that the aged feel human still. Is the scene painted here the mere nostalgia of an old prophet? Is there no place for a community where children play in traffic-free streets and where old people can sit and enjoy the scene, converse at leisure or just sit? As in Isaiah, there is a hope that people of all generations might be freed to act their age, and in most cases this runs counter to the expectations of those who are powerful and influential. 'Whoever does not accept the kingdom of God as a little child...' (Luke 18.17). Maybe that also means that in our assuming the open attitude of a child to learn and explore, we are coming to our senses!

✳ *Lord, give me strength*
to resist being what I think others want me to be.
Make me confident in Christ to be myself at all cost.

Thursday November 16   *Mark 4.1-9*

Seeds of hope

The seed is the ultimate symbol of hope, despite all that appears to frustrate its growth. Think of the times when we have allowed the birds of avarice and self-interest to pluck from the ground – almost on impact – the cries of the poor for decent wages. Has not enthusiasm for good stewardship of the earth's resources been scorched by our reluctance to exercise self-control if not self-denial? How often have we abused those who cry for justice and peace for all creation by smothering their cries with a forest of demands for our own well-being?

Yet nature has a resilience: frustrate it how we may, it will go on dying and rising in many ways to challenge us to hear and respond as partners with all creation to bring to fruition the paradise God designed. And God's Kingdom on earth is glimpsed where we see the culmination of creation's promise fulfilled in Christ who makes ALL things new – not just people but the environment which reflects who we are and the way we treat it.

✳ *Lord, help me to find my whole self*
As I discover wholeness with my neighbour
And with the land on which I dwell.

Friday November 17   *Hebrews 9.24-28**

Point of hope

The writer of this letter speaks of a once for all sacrifice to remove sin, of Christ's giving that others might live. In a way, this echoes the pattern of all creation in its 'natural' state: 'unless a grain of wheat falls into the earth and dies...'

Sacrifice, like obedience, is not a favoured word in a new century, but it is still a reality for many people. And, like death, sacrifice is something we tend to want to eliminate rather than accept as a fact of life – a law of nature.

Christ's sacrifice has purpose: it offers hope, new life: death to alienation, disintegration, apart-ment, sin... and welcome to reconciliation, integration and at-one-ment.

So, in verse 28, we have a picture of a Second Coming, not for judgement, but for reunion. What a gloriously positive vision, a hope worth living and dying for, a point to hope.

✳ *I know what I am worth to you, Lord,*
More than words can say: you have said it in action.
But what are you worth to me?
Only my love, deeds and sacrifice will tell.

Saturday November 18   *Revelation 22.1-5*
Vision of hope

No more night! The Russian space station Mir has been experimenting with giant mirrors in space. These will reflect sunlight onto the darker areas of the earth and release it from night! It sounds good at first sight, but what about the life-cycle of all those plants and animals, including humans, which have developed ways to cope with darkness? When do you get your rest? Do we always know what's right?

No more night! The Lord God will be their light: not so much an energy source – more a way to life. Go back, if you will, to the Upper Room. There, John gives us a picture of Judas about to alienate himself from Jesus and his other friends. As Judas leaves those with whom he had shared so much, John adds: 'And it was night'.

Darkness isolates. Revelation gives us the hope of no more isolation. We are no longer to be at odds with God, each other and the world. No more night. Enough! Our hope is not with space stations and pie in the sky. Our hope is in the Lord in whose image – of three in at-one-ment – we were made.

✳ *Forgive us, Lord, for all which keeps us apart from each other.*
Put right our minds within
and be with us in creating right relationships around us.

FOR REFLECTION – alone or with others

● How far are you able to be yourself?
● Who, or what, is stopping you?
● Does your church offer a hospitable space where children can be themselves?
● Has your community identified a local environmental issue which it could address?

FOR ACTION

Contact a campaigning agency and offer prayerful or practical support for its efforts to bring justice into an area of concern with which you can identify.

VOICES OF CREATION
5. Prayer

Notes based on the New Revised Standard Version by
Melvyn Matthews

Melvyn Matthews is the Canon Chancellor of Wells Cathedral in Somerset where he has responsibility for education and theology. He is also responsible for a Ministry of Welcome to over 300,000 visitors to the earliest Gothic Cathedral in England. He has been a University Chaplain and taught for a while at the University of Nairobi in Kenya. He is the author of a number of books on Spirituality, the latest being 'Rediscovering Holiness' (SPCK).

When we say that prayer is 'mystical' most people think that means some sort of experience where the soul is united with God. But the word 'mystical' comes from the Greek *muo* which really means 'to hide', and in the earliest years of the Church 'mystical' really meant 'hidden'. For example, it was used of the liturgy, which was called 'the holy mysteries', to show that the liturgy puts us all in touch with the unknown or 'hidden' reality of God. It is only in modern times that it has come to mean something like a particularly profound personal or individual experience. This is misleading as it implies that mysticism is only for those who have had special experiences of God. Prayer has become far too much associated with personal and private experience, and we need a fresh look at it in order for it to become what it should be for modern men and women. The use of the word 'mystical' in its original sense will go a long way towards that, so that we can recover something of the true meaning of prayer in our own day.

The readings are almost all from the Hebrew Scriptures and begin with the lovely stories of Hannah and Samuel before moving through two beautiful psalms. We then dwell for a while on the anguish of the prophet Jeremiah. The sequence finally comes to rest in the vision of God found in the two apocalyptic books, Daniel and Revelation. What emerges is that prayer is an expressed desire or yearning for the hiddenness of God.

Sunday November 19   *1 Samuel 1.4-20**
Accepting what is hidden
My wife and I recently spent several days in the French Alps staying in a friend's flat facing across the valley towards Mont

Blanc, the highest mountain in Europe. Mont Blanc is always snow covered and we had been looking forward to seeing this great mountain at such close range and to walking in the summer alpine meadows several thousand metres above sea level. We had been promised stunning views, especially in the early morning and late evening. Unfortunately on our arrival a deep depression swept across France and the mountain was hidden in thick mist. We had to wait several days before it cleared and we were able to see what we longed for. We had to learn to let go until we were eventually given the glory of the mountain.

In the lovely story of Hannah and her desire for a son the same thing happens. Hannah has a frustrated desire for a child. She is also the subject of ridicule by Elkanah's other wives because of her barrenness. But there comes a point in the story where, having brought her concerns to the Lord, she is able to let go. This moment occurs at the end of her conversation with Eli, the priest. 'And she said, "Let your servant find favour in your sight"' (1.18). Hannah then went to her quarters, ate and drank with her husband and her countenance was no longer sad. But it is in fact only much later that her petition is granted, after she has returned to Ramah, her home, and there she conceives.

This theme of reaching out and being prepared to accept what is hidden and therefore unknown, as Hannah does – even if it turns out to be not what we originally may have desired – is central to the reality of prayer. Faithful prayer involves a letting go and a waiting to be shown what the hidden will of the Lord is. But we will not find that will and be content with it while our own personal longings are imposed upon God.

✳ *God, give us grace to place our lives into your hands,*
even when we fear that what we want will never come about.

Monday November 20   *1 Samuel 2.1-10**

Magnificat

'My soul doth magnify the Lord...' Almost word for word, sentiment for sentiment, Hannah's prayer prefigures that of Mary, the mother of Jesus (Luke 1.46-55). Both mothers have been given something totally unexpected, and both mothers know that their sons are destined for God, in the case of Samuel in lifelong service in the temple of God at Shiloh. It is interesting to remember that this custom of dedicating a young child to the service of God was also followed in the Celtic church where children were given to the monasteries at a very young age. So we can also imagine many other mothers, particularly during the early days of the Church in Ireland, praying similar prayers.

This lovely prayer, which comes to the surface every now and again throughout the history of the people of God, seems to be a prayer which is hidden deep within the consciousness of God's people and which may be released by certain events. It is a hidden prayer which gives thanks for the mystery of life and the hidden things of God.

These hidden things are twofold. One is the awareness of something unexpected: that God has confused by his action the apparently normal processes by which the rich and powerful are blessed and made it clear that his constant hidden activity is to lift the poor and needy out of the dust. Second, the prayer, both of Hannah and of Mary, looks forward to the hidden, at present unknown, activity of God in the child who has been given to them. There is more to be revealed.

Too much prayer focuses on the visible power of God and refuses to trust in his invisible, hidden, but surprising blessing.

✳ *God, give us grace to bless your name, like Hannah and Mary,*
not just for what we know, but even more
for what we do not know of your constant love. Amen

Tuesday November 21   *1 Samuel 3.1-21*
What is really going on?
I am often present with my wife at a social function and on the way home my wife will say, 'Didn't you realize what was going on?' and interpret the evening's events to me in a way which I had not understood. Knowing the difference between 'what is happening' and 'what is really going on' is sometimes essential in public life.

Samuel is still very young and obviously has to be taught by Eli how to discern what is really going on in his life. He thinks he hears Eli calling. What is really going on is that God is speaking to him at a very deep level. Prayer, therefore, is the practice of attention to what is really being said. So much prayer is superficial, simply trying to involve God in what is happening rather than perceiving what is really going on. Our prayer needs the deepening that Eli gives to Samuel's response. Iris Murdoch, the novelist and philosopher said, 'prayer is a form of attention'. By this I think she means that it is a sort of 'tuning in' to what God is saying or has been saying for a very long time.

✱ *God, may our prayers be attentive to your presence*
   so that we may hear your voice
   in the deepest places of our souls. Amen

Wednesday November 22   *Isaiah 42.14-20*

Seeing in the dark

Isaiah is someone who sees in the dark. He sees what is really going on and describes it. His gift is to describe this to his fellow patriots, to allow them to see that there is hope for the future and that God is at work in hidden ways. He talks of God as a pregnant woman who has had a long confinement, kept her peace, but is now in labour, about to cry out and deliver her child. This image is remarkable not simply because it uses feminine imagery – which many even now shrink from using – but also because it expresses the hidden truth of the situation of the exiles which they had not been able to discern. They have been waiting, doubtful, perhaps, for the reality of the justice of God, their minds dark and resentful and so unable to see what was really going on. But, says Isaiah, what is about to happen has been like a secret hidden in the womb and now, even now, God is ready to deliver her people from the bondage of captivity, from the captivity of the womb, into a new future.

✱ *God, you are in labour from the beginning of time,*
   bringing forth your justice and your freedom.
   May we be reborn
   so that we too may participate in your new life. Amen

Thursday November 23   *Psalm 65*

'Teaching a stone to talk'

The American writer Annie Dillard, in an essay 'Teaching a Stone to Talk', portrays a strange young man who has a stone on his mantelpiece. Every day he uncovers it and gives it lessons, trying to teach it to talk as if it were a parrot or even a child. At first this appears very strange and we are puzzled and tempted to dismiss the essay. But Annie Dillard points out that this is our heritage. We are faced with the silence of the universe ever since we heard God speaking at Sinai and were so frightened we asked him never to speak to us again, 'Let not God speak with us, lest we die'. And the record shows that God agreed and sent us back to our tents and a silence that ever since we have found unbearable. Hence the torture of the strange man who tries to make a stone talk.

Every now and again, we receive a glimpse into the hidden reality: that the universe is not silent, but full of noises. We learn of the song of whales, which can be heard by other whales thousands of miles away but not by us. We learn of the noise of the cosmos, the strange sounds which other planets utter but which only very expensive equipment can hear, but not understand. And then we read the psalms and find that the psalmist knew about it all along, that there is a speech in creation – 'the valleys shout and sing together for joy'.

All this makes us aware of the great gap that there is between post-enlightenment thinking – when we regard nature as neutral or dead, speechless, and consequently 'ours' – and pre-enlightenment thinking when the creation was naturally understood to be alive with the praise of God. The early Fathers used to say that creation 'prays'. Annie Dillard's strange man would have agreed and wanted to hear what the prayer was all about.

✳ *God, open our ears to the sounds which your universe utters and free our tongues to sing your praise. Amen*

Friday November 24   *Psalm 84*

The valley of Baca

No one knows the actual location of the 'valley of Baca'. Perhaps it was 'a place of dryness on the pilgrim route to Jerusalem'. On the other hand, everyone knows its reality, and that is preserved in Miles Coverdale's translation of the Psalms – still to be found in the *Book of Common Prayer* of the Church of England, where verse 6 reads 'who, going through the vale of misery, use it for a well, and the pools are filled with water'. It is a place where we feel that there can be no hope. It is like that place on the East African coast where slaves came, just before they were put in ships for Europe, which they called in Swahili, *Bagomoyo* – 'Lay down your heart'.

But even in this place there is a hidden secret, for sorrow actually enlarges rather than destroys the heart, and an enlarged heart can then take on the sorrows of others. The place of apparent sorrow can, if we are brave enough and open enough, become the place where we hear more clearly the word of God which is speaking to us in our sorrow, but which our preoccupation with our own grief prevents us from hearing. If we are courageous enough, 'the Valley of Baca' can become the place where we know the love of God more surely than before, and 'its pools will be filled with water'.

✳ *God, when our hearts are dry,*
pour upon us the rain of your grace
and fill our empty pools
with the life-giving water of your love. Amen

Saturday November 25   Hebrews 10.11-14*

No more victims

All societies are sacrificial even if they say they have done away
with such barbaric practices as the sacrifice of animals. Certainly
most societies claim victims or make victims of different groups of
people, even saying that the good of all requires that some suffer.
This is certainly the case in western market economies where it is
claimed that unemployment, for example, is a necessary part of
economic growth. This is only sacrifice under another, apparently
acceptable, name. The Christian teaching has always been that we
do not need to live by means of sacrifice any longer. Since the
death of Christ – that 'single sacrifice' – no further sacrifice is
necessary. Christ's death shows us that victims are no longer
needed. We do not need to dispense with certain groups in order to
make the universe work better. So we do not need to ask people to
be unemployed. We do not need to find victims for society's ills, or
to ask for vengeance – as so many people are now doing,
especially outside courtrooms and at the trials of people we think
we do not want. That way is no longer necessary because God has
borne, and is bearing, all the ills of the world in Christ and will
continue to do so. Those who are broken and unwanted can 'hide'
in the cross of Christ, the point at which the love of God reaches
into our world. We are not the ones who have to make things work.
We do not need to create any more victims as if the brokenness of
the world was ours to mend. That sacrifice is now no longer needed
since Christ's death. Christ has done the work for us.

✳ *God, give us the courage and the grace*
so to trust in your hidden love that we,
like Jesus, can live without making anybody a victim. Amen

FOR REFLECTION – alone or with a group

● Are your prayers like Hannah's or do you simply try to
   manipulate God?
● How can your prayer become part of the music of creation?
● Do you just pray for those who are victims, or does your prayer
   call you to place yourself alongside them more effectively?

Prayer is 'Primary Speech'

The last words of David, at least as recorded here, bear an uncanny resemblance to the first sermon of Jesus. David says, 'The Spirit of the Lord speaks through me, his word is upon my tongue' (verse 2), while Jesus says, 'The Spirit of the Lord is upon me, because he has anointed me...' (Luke 4.18).

Prayer is not our own work. It is the work of the Spirit, God's speech within us. Much of the time we think prayer is some sort of work which we have to do, rather like mowing the lawn on a Sunday afternoon when we would rather be snoozing or reading a good book. Certainly we have to choose to pray but prayer is much deeper than something which we do: it is an entering into the speech of the Spirit. Two writers on prayer have called it 'Primary Speech' and say, 'Prayer is that primordial discourse in which we assert, however clumsily or eloquently, our own being' (Ann and Barry Ulanov, *Primary Speech* – SCM Press). The early Fathers said that prayer was a participation in the language of the Trinity, for the converse of God is the original speech which makes all things and in which our prayer participates. We pray too superficially, with words from our false, rather than our real, selves. David's and Jesus' words remind us of what we are doing.

✳ *God, we are always surprised when you tell us you speak in us.*
Give us grace to be glad that this is so
and to allow our feeble prayers to be joined with yours
in the depths of our being. Amen

Water from God

Jeremiah – from whose prophecies the passages for this week are taken – lived and wrote at a time when the Assyrian empire was in decline, and the power and influence of Babylon was growing. Within Judah there was a resurgent nationalism which was often supported by other nation states such as Egypt. Jeremiah was accused of being 'a Jeremiah' because he proclaimed that this new-found confidence of Judah was ill-founded and would bring disaster. He said it was the equivalent of abandoning God. Of course he was vilified and imprisoned for his words, but he remains a witness to the necessity of reliance upon God alone.

In this passage, he says that the people have abandoned God who is 'a fountain of living water'. They have dug empty cisterns for themselves, cisterns which are cracked. Teresa of Avila, writing many hundreds of years later, comments that 'heavenly water begins to rise from a spring that is deep within us, it swells and expands our whole interior being'. This water, she says, 'comes from its own source, which is God.' Jeremiah asked his people to rely on this source of life alone, but they could not. In these days, when national security and identity are also highly valued, can we?

✳ *God, your Christ said, 'Out of the believer's heart*
   shall flow rivers of living water.'
   Open our hearts by your grace
   that we may drink of the water of eternal life. Amen

Tuesday November 28   *Jeremiah 10.12-16*
God's storehouses
This passage is very much in the Wisdom tradition of the Hebrew Scriptures and resembles a number of other passages from the Psalms and elsewhere. It is very similar to the concluding chapters of Job, where God also speaks of his 'storehouses' (38.22). These are the sources of creation. In Job they are also referred to as 'recesses' or 'springs' (38.16), and even the term 'womb' is used at one point (38.8). All these terms describe the hidden dwelling place of God, the place where the wisdom of God dwells. In Proverbs 8 the word of God dwells in this place and God speaks his word of creation there. God speaks, indeed has already spoken, his word in each person as well as in the whole of creation. This 'hidden' word is a spring, a storehouse within us. There is a ground, a basic point where God dwells and speaks, and all of us have to listen to that and live from that point. We have to live out of that storehouse and not from some accumulated wealth of our own. We are already spoken and the word lives within us.

✳ *Your word, God, is from all time*
   and is spoken in us as your children. May this
   storehouse of your love be the food of our lives. Amen

Wednesday, November 29   *Jeremiah 12.1-13*
The beloved of my heart
Jeremiah laments that Judah has become lost, relying upon herself and not on the Lord. This is like a betrayal, he says. He

then uses a very striking image and says, 'I have given the beloved of my heart into the hands of her enemies' (12.7). This 'beloved of my heart' is also described as 'my heritage', or 'my vineyard', or 'my pleasant portion'. In one sense these terms all refer to the land of Judah, the nation, but the phrase 'the beloved of my heart' shows that it is more than that which is at stake. This 'beloved of the heart' is like an interior secret, a deep point of life and source of love which has been given away, betrayed.

The thirteenth century Dutch Beguine writer Hadewich uses the term *Minne* to describe something similar. This is a very evocative word which means much more than the English equivalent, 'mine'. '*Minne*', one writer says,' is the intimate presence of the one we love within us arousing us towards the very source of our desire...the source of our desire is also where we will find the truth of who we are created to become.' God is *'Minne'*, mine within, 'the beloved of my heart', and calls us to live with her in deepest intimacy. For Jeremiah, the ultimate betrayal was to deny that possibility and to give what was intimately and ultimately God's into the hands of others for whom it was not 'mine'.

✳ *God, you are mine and I am yours.*
May you be mine and I yours, for ever. Amen

Thursday November 30   *Jeremiah 18.1-12*
The potter's wheel
In the early days of television in Britain, there were often gaps of several minutes between programmes, and these gaps were filled with short films with the word 'Interlude' superimposed on the screen. One of them is still well remembered – it was a film of a potter's wheel and showed the potter's hands shaping the clay into a vessel. It reminded you to be patient and wait, to remember that things were in good hands and the film you were waiting to see would come in due time. We might not have thought of it at the time, but it was really a commentary on Jeremiah 18. Jeremiah uses the image of the potter in his prophecy about the state of the nation. The potter is God and the pot is in God's hands, being shaped and directed by him. If God wants to make this particular shape a pot he will do so; if he wants to break that pot down and use it to make another shaped pot he will do that as well. There are forces at work which are totally beyond our control because they belong to God. The leaders of the nation in Jeremiah's day were reluctant to recognize the truth of that. They

felt they were in control; they wanted to keep things together in their own way. They resisted the call to rest in the hidden wisdom of God.

All of the spiritual teachers speak of the need for human beings at some point in their lives to let go and let God be God in them. We have to trust the processes of the potter, otherwise we are faithless.

✳ *God, when we are afraid,*
help us to imagine that your hands hold us,
like the hands of a potter, like the hands even of a lover,
caressing our being and drawing us to become
what only you know we can be. Amen

Friday December 1   *Daniel 7.9-10; 13-14**

Uncovering what is hidden

The apocalyptic visions of Daniel are uncoverings of what is normally hidden from our eyes. The very word 'apocalyptic' means 'unveiling', and Daniel claims that in his dreams he sees what is really going on in the world of human affairs: that 'what is happening' has been peeled away and he can see the truth behind events. His vision is a vision first of God and then of the Son of Man, the one who carries the authority of God to, and in, the world of human beings.

All prayer is a doorway into what is really going on, a window into the reality of God's activity. The pity is that we do not treat it as a doorway, a place where we must quietly wait to see what it is we are being told or what it is that God is doing with us and for us. Instead we tend to use it as a means of persuasion, a lever by which we can alter the course of events. This is really a very secular way of understanding prayer and reduces God to the level of the genie in *Aladdin*, who simply does what we wish, provided we wish hard enough. Prayer is rather a means by which we can be changed, the means by which we attend to the hidden but loving purposes of God and then, slowly but surely, come to ask that those purposes be done, 'disclosed' if you like, in us. Then we become the place where God's hidden purposes of love are revealed. This is illustrated by the Lord's Prayer, where the words 'Thy kingdom come, thy will be done, on earth as it is in heaven...' call us to ask that what is actually the case from God's viewpoint be released, uncovered, revealed to be the case in the reality we inhabit.

✷ God, hold back our desire to change you
and release in us the contentment
to be part of your purposes for all things. Amen

Saturday December 2   *Revelation 1.4b-8**

Scales over our eyes?

In C S Lewis' book *The Great Divorce,* the story tells of a bus journey from earth to heaven. It begins on a foggy evening where you cannot see very far but ends in a place where the light is so clear, and everything is so real, that it becomes frightening to some passengers who thought they were being taken somewhere comfortable and undisturbing. Some of them get back in the bus and ask to be taken back home.

This is a powerful parable of the coming of Christ, spoken about in this passage. The coming of Christ is not something which will remove us from difficulty to comfort. It is rather the opposite: it enables us to see what we could not see before because our inner eye, the eye which sees the truth, was closed and we were content with the half reality, the hazy comfort of where we are now. There is a real sense in which modernity lulls us to sleep; it takes away our capacity to see what is really the case and says that everything is all right, we have everything we need, and we don't need to do anything. This falseness of modernity puts scales over our eyes and prevents us from seeing easily what is happening to God's poor, what is happening to the victims, what is happening to all of us.

The coming of Christ is a forcible opening of our eyes to the truth and a call to repentance and faith. The Revelation of St John is not so much a book about the future, about what will come to pass, but a book about the necessity for readiness and openness now, so that we can see what is going on with the eyes of God.

✷ God, take away the scales from our eyes and open them
to what is real but hidden from us by our selfishness. Amen

FOR REFLECTION – alone or with a group

- Try to find a copy of *The Interior Castle* by Teresa of Avila and read what she says about the spring of water which rises within us in the Fourth Mansion. Compare it to John 7.38.
- Reflect on how prayer is 'a window into the activity of God' and ask yourself whether the noise of your prayer is so loud that you cannot hear what is being said to you.
- What is central to your heart's desire?

FOR ACTION

Every time you go to a prayer meeting ask yourself whether that meeting has served to clarify a course of action for you or one or more of the members of the group. If your prayers are not a means of clarifying one or more courses of action for the Kingdom ask yourself why this is and challenge the group to discuss this problem. Dag Hammerskjold, who was Secretary General of the United Nations and a devout man, said, 'In our day, the road to holiness passes through the world of action.'

Is that true for your group? If not, why not? Study the life of Teresa of Avila to see how spiritual growth and action for the Kingdom of God were related in her busy life.

ADVENT – GOD IS WITH US
1. God's Kingdom

Paraphrases, notes and prayers by
John Vincent

John Vincent is a theologian and lecturer. His most recent books are 'Seeds in the City' (Epworth Press), which reflects on his work in the Sheffield Inner City Ecumenical Mission, and 'Gospel from the City' and 'Liberation Spirituality' (Urban Theology Unit), which he co-edited.

'God is with us' is the meaning of two great words in the Christian world: **Emmanuel,** which means 'God (El) immanent in', 'present in'; and **Incarnation**, which means '(God) in the form of humanity', 'God in flesh'.

The result of God's presence in the world is in the presence of God's Kingdom. Right at the beginning of the Gospel, Jesus declares: 'The *Kairos* (decisive time) has arrived. The Kingdom of God is now present. Change yourselves completely and trust yourselves to the Good News' (Mark 1.15). So God's Kingdom is the new situation resulting from the coming of Jesus. Advent announces each year his Coming, his Appearing, and his Kingdom.

We need to gear ourselves up for some surprises, though, as to what that Kingdom actually is.

1st Sunday of Advent, December 3   *Jeremiah 33.14-16**
The Kingdom is Righteousness

The Advent is the Coming,
the fulfilment of God's promise (verse 14)
a righteous Branch springing up for David
justice and righteousness in all the land (verse 15)
salvation and security for Judah and Jerusalem.
And its Name? The Lord is our Righteousness (verse 16).

The whole passage is about Righteousness. And the new beginning for human beings, 'to be saved' and 'to live in safety', is the result of this Righteousness.

'Righteousness' is 'the state of being right', or 'in the right'. God's righteousness is God's own 'upright conduct' in bringing people and situations into a state of rightness. This God can only

280

do by rescuing people and putting them in the situation which they cannot themselves attain – hence the link with 'saving' (verse 16).

A single new shoot is to transform everything, and bring righteousness, justice, security and salvation!

The hopes and fears of all the years, now this year again, meet in the unknown one who is 'The Lord our Righteousness'.

✳ *Lord our Righteousness,*
Messiah and Justice,
Lord our Rock,
Jesus our Salvation,
Let us cling to the promise
As if we had never heard it before,
And see its coming
In places where it had never been. Amen

Monday December 4   *Psalm 25.1-10**

The Kingdom is faithfulness

I'm betting on the eternal One;
I'm trusting myself to Jehovah (verses 1-3);
I'm setting out on paths and ways,
Truths and readings (verses 4-5);
I'm not the first to find them all
Loving and faithful (verses 6-10).

A psalm like this can work for wildly disparate people and situations. It can be a calm and assuring statement of trust, perhaps a simple self-confirming promise at the end of a day, or a meditation to get my head right and put me back to where I inwardly already am, with my hopes where they should be.

Or it can be a cry and protest of pain. Don't remember my rebellious ways. Don't let me be put to shame. Don't let my enemies triumph over me. Put your enemies to shame, not me. Reduce me to a proper humility.

A psalm like this cannot, though, be neutral. It's either a comfort or a protest. How is it for you?

✳ *Caller, Reality, Rock and Judge,*
Lover, Faithful, Forgiver and Teacher,
Let the multitude of your Faces
See me as I am and minister to me as I need. Amen

The Kingdom is attitude

The poor in spirit, the mourners,
The meek, the desperate, the merciful
Get Kingdom and comfort,
    the earth, fullness and mercy.

It's probably a single type of disciple – or human being – that is being declared 'blessed' – a type of person that is modest, self-effacing, un-pushing, always looking for justice, merciful to others. And it's probably also a single state of blessedness that is indicated – getting the Kingdom, being comforted, inheriting the earth, being filled, and being shown mercy.

In other words, we don't have one group getting one set of goodies, and other groups getting different goodies. The disciple picture comprises aspects of a single portrait, and the blessings are circumlocutions for a single reality – the Kingdom, the place of shalom, justice, wholeness and ultimate mercy.

✳ *O for the Kingdom*
    for which my spirit yearns;
O for the comforting
    for which my emptiness mourns;
O for the earth's inheritance
    for which every creature longs;
O for the fullness of righteousness
    for which we hunger and thirst;
O for the divine mercy
    of which the gentle have part. Amen

The Kingdom is action

The pure, the peacemakers, the persecuted,
The insulted and the slandered,
See God, are his children, get the Kingdom,
Belong to the faithful warriors for God.

Again, it looks like a single type – the type of a simple person, living at peace, persecuted by others, falsely accused.

And it looks like a single condition of blessedness – seeing God, being called God's children, receiving the Kingdom, belonging to those who can rejoice because in the end they will be shown to be God's beloved ones.

These verses emphasize the ultimate significance of 'this-worldly' activities – not being impure, making peace, being insulted, being slandered. They are pieces of human practice – active or passive – perhaps as distinct from verses 3-7 which were more in terms of attitudes.

✳ *This day, this day, give me to be pure;*
   Give me to create peace;
   Give me not to return evil for evil,
   But to manifest in all I do your peaceable reign,
   Your radical Kingdom. Amen

Thursday December 7   *Matthew 7.21-27*

The Kingdom is embodiment

God's Kingdom is for actors, practitioners,
Not sayers of 'Lord, Lord' (verse 21);
God's Kingdom is for those who go about doing good,
Not those making a show of miracles (verses 22-23);
God's Kingdom is the Rock on which to build,
It makes Jesus' words its foundation (verses 24-27).

The Beatitudes of Matthew 5.3-12 have often been thought of as descriptions of aspects of Jesus' own character and activity. Jesus embodies the Kingdom which the disciples are to receive. It is, therefore, the practical and physical embodiment of Kingdom behaviour and disposition in the disciples which characterizes the disciple's being in the Kingdom.

As Jesus went about doing good (Acts 10.38), so must the disciple. As Jesus offers his whole life as an offering (Hebrews 10.10), so must the disciple. The Rock to be built upon is the whole gospel pattern of words and deeds epitomized and manifested in Jesus.

The picture of the wise and foolish builders seems to be about survival through storms in this life, rather than in any future situation. It is about how to build your life, here and now. Is it right? Does it work?

✳ *Let me build my life on words faithful and true.*
   Let me embody the Christ in deeds faithful and bold.
   Let me do the good I can
   In the body of the altogether good. Amen

The Kingdom is relationship

The apostle glories in the followers
and prays for their fullness in faith (verses 9-10),
'May your love increase for everyone,
May your hearts strengthen before God' (verses 11-13).

The Movement of Jesus has arrived in a very alien world. As the preceding chapters show, Paul had promised them trouble if they became believers, and trouble had certainly come. Paul had been persecuted, and so have they been. But they had remained faithful, as an excited Timothy had just reported back to Paul (verse 6).

The Kingdom has created a community of believers, followers, people of the Way, men and women who hold to Jesus despite the ridicule of their contemporaries – just as Jewish Christians had suffered from theirs (2.14). But they have kept the faith, and continue to live worthy of the God who 'calls us into his Kingdom and his glory' (2.12).

✳ *I belong to brothers and sisters*
   Who have learned from me,
   and from whom I learn,
   Who love and care and agonize for me
   as I love and care and agonize for them;
   Who hold me precious as a Kingdom traveller
   And stand by me in my Kingdom life.
      Hallelujah! Amen

The Kingdom is unpredictable

Wars and revolutions will come
But they are not the Kingdom (verse 9);
International conflict and natural disasters will come
But they are not the Kingdom (verses 10-11);
Imprisonment and trials will come
But they will only be your witness stands (verses 12-13).

If the Kingdom is mainly a this-worldly reality, as it plainly is from our readings this week, then there will always be the temptation to look at this or that secular event, and seek to find its relevance to the Kingdom, and to say, 'Lo here', or 'Lo, there' (Matthew 24.23).

Rather, the Kingdom, it seems to me, is always a dynamic, sudden, unpredictable happening. It can be an unexpected radical appearance of some Kingdom value. It can be the appearance of some activity or people which only makes sense in the light of the Kingdom. It can be the manifestation of some new reality that reverses the expectations of background, environment, culture or history. Inevitably we say, 'Lo, here' – 'by the grace of God, lo here'. But then we cannot build on it, much less can we 'build the Kingdom'. But we can prepare for it, service it, and celebrate its appearing.

✳ *Let your Kingdom come,*
  Let it appear before me today.
  Let me prepare for it tomorrow,
  Let me celebrate it at all times,
  And keep us as your Kingdom people,
  Now and always. Amen

FOR REFLECTION – alone or with a group

● The Kingdom comes over as something which is present but not present, possible but impossible – a sudden happening, but unpredictable. How can we use the reality of the Kingdom responsibly?

● What is the point at which the Kingdom becomes present or possible for you? My colleague, Jane Grinonneau, says, 'Kindom', not 'Kingdom'. Is that it?

FOR ACTION

Think up a Kingdom action to do in your own neighbourhood this Christmas. Find out the facts, who is in need, who would help, what you could do. For example, find out who will have no Christmas Day dinner, and plan a way to deal with the problem.

ADVENT – GOD IS WITH US
2. God's messengers

Notes based on the Revised English Bible by
Jean Mortimer

Jean Mortimer has been a minister of the United Reformed Church (formerly Congregational) for 32 years. Much of her pastoral ministry was concerned with young people in inner city areas. In 'active retirement' she has taught New Testament Greek in the University of Leeds and is currently involved in theological education via the Scottish Churches Open College in Edinburgh. She is a published writer of prayers and other liturgical material and her research interests are in the area of 'Health and Salvation'. In her 'spare time' she writes poetry and short stories, paints and flies a variety of kites both real and metaphorical!

God's messengers

God's messages are often delivered by the most unlikely people in the most unexpected ways. Some bring hope and encouragement. Others are disturbing because they require us to respond with obedience, self-sacrifice, trust or a change of heart or direction. The Greek word for messenger is *angelos*. Not all 'angels' have haloes and wings! In highlighting some of the less frequently explored aspects of the familiar passages set for this week, I hope that their message will be heard, applied and passed on with clarity and contemporary relevance.

2nd Sunday of Advent, December 10   Malachi 3.1-4*

'Don't shoot the messenger'

The old saying, 'Don't shoot the messenger if you don't like the message' comes sharply to mind on this, Human Rights Day. Those who have no freedom to express their thoughts or beliefs without fear of reprisal – no home, no comfort, no liberty to be themselves, no hope, no love – are disturbing and challenging messengers of God to all of us as we prepare for Christmas. How can we allow ourselves the indulgence of basking in the warm glow of a comfortable hearth and home, wrapping gifts to be exchanged with family and friends, if we are not prepared to be exposed to the white-hot furnace heat of God's judgement, exposing and refining our motives and aspirations? How can we sleep easily between the crisp, smooth sheets of privilege and so-called respectability, or snuggle down under a blanket of complacency, if we are not ready to have our most self-centred or sordid thoughts and intentions scrubbed till they are squeaky clean?

✴ *Advent God, bringer of purity and judgement,*
  refiner of base motives, selfish actions and intentions,
  cleanser of soiled hands and hearts,
  help us to hear and heed all your messengers
  especially those whose unjust suffering disturbs
  our complacency. Amen

Monday December 11   *Luke 1.5-25*

Don't doubt the messenger

Barrenness can take many forms. Lives which appear useful and purposeful on the surface may conceal emptiness and lack of fulfilment. Has anyone ever tried to persuade you that a long cherished hope or ambition might be realized? How did you respond? With joyful acceptance and confidence...or were you dumbstruck with doubt...paralyzed by fear? Do you know people whose lives feel wasted or empty? Think of infertile couples who long for a child; those who are harshly labelled as 'selfish' or 'unnatural' and made to feel worthless because they have decided not to have children; old people whose youthful aspirations seem to have borne little fruit; young people who have never had paid work or who have grown old too soon in the child labour or child prostitution markets of the world. How can you be a messenger of hope and encouragement to them?

✴ *Gracious God, we thank you for John,*
  your gift of hope in barrenness, doubt and despair;
  your gift of courage in the face of fear;
  your messenger of the saving one, coming into the world.
  May all who are disabled by disappointment,
  diminished by real or imagined disgrace find,
  in the story of his birth, your promise of wholeness.
  Help all your people to hear your messengers of hope today
  and proclaim your promises. Amen

Tuesday December 12   *Luke 1.26-38*

Say 'Amen' to the messenger

Charles Causley's 'Ballad of the Bread Man' offers challenging insights on this story. Mary is in the kitchen baking bread when the angel appears to announce that God has a job for her. Although cooking has traditionally been regarded as women's work, pregnancy and birthing are not normally regarded as a job, notwithstanding the use of the term 'labour' in this context! Joseph is mentioned in passing, as in Luke. He is 'planing a piece of wood' – getting on with men's work – and is given no further role in the drama. The neighbours react with cynical disbelief. 'The old man's past it.' 'That girl's been up to no good.'

What does Causley's slant on the story say to you about how women and men can co-operate in saying 'Amen' to God's messengers when they are called to bring to birth new ways of being, new patterns of living, new role models, new job descriptions for the work God gives each one of us to do? How can we help one another to achieve this, even in the face of hostility and suspicion?

∗ *'With God, nothing will be impossible.'*
  As servants of the Lord, let it be to us according
  to his word. Amen

Wednesday December 13   *Luke 1.39-45*
Solidarity in confirming the message
Despite her words of acceptance, Mary still needs reassurance so she visits Elizabeth to check the angel's story. When they meet, Elizabeth's formerly tentative acceptance – 'for five months she lived in seclusion' (verse 24) becomes complete as her baby kicks in her womb. Was this the first time she had felt the thrill of his movement, or perhaps the first time she had allowed herself to trust what she had already begun to feel? She, too, needed reassurance. Her joyful and affirming response to Mary, which assumes that the younger woman had not experienced her doubts and fears, unwittingly provides Mary with the confirmation she has come to find. How can this story of solidarity and sisterhood help women of all ages and cultures to support one another in bearing messages of hope and affirmation in the barren places of the world where women are still exploited, marginalized or dismissed? List ways in which your attitude to yourself as a woman, or to women if you are a man, has been challenged or changed during the World Council of Churches' ecumenical decade, 'Churches in solidarity with women' (1988-1998).

∗ *Spirit, our Sister,*
  our midwife,
  make the Church your birthing room,

where new women,
new men,
are delivered and cradled
to bring new life to the world. Amen

Thursday December 14   *Luke 1.46-56*

Solidarity in sharing the message

An ancient tradition ascribes the *Magnificat* to Elizabeth and if we compare it with the words of Hannah (see I Samuel 2.1-10) when she offered Samuel, the child of her old age, to the Lord, the striking similarities lend weight to this theory. A feminist lectionary and Psalter, Marie Thérèse Winter's *Womanword*, has dealt with this difficulty by interweaving the stories of Elizabeth and Mary and making the Magnificat a psalm of praise for two voices. How can we make it a psalm of praise and affirmation for all women, for all who are oppressed, all who are powerless, all who are hungry, all who are poor, regardless of gender or ethnicity? Offer this prayer in company with others on their behalf:

✷ *When the lowest of the low are honoured;*
When 'the curse' of womanhood is seen as blessing;
When the proud are put down;
When the power-crazy are usurped;
When the powerless are raised up high;
When the hungry are enabled to prepare their own banquet
and the rich are not summoned to the feast;
When everyone remembers God's mercy
and delights in sharing God's promises,
Then my soul will magnify the Lord
and my spirit will rejoice in God, my Saviour. Amen
            Prayer inspired by Marie Thérèse Winter, Womanword
                   (Collins Dove, HarperCollins, Australia 1990)

Friday December 15   *Luke 1.57-80**

Strength to speak a surprising message

It is Elizabeth, not her husband, who first finds the strength to stand out against custom and convention in naming their child. Zechariah's ability to speak is only restored after he has supported her initiative. In bringing to birth real equality of status and opportunity in the Church and the world, women and men are increasingly called to run the risks inherent in such role reversals and naming. Give thanks for those moments when your ability to speak an unexpected truth has taken you, or others, by surprise. Give thanks for those who have accepted God's word to remain silent so that you might find and articulate your own words. Give thanks for those who have underlined your right to speak in this way. Be prepared for your ideas and initiatives to undergo a period 'in the wilderness' until the time is right for their full acceptance. Nurture and strengthen all who stand with you in preparing the way.

✳ *God of the unexpected,*
   speaking to us through an old woman
   who found a new voice and a new role;
   through an old man
   who heard your word in unaccustomed silence;
   through an unconventional prophet
   with strident manner and unusual ways.
   Keep on surprising us in the people you choose to deliver
   your messages. Keep on calling us to respond in
   equally unexpected ways. Amen

Saturday December 16   *Philippians 1.3-11**

Remembering fellow messengers

How appropriate that this study of God's messengers should conclude with part of Paul's letter to his partners in the gospel at Philippi. Even though he yearns for the support and comfort of his friends in the loneliness and uncertainty of his imprisonment, he is able to put their spiritual development before his own needs. Would that all of us in the community of the Church today might be enabled to follow his example. Call to mind a time in your life when you felt isolated or unsupported. Was this a direct result of your defence of the gospel in a situation where this called you to deliver an unpopular message? How far do you think you may have contributed to your sense of rejection and isolation? To what extent were other people responsible? Did anyone help you? Did you feel able to ask for help? If not, why not? Did anyone or anything that you remembered at this time help you to get through it? What kind of prayers did you offer?

✳ *Ever present God,*
   I thank you for the encouragement of . . . .
   (insert a name or names)
   my partner(s) in proclaiming your message.
   Help me to be a partner in the gospel to others. Amen

FOR REFLECTION – alone or with a group

With which of the messengers do you feel most able and least able to identify? Make a list of your reasons.

FOR ACTION

Select one of the messengers. Write, on a postcard, a brief paraphrase of his/her words and identify one situation in which you feel you would be able to speak them.

Post the card to yourself as a spur to action.

ADVENT – GOD IS WITH US
3. God's judgement and promise

Notes based on the Revised Standard Version by
Jane Ella Montenegro

Jane Ella Montenegro is a lay pastor and Christian Education worker involved in empowerment programmes with and among women, youth, children and rural churches. She also writes educational materials for the National Council of Churches in the Philippines and is a member of the Asian Women's Resource Centre for Culture and Theology.

This advent, God's judgement convicts us once again where we have failed in following God's justice and righteousness. Also, God's promise of joy, freedom and peace through Jesus Christ lifts us up to keep hoping for this vision. May the Spirit of the cosmic Christ humble us to accept God's judgement, make us dance with joy in spite of our pains, and empower us to trust in God's wisdom and strength in all circumstances.

3rd Sunday of Advent, December 17   *Zephaniah 3.14-20**
God's promise of joy

It is about 2,400 years since the prophet Zephaniah spoke these words. Yet the promise of God today includes all daughters: not only those of Jerusalem, but all the women of the world.

Take heart, O women, even though violence against children and women is one of the best kept secrets of the Church today; a God of justice will deal with the oppressors – someday.

Take heart, O children and women, even though you are the hardest hit by the brunt of global economic crisis today; a gentle God will embrace the lame and the outcast – someday.

Take heart, O working mothers and daughters, enslaved fathers and sons, even though you are scattered over the face of the earth, a compassionate God will gather you home – someday.

Take heart, O women, even though men destroy each other by conflicts and wars, ravage nature and leave you widows, orphans and objects of pleasure today; a loving, forgiving God will change your shame into praise – someday.

✶ *O God of hope, in the midst of all our tears,*
we shall sing and shout, smile and dance with all our being.
As in a time of festival, so we may claim
your promise of freedom and joy as early as today.

Monday December 18   *Luke 3.1-6**
God's gift of forgiveness
Some high school students in a mountain church were excited as they began to make plans to exchange gifts and solicit prizes for the games at the Christmas Eve celebration in church. The visiting preacher, however, was firm. The banana plants with ripened fruits and the tall, bamboo grass were appropriate for the manger scene. The exchanging of gifts was not necessary. Gifts of food could be offered voluntarily by families, including the prizes. But no one must feel pressurized to celebrate Christmas in a particular way.

Then he affirmed the message from Isaiah: Out of the solitude of the wilderness, God's quiet, persistent voice is heard. Out of the gifts of the seas and farmlands, God's daily provision is shared among simple folk. Out of the utterance of people from high and low places, God's Word judges all – without exclusion. God's gift of forgiveness is for young and old, rich and poor alike; it is for anyone who repents. The elderly peasants heaved a sigh of relief and acceptance, and the young realized that the Advent message is not found in the glitter of Christmas.

✶ *Forgive us, O God,*
for falling easily into the trappings of Christmas,
forgetting that it's you we need, most of all.

Tuesday December 19   *Luke 3.7-9**
God's judgement by fire
John's call to repentance is harsh, cursing and merciless. Was it possible that people came to be baptized out of fear of God's wrath? It is so much like the fiery sermons of evangelistic crusaders who vividly portray hell, fire and brimstone and make young people raise their hands out of fear and shame as they accept Jesus Christ as Saviour. Everyone and everything on the face of the earth will be annihilated, they say, and they live in fear, awaiting such a time. One faith community in the Philippines believes in this purification by God's fire, but God's fiery path will not hurt nor destroy them in the end-time. Instead, they will meet

God face to face. But for the evil-doers and arrogant, the excruciating pain and horror will surely be a punishment.

But simple peasant Christians live humbly without fear. They care deeply for the earth, respect the spirits, share resources and wait patiently for God's judgement.

✳ *Help us truly to repent, O God, this Advent time,*
not out of fear of your judgement,
but out of our failure to do justly,
to love mercy and to live humbly in your presence.

Wednesday December 20   *Luke 3.10-20**

God's news

In the midst of a commercialized Christmas and materialistic Christians, John shakes us and challenges us to bear good fruit. What good news could he possibly say to our Christmas holidaying, partying, expensive gifts, glittering decorations and even Santa Claus as the ills of our society deepen? For truly, we ought to be ashamed of our thousands of Filipino street children who shiver on cold pavements while the rich bask in beach resorts. We ought to be ashamed of certain lawyers and government officials who 'arrange secret deals' and are able to get away with it. We ought to be ashamed of those in uniform who kidnap for ransom and somehow escape from being penalized.

Still the good news is – John did not preach in vain. Today, many young women and men speak out against human rights violations at church and public rallies. A boy of ten testified recently against a drunken adult neighbour who shot a child who was enjoying his kite. A girl of fifteen points her accusing finger at a famous congressman who molested her. A cab driver stands in court as accomplice to an illegal drug business.

✳ *Help us to realize, O God, that your good news,*
this Christmas time, is putting right
what is inappropriate, excessive and evil in our society.

Thursday December 21   *Philippians 4.4-7**

God's peace

A young woman from the seminary excitedly prepared her lectures for the Christmas conference. She opened her suitcase of books and proceeded to read her materials. She was interrupted, however, by her room mate. With a disarming smile, her room mate remarked quickly, 'Oh, you must be one of those intelligent women who can preach stirring sermons. How I admire your courage. Will you let me touch the covers of your books? You know, I never had a chance to go to school. I don't even know how to read and write. My husband teaches me the alphabet, using the Bible as my text-book. One big lesson I have learned is to thank God in all circumstances. And so, whether I am ridiculed or praised – these are all the same to me.'

This encounter took place 50 years ago, opening up a friendship that was to last a lifetime. One learned from the books, and the other was nurtured from her daily sharing with her friend the words of the Bible.

✷ *Let my thanksgiving be deepened, O God,*
whether in humiliation of my pride
or in the joy of unexpected renewal,
and so may I attain the peace of Christ Jesus.

Friday December 22   *Isaiah 9.2-7**
God's child
When we were young, we sang with pride the anthem, 'The people who walked in darkness have seen a great light...' That was before we linked Israel's slavery with suffering in our own context. Today, as a Third World country chained to more powerful countries and the World Bank, we now understand Isaiah's vision of a Prince of Peace for Judah. Would we in the Philippines not long for one who would also bring peace, justice and righteousness to our land and people? Any child of God?

Many Filipino Christians believe that God answered their prayers for a change of ruler when, just over a decade ago, a gentle, smiling Cory Aquino graced the predominantly male decision-making structures of our government. She was far from perfect, but was a prayerful Christian woman, supported by a praying faith community.

This Advent we can sing this anthem again in deep thanksgiving because we have had a glimpse of justice and righteousness even for a brief time with God's child, a daughter of peace.

✷ *O God, remind us, through your child Jesus,*
of the precious gifts and vision
of justice, righteousness and peace.

God's wisdom and strength

From time immemorial, amusements and armaments have seemed to be the main pre-occupations of humankind. Rich countries today maintain their security and economy through weaponry, while wealthy families secure themselves with human and animal guards and high-tech gadgetry. But peace remains unattainable.

The prophet Micah envisions peace as God's peace. A ruler who comes from humble ancestry will act according to God's wisdom. He will be completely dependent upon God's strength. Through him, people will find security and peace in God.

The tragedy of Christianity is that it was brought to our country by gun-wielding colonizers. So hundreds of Filipino Christians who migrated to non-Christian communities within the archipelago have imitated them. They arm themselves and apply better techniques of farming. This century, in less than 50 years, schools and churches have sprouted up in many villages and towns, marginalizing countless indigenous communities to anonymity and extreme poverty. Also today, mission orders are perpetuated through warfare in the name of peace, and in the name of Jesus Christ. And various Christian sects continue to proliferate out of personal conflicts and power games.

✳ *Forgive us, O God, for failing again to learn*
that your wisdom and strength are the well-spring of peace.

FOR REFLECTION – alone or with a group

- In what ways have Christians perpetuated the commercialization and materialism of the Christian celebration?
- What aspects/areas of the church's structures and ministries need to be changed so that we can 'do justly, love mercy and walk humbly with God' today?

FOR ACTION

Write a play or prepare a contemporary manger scene that is ecologically and politically Third World-friendly.

CHRISTMAS – GOD IS WITH US
4. Come and worship

Notes based on the Revised English Bible by
Jim Cotter

Jim Cotter is a wordsmith and godstriver, a presbyter of the Church of England, a cairnbuilder and webtrembler who enables Cairns Publications and the Cairns Network, with their background spirituality of commitment to the earth, wrestling with faith, daring to contemplate, and having the courage to be creative. He lives in Sheffield, and relishes theatre, music, hills and friends.

In these comments, the writer is imagining how an inhabitant of Nazareth might have responded to these passages of Scripture if he had come across them in the forties of the first century. Of course, only the readings from Isaiah would have been available to him: no Letters or Gospels had yet been written. The reader is being encouraged to engage both with the writer and with the Scriptures themselves – to question, to ponder, to argue, and so to discern the *living* words of God for us today. Let your praying each day emerge from that process, *in your own words*.

I have recently become a follower of the Way. I live in Nazareth where most of us remember Jesus. It is more than ten years since Pilate authorized his execution. I am of course Jewish, always have been, always expect to be. But now I find myself arguing with my fellow Jews: you know the old story of where there are two Jews there are three points of view! I want them to understand the impact that Jesus has had upon my Jewish faith. I am convinced that he is still alive and present – in me, in my neighbour, in our bread-breaking. I believe he was indeed God's Messiah and lived, taught, and practised the Way of the Kingdom of God among us. It is beginning to dawn on me that Jesus began breaking down every kind of division among human beings, even religious divisions among Jews. I think he was 'anointed by God' to show us that God welcomes Gentiles (even enemies, even the Romans) as well as Jews (even those who claim to have got it right, like the Zealot Jews and the Pharisee Jews, let alone the Samaritans). God includes everybody in a great embrace of justice and compassion.

We have begun to search our Scriptures to find clues to persuade our fellow Jews to respond to Jesus as we have done. They need a lot of convincing that a human failure was indeed sent by God. And I have begun to hear stories about his birth. Over the years I have quite often walked the four miles to Sepphoris and heard Greek stories in the market place about divine sons, about gods who come down to earth and produce offspring with young women, about the connections that the Greeks make in this way between the human and the divine. One of my new 'adopted' brothers in Jesus has told a story about an archangel and a young woman from among the humble poor. I can understand why. It will remind us that when we think about Jesus we can't help thinking about God, and when we think about God we can't help thinking about Jesus. They seem inseparable.

I have also begun to share these thoughts with my son, who may one day make friends with a clever writer who will put it all together. This sense of wonder overcomes me when I realize what Jesus has come to mean for me, from inner freedom to treating everyone I meet as adopted brothers and sisters. This awe and this gratitude are spilling over into arguments and tales that my descendants will use to cloak even the moment of his birth. And a long time in the future will they have a special day of the year to celebrate? What will they call it? – a Christfeast?

Christmas Eve, December 24   *Luke 2.1-7**

Come and worship...because Jesus was homeless

No question here: Jesus was definitely Jewish. His ancestry was impeccable. And if he is the messenger of God for us, showing us that God is for every human being, it wouldn't make sense to tell a story of his birth that placed him in a king's court. If I can believe he was born to poor folks trying to make a respectable living, then I'll give his message a hearing. He couldn't be one of the privileged and powerful minority who burden us so. And I like the thought of his being born 'of no fixed abode'. He identified so much with the destitute, with those who have no nest or den. Don't you just love him for that – and want to worship the very ground he walked on? Sorry – but my enthusiasm carries me away!

Think: In what ways am I 'not at home', homeless, without roots, destitute, stigmatized? And simply pray:

✳ *Bless me and all humankind this Christmas Eve.*

Christmas Day, December 25   *Luke 2.8-20**

...because Jesus embraced the disreputable

Yes! I like the idea of shepherds being the first to hear of his birth. They've always been disreputable. They keep such irregular hours that they can't keep the ritual rules of cleanliness. I know I mustn't think myself superior to them (another lesson Jesus taught us), but it's hard sometimes: such a smelly lot. But of course we rely on them for lambs for sacrifices – and for a good meal. Typical double thinking: I wouldn't be seen dead in a slaughter house but I love 'the fatted calf' on the table! But if shepherds are invited round the table, what a strange party! Awesome I call it. What was that? The new-born *King*? That really *is* being over-enthusiastic. Hardly the kind of king we know about.

Think: Who are the people I exclude from my heart and life? And simply pray:

✳ **Enlarge my heart this Christmas Day,
and through all the ordinary days.**

Tuesday December 26　　　　　　　　　　　　　　　　*Titus 2.11-14**

...because Jesus healed as well as cured

Here he comes. There's one in every synagogue. He's happy in his misery. Casts a pall of gloom on every festivity. Thank God there are enough of us to let cheerfulness keep breaking through. And yes, all right, we need reminding not to give in to gluttony or any other kind of excess. And my head is thumping anyway after yesterday's feast. Don't make it worse. Ah! Now that bit is true enough – at least as a vision, and Jesus did practise what he preached – healing for all humankind. A sobering and joyful thought, and one that evokes my sense of wonder. You see, he not only cured people – he had the touch – but the touch meant something much, much more. He touched the untouchables and shared meals with them: they knew they were honoured and not shamed. Wonder-full!

Think: When am I gloomy, and when am I full of wonder? And simply pray:

✳ **Lift my gloom and expand my sense of wonder.**

Wednesday December 27　　　　　　　　　　　　　　　*Titus 3.4-7**

...because Jesus lived the generosity of God

Yes, I recognize Jesus here. Kindness, generosity, lavish gifts. If I matter *that much* to God, well, that's a God worth worshipping. And we do practise it at times – not least when we find ourselves spontaneously generous at festivals. It makes me realize I can never *claim* another person's generosity as my right – whether because of my virtue (my family will fill you in on that one) or my status (always struggling to pay the rent in time). It is because I have nothing much to offer that Jesus' overwhelming love and acceptance touched me so deeply in the first place. Letting myself bask in it from time to time – I think that's part of worship. And yes, I'm also an heir: I'm assured that the gift is for ever, that the quality of life I have experienced with others *through* Jesus *in* God is eternal – the deep knowledge that nothing can separate us from one another in the divine mystery.

Think: How generous am I? And simply pray:

✳ **Let me receive and give with great generosity.**

Thursday December 28   *Hebrews 1.1-12**

...because Jesus overturned the usual understanding of worship

My studious friend (a bit too clever for me) is so enthusiastic about this letter. He's pointed out to me all the references (bored me, if I'm honest, with his precise scholarly ways – Scrollworm is my nickname for him). And I have to admit that I love the Psalms too – though I don't know them half as well as he does. He can quote from memory, and I can see that there are hints of some of the books of Wisdom and of History. Our ancestors seem to have written about more than they knew, but he tells me that poets and the wise often do this: later generations find more truth spring to light from their words. With more help like this letter, we'll win the argument yet! Bring on the trumpets and drums. We'll be falling down and worshipping Jesus at God's right hand in majesty. Alleluia! Wait a minute though. I'm getting carried away again. Will shepherds still be welcome? Is this the same Jesus that shocked his first followers by washing their feet, becoming a slave woman in their sight?

Think: Do I find it easier to lift up my hands or to use them to bend down and serve others? And simply pray:

✳ **May my worship be without taint**
 of triumph at the expense of others.

Friday December 29   *Isaiah 52.7-10**

...because Jesus embodies *shalom*

Isaiah, now. Yes, he was very good on justice. Justice for all, not only those who can afford the best lawyers, not for the few at the expense of the many. I like the vision here, and I think Jesus practised it: 'inaugurated the Kingdom' is the way Scrollworm puts it. All of us human beings together are reconciled with one another and with God. Relationships that have gone wrong are put right, made right, have come right. There is harmony at last. *Shalom* is the great word we use. Generous blessings, abundant life – for the whole creation. The message of those who keep watch and are breathless with joy. Jerusalem at last a city of peace. Again, I'm awe-struck. I adore.

Think: What in my life hasn't come right yet? And simply pray:

✳ ***May shalom in me spread to help create shalom in everyone.***

Saturday December 30   *Isaiah 62.6-12**

...because Jesus imagined a house of prayer for all peoples

Brought down to earth again. The vision of Jerusalem – but not as it is now. I've been there – only once, and it is so very beautiful, especially the Temple. Part of me wants to believe Isaiah: the promise that all those awful foreigners, oppressors, colonialists, will one day be driven out, and Jerusalem will be ours and nobody else's. No longer will they have the best of my crops. But I can't help remembering that I was told that Jesus wept over Jerusalem. And if you look at the Temple from the angle of those who exercise power over us, dominating our religious as well as our economic lives, you can understand why he said that not one stone would be left standing upon another. Within a generation – perhaps in my lifetime – it will be flattened. I am so susceptible to glorious rhetoric, like Isaiah's. I must be very, very careful how I think about Jerusalem. I am glad that the multitudes will come and worship. But how? With what? And what kind of God are we worshipping?

Think: Who would I throw out of my church? And simply pray:

✳ ***Protect us from all who would harm us,***
and protect others from the way in which I harm them.
Show us how to welcome
and keep close to those who trouble us most.

1st Sunday after Christmas, December 31   *Revelation 5.1-14*

...because Jesus turned the throne room into a banqueting hall

Now this passage seems a very long way from my little home in Nazareth, comforted as I am by these new stories of shepherds and a frightened family far from their home. I think they'd be out of place in the emperor's court. I certainly would. Completely tongue-tied. What a vision – thousands round the throne, all prostrating themselves, worship taken over again by the wealthy and powerful. Well, all right, I know it shows a *lamb* before which they fall on their faces. And yes, the universe is in harmony at last. And the music sounds wonderful. But I still prefer the banqueting scene – even if I do sit next to the local tax man. If together we receive the bread from the waiter, I wonder who we shall recognize in each other? Wonder again, and worship.

Think: When have I been tongue-tied in the presence of someone more powerful than me? And simply pray:

✳ **Give me God-given confidence this New year,**
   and loosen my tongue.

FOR REFLECTION – alone or with a group

- Do you feel comfortable with this approach of engaging thoughtfully with our ancestors of faith, even if you find yourself arguing with the words of Scripture?
- Keep on asking whether pictures derived from scenes of worldly power are appropriate for our understanding of worship *through* Jesus. A recognition of the presence of God among us with awe, gratitude, and love may not be dependent on the kind of bowing down which is given to the Biggest and Grandest Emperor of them all.

FOR ACTION

Challenge leaders of your church with these subversive questions. After all, the presence of Jesus born in us and among us as the human face of God has implications for corporate justice as well as for acts of individual kindness and compassion.

IBRA scheme of readings for 2001

1. **God's new world**
   Gospel stories today
   Psalms for today

2. **Dare to be different**

3. **LENT to EASTER Journey with Christ**
   Which way? – The cost – Time for God –
   New beginnings – Knowing what lies ahead
   Who cares? – Emptiness and triumph

4. **New roads in mission** (*Acts & Galatians*)

5. **Suffering and a God of love**
   Why have you abandoned me?
   Weep with those who weep
   God of healing
   The healing Church
   Joy and sorrow

6. **God of love and anger** *(Hosea)*

7. **The power of dreaming**
   Dreams, fantasies or nightmares?
   Discerning the message
   God's dreams – A green apocalypse?
   When do dreams come true?
   God in our dreaming

8. **Challenges for change**
   What's wrong with society? – Hear the cries of the poor
   Change is possible – Pray for change
   A new respect *(Ruth)*

9. **Letters to the Thessalonians**

10. **Profile – King David** (*1 & 2 Samuel*)

11. **Advent & Christmas – God with us**
    David's descendant – Words for today
    The unshakeable prophet – Born of God

The themes and books studied each year are linked with the Revised Common Lectionary.

Order your copy now through your local bookseller, your local church representative, or direct from IBRA using the booking form on page 217.